INDIGENISING AND DECOLONISING SOCIAL WORK EDUCATION

About the Editors

Dr. Bishnu Mohan Dash, M.S.W. (Visva-Bharati), M.Phil. (University of Delhi), Ph.D. (University of Delhi), ICSSR Post-Doctoral fellow Associate Professor in the Department of Social Work in Bhim Rao Ambedkar College, University of Delhi. He is the recipient of Best Teacher Award from Government of Delhi, 2019-20 and the prestigious Delhi University Excellence Award teachers in the year 2021. He is also engaged in promoting for Indianisation of social work education in India. He is also an editorial board member/Advisory member in several national and international journals. He has also authored/co-authored/edited 14 books and has published more than forty papers in various reputed National and International journals and frequently contributes in leading national newspapers. He has presented papers and chaired sessions in various national/international conferences including Canada, Japan, and Sri Lanka and delivered invited lectures in various academic forums. He was also member of the Expert committee in the course Revision/Member, School Board, Academic Council, Indira Gandhi National Open University, New Delhi; Orissa State Open University, Mahatma Gandhi Antarrashtriya Hindi Vishwa Vidyalaya, Maharashtra, BPS University, Sonepat and Member, Board of Studies in Social Work, Indore School of Social Work, Indore and Jagadguru Rambhacharya Divyanga University, Chitrakoot. He has completed a number of research projects sponsored by ICSSR and UGC and organized various workshops and seminars. His areas of interest are Rural Development, Child welfare, social work education.

Dr. Mithilesh Kumar is working as a Senior Assistant Professor in Wardha Samaj Karya Sansthan, Mahatma Gandhi Antarrashtriya Hindi Vishwavidyalaya, Wardha. His Area of Specialisations are Human Rights, Research Methodology and Gandhian/ Indian Social Work. He has written/edited 18 Books including Indian Social Work *(*Routledge, Taylor and Francis*)*, Social Work in India: Indigenous Models and Approaches, Nanaji Deshmukh: An epitome of Indian Social Work (Concept Publishing Company), New Frontier in Social Work Practice: Bhartiya Context, Perspective and Experiences and 21 Research Papers in reputed national/ international Journals. He is a recipient of the Social Work Education and Promotion Award by International Association for World Peace (Affiliated with ECOSOC of United Nations, DPI, UNICEF, and UNESCO). He is also working as Joint Secretary, Bhartiya Samaj Karya Parishad, a national level professional Social Worker Organisation for the promotion of Indigenous Social Work/Bhartiyakaran of Social Work.

INDIGENISING AND DECOLONISING SOCIAL WORK EDUCATION

Edited by
Bishnu Mohan Dash
Mithilesh Kumar

CONCEPT PUBLISHING COMPANY PVT. LTD.
NEW DELHI - 110 059

ISBN: 978-93-5594-627-0

First Published 2023

Published and Printed by

Concept Since 1974

Concept Publishing Company Pvt. Ltd.
A/15-16, Commercial Block, Mohan Garden
New Delhi-110059 (India)
T: +91-11-41101460
E: publishing@conceptpub.com, *W*: www.conceptpub.com

Cataloging in Publication--Courtesy: D.K. Agencies (P) Ltd. <docinfo@dkagencies.com>

Indigenising and decolonising social work education / edited by Bishnu Mohan Dash, Mithilesh Kumar.
pages cm
Contributed articles.
Includes bibliographical references and index.
ISBN 9789355946270

1. Social work education--India. 2. Social service--Practice--India. 3. Hindu philosophy. 4. Social work with indigenous peoples--India. 5. Decolonization--India. I. Dash, Bishnu Mohan, editor. II. Kumar, Mithilesh (Assistant professor of social work), editor.

LCC HV11.8.I4I53 2023 | DDC 361.30710954 23

Prologue

The concept of Indianisation and decolonisation are two different things and are not synonymous. But whenever we discuss about decolonisation, it is important to change the mindset and decolonise the methods. Despite various efforts undertaken to Indianise the concept and approach, the contemporary world is very much dominated by Euro-centric ideas and the field of social work is mainly dominated by the philosophical concepts and methods and approaches of the United States of America. All dominant branches of knowledge are Euro-centric, but in case of social work education there has been shift of approaches from Europe to America. The decolonisation and Indianisation aims at liberation from the Euro-American centric knowledge in Asian and African countries. The movement of Bharatiyakaran of social work education has attempted to get freedom and achieve proper freedom from the academic dominance of Euro-American Knowledge systems.

Therefore, there is a great need for decolonising the colonial legacy in social work education, rediscover Indic knowledge system, conduct original research, develop relevant models and restructure the social work curriculum in India. The literature, social systems, social service, social reform movements and cultural and ethnic diversity in India have enough potential for original research that may contribute significantly in the pool of the universal knowledge of social work for the planet earth.

'Bhartiyakaran' of Social Work does not mean indigenisation. Being indigenous is different from being classic. Bhartiyakaran is not localisation. If Bhartiyakaran is understood to mean that, the spatiality is to be amplified, and then this interpretation is not correct. Instead, it is the effort and an enterprise to develop, invent and revive the lost methodology and models of community development and social work by understanding the true nature of Indian society and the eternal interrelationship between society and individual.

The social work education in India should be free from Euro-American paradigms. It should be Indianised, naturalised, indigenous and contextual and should be free from any kind of colonial hegemony. Emphasis should be given to Indian culture, tradition, civilisational vision and wisdom. The social work curriculum should be redesigned in a war footing so that it will not only improve the standards and quality of social work education but also it will definitely make the society better as social workers can be able to utilize their skills and resources for the well-being of its citizens and nations.

Social work has an ancient history rooted in the Indian tradition. On examining the vital elements of Indian society as found in the old scriptures of India, we find that the practice of social work is embedded in India from the outset. Now the question arises, Is social work a charity or a profession? Or a profession in which the charity is embedded, or a charity in which a profession and charity are reciprocal? The way Europe determined the nature of society after the Renaissance or Industrial Revolution, it is clear that it assumed that society is an enterprise and if society is an enterprise, then the actions of society are based on the intent of profit. Europe assumed that society is the outcome of a contract where individuals created it to protect their interests. In both ways, it is believed as an artificial creation. Creation is always based on intelligence. Is Indian society really like this?

The concept of society in India was neither based on contract nor based on purpose. The principles of the origin of society which Europe had built up is dogmatic, whereas the USA adopted the principle of purposefulness as the basis for the profession of social work is not useful in the context of Indian society. Indeed, over a period of time, what began as an applied form of sociology and finally as an academic discipline, social work profession is utterly independent of sociology, and has been taught in many countries of the world as a professional discipline.

However, in the Indian context, society is not dependent on the state. Society is not controlled and regulated even by the individual. It is controlled and regulated by *Dharma*. Indian sociology is the study of *Dharmashastra*. It is not theology. Therefore, it cannot be understood by theology, and it was the biggest mistake of Indian society to understand it as theological studies. Due to which the original form of social work could not emerge in India till Independence. It did not appear before Gandhi that social work can have a theoretical background from the Indian point of view. Vivekananda had also presented all the theoretical grounds on which the social work later evolved and appeared in the form of the Swadeshi movement in Bengal.

In the Indian context, social work is neither charity nor profession but it is the nature of human being, i.e. *Dharma* or Moral Code of Conduct of human being. So, the problem arises when we try to establish some norms for social work without understanding these contexts, and build a society based on those norms, then there is a difficulty. Like state governments have undertaken many efforts for social welfare which are proved to be unsuccessful because these programmes were not in conformity with the social values of the groups for which they had strived. So, without understanding social values and foundation of society, the welfare programmes implemented by the government does not yield effective results.

Combination of theory into practice is a central goal for all professions, the question of how to bridge the gap between theory and practice and between the classroom and the fieldwork practice is one which has preoccupied social work education since its very beginnings. So it is necessary to adopt and practice Indian models of community development. The life and work of Nanaji Deshmukh is most appropriate for addressing these concerns. He constructed the necessary foundation for this work in the form of Deendayal Research Foundation apart from making the first attempt of professionalisation in India. He worked relentlessly for poverty eradication, minimum needs programme, cottage industry and agriculture. He successfully carried out the social restructuring programme in more than 500 villages of Uttar Pradesh and Madhya Pradesh. The present and future social worker need to learn a lot from the works of Nanaji and many more Indian Social Workers. So, in order to improvise the social work profession, we need to learn from our Indic models, experiences which will be a significant attempt towards indigenisation and decolonisation of social work education. I hope that this book will be indispensable to every member of the academic and professional community of social work.

Rajaneesh Kumar Shukla
Vice-Chancellor
Mahatma Gandhi Antarrashtriya
Hindi Vishwavidyalaya,
Wardha, Maharashtra, India

Foreword

In the first one and a half millennia of the Common Era, i.e. till CE 1500 from the beginning, India's contribution to World GDP was around 43 per cent. During that time, lifestyle at the village levels contributed to the economic progress and share of world GDP was impressive. Compared to the timeline given byAngus Maddison in his book '*Economic History of the World: a Millennial Perspective*', we can comfortably conclude that India lost her economic progress by the time Britishers started colonising the mind.

During the period of British India, Lord Macaulay implemented the Downward Filtration Theory in education. The Downward Filtration theory focuses on indoctrination from top to bottom, i.e. from the revered class to the common people. It premised that if the socially dominant class is educated in the foreign way, then others who follow them will also emulate them. The colonisation of educated minds during the British Period resulted in the more scientific ancient model of education becoming secondary and sidelined. As part of British Policy, education was controlled by the Government and subsequently the curriculum and pedagogy was decided by them. As a result, the Indic wisdom got sidelined and neglected and British pattern education became mainstream gradually. During educational surveys done between 1823 and 1826 by the British revenue officers, we find astonishing facts that, the literacy rate in most parts of the country was almost 100 per cent; however, by the time of Independence in 1947, it dropped significantly low to 12 per cent. It shows that 88 per cent of the masses were de-educated, their ideas, languages, educational culture lost.

Thus, there is an urgent need for decolonising the mindset of teachers and students towards importance of indigenising and decolonising education in general and particularly social work education in this context, as it has remained completely Euro American Centric. Even at the global level, there is renewed interest towards indigenisation and decolonisation of social work education. Mahatma Gandhi also wanted to get rid of from Western hegemony in education and advocated contextualising education based on indigenous culture and language. Renowned Political Philosopher Prof. Dharmapal emphasized that contextualisation of education alone will help to liberate the colonized minds. Even after 75 years of Indian Independence, *status quo* is maintained in this regard. The aspiration to establish self-reliant India, demands urgent decolonisation of minds—financially, politically, culturally.

Reclaiming knowledge treasure in the field of social work is a constant struggle. *Bharatiyakaran* of Social work curriculum is need of the hour to complete the idea of social work as a profession. *Bharatiyakaran* stands for scientific, contextual, logical, holistic and integrated as well as multidisciplinary approach. It relates the content from societal point of view, taking into consideration local needs of the community in order to improve skills and efficiency of the social work professionals. *Bharatiyakaran* does not refer only to the glorious past; rather taking inspirations from the experience of ages solves the present problems. The Chhandogya Upanishad mentions service as a means to achieve the divinity within. Sage Aushastipada's verses about the service of humanity described as worship of divinity as '*Vaishwanar Sadhana*' is an eternal inspiration for modern social work not taking back to the 12th century. *Bharatiyakaran* is a forward-looking approach. Prime Minister Narendra Modi exhorts all to be 'Vocal for Local' and former US President Donald Trump also gave a call—'Be American buy American'. The whole world is virtually gravitating to the idea of *Swadeshi* (Self-Reliant Model of Economy). Hence, contextual thinking be it social work education, rural development or economy is very important and timely. There is also need to widen the spread of the concept and propogating the urgent need of *Bharatiyakaran* of Social work education in other Asian countries. This is the only way to liberate the social work curriculum from Western hegemony as the world has now realised that—one size does not fit all. Be it Economics, entrepreneurship or health sector; theories or models that are suitable in West may not work in the East. Thus, indigenous perspective is most appropriate as it considers the needs of indigenous population. Social work education has to be contextualized in a more decentralized manner to acclimatize with the trust, faith and way of life of the diverse masses, their indigenous working style and behaviour. Contextualisation of social work has to happen according to the needs of the society at local level.

The Concept of *Bharatiyakaran* is also on the lines of modernisation. Modernisation is not to be understood synonymous to

Westernisation. Modernisation is being contemporary and being able to adopt and address the context according to time. Contextualisation per se is not anti-Western. Contextualisation is keeping West to West. Decolonising the mind is much difficult in India as it has gone through tragic history of almost 200 years of colonisation. Europeans may have genuinely thought that uniformity is the only way. They even coined terms like 'white man's burden' claiming it to be their religious duty to civilize the whole world. Accordingly, India became victim of European cultural hegemony.

Bharatiyakaran of social work will have a much larger implication preserving all those Indic knowledge and traditions and is a positive attempt towards indigenising and decolonising social work education. I am sure this book '*Indigenising and Decolonising Social Work Education*' is a significant contribution for global social work fraternity and will be an essential reading for social work educators, researchers, students and practitioners and policy-makers.

Mukul Kanitkar
Eminent Academician and
Organising Secretary,
Bharatiya Shikshan Mandal,
Nagpur, India

Preface

Social Work profession, by and large, is a way of helping people who is in need. Social Work emerged as an academic discipline globally during the period of industrial revolution in United Kingdom and United States of America to address the dire needs of people who were the victims of new social order. With the passage of time, American-Euro-centric knowledge and western perspectives are meticulously enforced in the existing literature for Social Work curriculum offered all over the world. As a result, social work researches are bound to employ the western perspectives to understand the problems of native and consequently fail to capture the actual issues. It further undermines popular and indigenous knowledge systems. However, the debate on indigenisation *vis-à-vis* universalisation of social work knowledge is progressing at global level. The movement for Bharatiyakaran of Social work education aims at indigenising the social work education in Indian context.

Decolonisation does not stand completely against American-Euro centric knowledge base or even the Western paradigm of social work. It mainly rejects the Western world-view and the way of understanding society from the Western perspectives. It further challenges and critiques the Western hegemony, colonial legacy and professional imperialism in social work education. However, some South Asian countries and Africa have developed their own indigenous perspectives, drawing inspiration from their local rich cultural and philosophical wisdom. Indigenisation mainly strives to include indigenous wisdom and philosophies in the models, principles, values, and approaches to social work. The basic foundation of social work is humanism, which exist in every society. Therefore, the present volume has highlighted the need for indigenous literature of Social Work as a respond to the immediate needs by finding locally viable solutions to local problems. Even in India, the University Grants Commission review committee has also emphasized to introduce such syllabi of social work that engage more with Indian social realities.

So, to strengthen social work profession and its development, indigenisation and decolonisation of social work education is a conscious step to rejuvenate the social work education in South Asian and African countries. The book has made a modest attempt in highlighting various issues and perspectives towards Indigenising and Decolonising social work education from India and South African countries. The book has been divided into two sections. Section A delineates various approaches and theories of Indic Social work and Section B describes on indigenising social work education in India, Nepal and Africa.

In the first chapter of Section A, 'Roots of Indian Social Work', Rathore, Nagar and Dash have analyzed Indian concepts in the context of social work. This article has made a detailed analysis of Indian approaches such as the Indian *Karma* theory, *Tridosha-Trigun* theory, *Purushartha* theory, *Tri Reed* principle, the *Antah Karan Chatushthya*, the sixteen *sanskara* (rites),*aashramvyavstha* and the Indian family system etc. In the second chapter, Rathore in her chapter has highlighted that each and every religion in the world has unique ways of their own to deal with mental health problems and have long line of practices based on their experiences with humanity. She in this chapter has emphasized the relevance of spirituality in social case work practice. Kumar and Prakash in their chapter have shed light on Aurobindo's Integrated Model for Social Case work Practice. Besides that, in their chapter has also discussed Aurobindo's views on Integral yoga and integrated philosophy. Mishra in her chapter narrated the significance of indigenization in social work education. The chapter has also tried to examine the historical analysis of group work in social work practice in the colonial era as well as presented the indigenous models of group work practice in India. Prakash in his chapter has described the Indian concept of Social work, '*Sewa*' as discussed in various Hindu scriptures. The Indian concept of social work is deeply rooted in the philosophy of oneness where the religion guides each one to immerse themselves with nature and other living beings. The concept of '*Daridra Narayana*' (Witnessing God in Poor) is the central concept of Hinduism which teaches each one that serving humanity should be done with the same fervour as serving the god. It is also promoted through the Upanishads which talks regarding the idea of universal prosperity and '*Vashudhaiv Kutumbakam*' (the whole world is a family) considering the whole world as a family. It echoes the moral values of a highly principled individual to not differentiate among people like mine and others. The same has been advised as the guiding principle for the relationship with nature. The Virtue of *sewa* guides a common Indian to live a life in harmony with society and nature to ensure the lowest negative environmental impact. Promoted through religion it gets the sanctity of God and is regarded as the unbreakable vows. It is important to explore the religious classical texts which form the foundation of social work and make it mandatory for everyone to perform the duty which takes the form of Dharma in texts. Prasad and Actovin in their chapter have described that in India, Religion has always played a significant part in all reform movements. The influence of religion is highly apparent, especially in the ongoing search for social and political correctness. In this chapter the authors have tried to give an overview of the inherent philosophy of Indian originated religions, i.e. Hinduism, Buddhism, Sikhism, and Jainism and its relationship with the growth of modern Social Work profession in India. In her chapter, Dimple Mishra has discussed the importance of '*Ashram*' in social work education. India is rich and resourceful country imbibed with various cultures, traditions, values and beliefs. With core age-based life stages, "*Ashram*" is one of the complex concepts of Dharma in Hinduism. It consists of four stages: *Brahmacharya, Grihastha, Vanprastha* and *Sannyas*. These stages are engrained with rich values of not only social work but various other values and beliefs, which stimulate the actual meaning of life. "*Ashrams*" are the guiding factors for individual functioning which in turn leads to proper societal operations. It is believed that if a person follows the path of "*Ashram*" rightly, he/she lives a healthy and contented life. "*Ashrams*" are divided into four parts with specific age limits prescribed in it and each stage is engrained with guiding values which shows us the correct and directional path in our lives. Rathore in her another chapter on *Triguna* theory of personality has discussed various types of personality structure and application of *Triguna* Theory of personality to balance the personality of human beings. Adhikary in his chapter develops a discussion and retrieval of Hindu concepts of *Purushartha, Varna ashram, Dharma, Karma, Papa* and *Punya* and extends them to bear upon the Indian Social Work Philosophy, as a broad context, as well as in a range of applications. It seeks to unpack the broadly vague Indian ethics and tradition into constituent parts and examines their role and relevance in the search of a resolution of the contemporary social problems from a social work practice perspective.Mahanty and Parmar in their chapter have highlighted the Sayajirao's contribution towards community development. Sayajirao ushered in progressive reforms in his Baroda model of development which is a great milestone in history of Social Work Education and Community Development in India.

In the first chapter of Section B, 'Sanskar, Religion and Region: Indigenising Social Work in Nepal', Lamichhane has discussed the sixteen rituals (*Sanskars*) of Hindu which is practiced and celebrated in almost all Hindu's life. In Hindu religion, *Sanskar* is the combination of culture, rituals, actions that serve as a means of passage and, also mark as the various *Ashrama* stages of life. *Ashrams* are the stages of the life of a human being. There are four *ashrams* that are mentioned in ancient texts, i.e. *Brahmacharya, Grihastha, Vanaprastha*, and *Sansyasha*. The *sanskar* is believed to aid people to attain peace of mind, spiritual nourishment and *moksha*. In Hindu religion, *Sanskaras* are the turning points of life and believed to be celebrated as festivals. Hence, celebrations are done in the major points of everyone's life since birth and also sometimes even in pre-birth. During the celebrations, people come together to convey their best regards and offer blessings to the concerned people giving *sanskar* the social flavour. This blends the social and religious actions to be a socio-religious ceremony. In her Chapter, Charity has discussed the challenges of the use of social work models because these models are primarily Western and are not relevant to African society. Social Work field education is an essential component of Social Work education. In this process, students learn in real-life settings and put into practice the theories and models taught in the classroom. Most of the models have foreign and European background. The students encounter problems and challenges in the application of the models. The results of her study showed that some of the methods used were family therapy, crisis intervention, and task-centred therapy. The challenges experienced by the students in the use of these models are culture, poverty, and inappropriate office settings as it is different from Western countries. Among other things, the study recommended that African Social Workers should strive and develop African-based models for social work intervention. In her chapter 'Building a Crime-Free Society Using African Traditional Parenting Model',Titilolaa highlights that Parenting is a great task; it is beyond feeding and clothing but the total well-being of a child: psychological, physical, physiological and spiritual. The best way to bring up a child favourably, distinctly and be resolute has to do with culture and tradition. Africa has a very rich culture which helps in the training to bring out disciplined individual. She has highlighted the parenting style in the context of Africa. She has emphasized that African parents have to look into the training of their children according to the cherished culture and tradition to curb crime in the society. Sahare in her chapter, 'African

Feminist Perspectives and Social Work Practice' describes that African feminism is a type of feminism innovated by African women that specially addresses the condition and needs of continental African women, specially, who reside not only on the African continent but also elsewhere. She has analyzed the present status of women in Africa. She has also discussed about the works of feminist women thinkers who have done social work for their welfare and betterment. African feminist thought is introduced, defined and examined as theoretical perspectives and model for professional social work practice. Developed by the African women, its utility may serve to alter the methods used with similar marginalized client population. In their chapter, Pavitra and Lokesh have attempted to explicate the role of social work intervention and people participation in the field of mental health. The chapter further represents the role of social work intervention that catered to the needs of the people with mental health issues on ground realities. In order to address the felt need among community people based on the findings of the study researcher organised participaory rural appraisal technique, community camp, one day workshop for lay counsellors, school mental health pogrammes and awareness programmes on mental health issues. All the programmes were envisioned to build a community where everyone has the first aid skills to support people with mental health issues. Pankaj and Jaspreet in their chapter have raised various challenges and concerns in indigenising social work education and practice in Indian context. Professional social work is evolving in India day by day. Social work as a profession need to deal with diverse groups of people. The needs, issues, problems, challenges, culture, beliefs and ideologies of the all the people is different. So is quite difficult to use the same model or approach to everyone. There is a lack of educational material and literature related to social work in the Indian context and those which are available have huge influence of West. As Indian social work curriculum is highly influenced by Western principles, ideologies, methods, approaches and practices, and hence not fully applicable in Indian society. Thus, the social work education and practice immediately demands complete changes and rely on visible indigenous solution for the local problems. Indigenous social work has recently become a popular term in social work literature, although very little empirical social work research inspired by Indigenous concepts and methodology can be seen in literature and in the last chapter, Jha has suggested various indigenous models of community development to cope with the ruins of Covid-19.

The book will be definitely be useful for social work academicians, practitioners, policy-makers and students of social work and other social science disciplines.

Bishnu Mohan Dash
Mithilesh Kumar

Contents

List of Contributors

Abhinav Prakash, Technical Secretary, Rashtriya Sewa, Bharati, Delhi. **Email:** abhinav.rsb@gmail.com

Adebowale, Titilola A., Ph.D., Department of Social work, Faculty of Education, University of Ibadan, Ibadan, Nigeria. **Email:** titade07@yahoo.com

Arul Actovin, Ph.D., Assistant Professor, Department of Social Work, Sri Ramakrishna Mission Vidyalaya, College of Arts and Science, Coimbatore. **Email:** arulactovin@gmail.com

Avnish Nagar, Ph.D., Associate Professor and Principal, Udaipur School of Social Work, Udaipur. **Email:** avnishnagar@gmail.com

Bhuvneshvari Poonam Rathore, Ph.D. Research Scholar, Udaipur School of Social Work, Udaipur. **Email:** bhuvneshwari9@gmail.com

Bishnu Mohan Dash, Ph.D., Associate Professor Department of Social Work, Dr. Bhim Rao Ambedkar College, University of Delhi, Delhi. **Email:** bishnudash2006@gmail.com

Charity Ngozi Uzuegbu, Ph.D., Senior Lecturer, Department of Social Work. University of Nigeria Nsukka, Enugu State, Nigeria. **Email:** charity.uzuegbu@unn.edu.ng

Chittaranjan Das Adhikary, Ph.D., Professor, Department of Sociology, Banaras Hindu University, Varanasi. **Email:** cdadhikary@gmail.com

Dimple Mishra, Ph.D., She has completed her Ph.D. from the School of Social Work, Indira Gandhi National Open University, New Delhi. **Email:** dm747542@gmail.com

Geeta Sahare, Ph.D., Professor, Department of Political Science, Lakhmibai College for Women, University of Delhi, Delhi. **Email:** geetasahare@yahoo.co.in

Jaspreet Singh, Ph.D., Research Scholar, Department of Social Work, Central University of Jammu. **Email:** jk.ladakh@gmail.com

Jayalaxmi R. Mohanty, Ph.D., Assistant Professor, Maharaja Sayajirao University of Baroda, Vadodara, Gujarat. **Email:** jaya8001@gmail.com

Lokesha, M.U., Ph.D., Associate Professor, Department of Social Work, Davanagere University, Karnataka. **Email:** lokeshmswtut@gmail.com

Mithilesh Kumar, Ph.D., Assistant Professor, Wardha Samaj Karya Sansthan, Mahatma Gandhi Antarrashtriya Hindi Vishwavidyalaya, Wardha. **Email:** mkt1980@gmail.com

M.N. Parmar, Professor, Maharaja Sayajirao University of Baroda, Vadodara, Gujarat. **Email:** mnp.msu@gmail.com

Mukul Kanitkar, Eminent Academician and Author. **Email:** madhyanchal@gmail.com

Pankaj Kumar, Ph.D., Scholar, Department of Sociology, Jamia Millia Islamia, New Delhi. **Email:** pankajnag04@gmail.com

Pavithra, A.V., Ph.D. Research Scholar, Department of Social Work, Davanagere University, Karnataka. **Email:** pavisprasad48@gmail.com

Pratik Sharma Lamichhane, Psychiatric Social Worker & Faculty Member, Department of Social Work, Tribhuvan University, Nepal. **Email:** pratik.sharma047@gmail.com

Rajan Prakash, Ph.D., Scholar, Department of Social Work, Jamia Millia Islamia, New Delhi. **Email:** rajanprakashssm@gmail.com

Rajaneesh Kumar Shukla, Vice Chancellor, Mahatma Gandhi Antarrashtriya Hindi Vishwavidyalaya, Wardha. **Email:** rksphilosophy@gmail.com

Shivani D. Mishra, Ph.D., Professor and Director, Department of Social Work, Sardar Patel University, Gujarat. **Email:** skdmishra1020@gmail.com

Sunil Prasad, Ph.D., Assistant Professor, Department of Social Work, University of Science and Technology, Meghalaya. **Email:** prasad.sunil17@gmail.com

Yugal Jha, Ph.D., Associate Professor and Head, Department of Political Science, KKM College, Pakur, Jharkhand. **Email:** yugaljha1@gmail.com

Section A

Indic Social Work: Theories and Approaches

1
Roots of Indian Social Work

Bhuvneshvari Poonam Kunwar Rathore, Avnish Nagar and
Bishnu Mohan Dash

With regard to the history of social work in India, almost everyone believes that it was only after the arrival of the British in India that the education of social work started in a systematic and scientific manner and that there was no Indian theory or practice for social work. There was no system, method, or model of social work in India. There were community services, but there were no trained social workers to do social work. Philanthropy was prevalent in India, but there was no formal and systematic arrangement for the maintenance and care of the needy and the underprivileged.

Social work in India had a philosophical background, but not a theoretical one. But, if the background of India is understood aesthetically, then in reality, these are only misleading assumptions. Indian society, social system, and civilization are not only the oldest in the world but are in continuous existence. Many ancient civilizations have disappeared from the world today, but Indian civilization is not only in existence but has also evolved over time.

It is, in some ways, a large and extremely complex society inhabited across a vast geographical area that has witnessed human life and its needs for thousands of years. How could it be possible that a society that has been trying to better the quality of human life, whose work can be observed even in subjects like *Kama Sutra* and *Arthashastra,* does nothing for social work?

That too, in a situation when a complex and diverse society needs it. India has also done a lot of work towards social work, but that work has not been recognised and given much importance because the approach to defining social work has been very limited. Certainly, every country in the world has its own unique ways and procedures for working for society. But when the theoretical basis of social work was being formally developed for modern education, not much attention was paid to the fact that the cultural and social background of each country is unique and its requirements would also vary accordingly.

Therefore, every country has unique approaches and methods that need to be recognised and accepted. By doing this, not only will this subject be enriched, but each country will get a syllabus tailored to the needs of society.

The Theoretical Foundation of Social Work in Ancient India

Western social work foundations and their experiments are altogether different in their nature from Indian social work foundations. They have been developed in India in such a way that they can blend well into Indian social life and develop into a sustainable, self-sufficient system for the people. so that no external power or organisation is required for their implementation. They were developed as a way of life.

In a dynamic society, when the principles of social work are in the hands of its people, they will keep improving and make changes in it from time to time according to their needs. While developing these types of living systems, their modalities will change, but their values will not be irrelevant. At the core of these principles were the values of maintaining, improvising, and developing society. Therefore, for improving systems and for reformers, this principle holds importance. Perhaps this is why many generations of social reformers had opportunities to work in India, and hence changes kept happening. So a significant thing that happened was that such social values took root in the core of Indian society.

The entire society believes in taking care of each other without any special formal education or training and constantly tries for it. Persistent efforts by individuals and organisations can be seen in Indian society for the deprived, aged, and people suffering from illnesses and disabilities. Efforts were made that no person in society should feel alone during a difficult time in life.

The aim of such traditions is to develop a sense of integration, love, and compassion, not only to live life organically but to give life a purpose, so that life does not become dull, cumbersome, and idolised. Many such clearly visible experiments are the result of ancient social theories in India. The only difference between Indian social work and the rest of the world is that India developed it and adopted it as a way of life, but did not document it nor promote it much as a theory.

Karma Theory

This theory has gained universal acceptance and significance. It has gained so much popularity in the whole world that it is called in public as an undeclared rule of justice. That "whatever you do, will turn around and come to yourself". In other words, what goes around comes around. Due to its influence, many religious sects have adopted and defined the Karma theory in their own way.

Its influence and importance in India can be accessed from the fact that, according to the rules of the sacred writings of Hindus, the Vedas are the most important religious texts. But today, if any ordinary Hindu is asked to mention the name of one of his most important spiritual texts, almost all of them will mention the *Shrimad Bhagavad Gita*, the small-sized book that is the best representative of *Karma theory*.

Though not as old as the *Vedas*, the *Gita* is considered the essence of the Vedas and Upanishads. If Karma theory is seen in its practical form, then it is the first social work principle in the world. It has also been adopted by religion, but at its core, it is a social work principle. The basic objective of social work is to develop a world where every person does good deeds, receives goodness and well-being, and creates an atmosphere of spreading wellness and helping the ones in need.

Karma principles teach every person not only their own responsibility but also motivate them to do good for themselves, which gives them reason and emotional and moral training to do something good for the world around them as well. The basic idea of Karma is that if everyone does everything with the right intention and right will, the world will become a better place.

To keep society going in the right direction and to maintain it, it is necessary to motivate it and make it capable of doing so itself more than any external system should. The aim of the Karma principle is to build a self-supporting, socially interdependent social base for human society.

If a person commits negative actions with anger, greed, hatred, violence etc. then these kinds of karmas cause misery, inequality, tension, conflict, jealousy, and disharmony in society. In the same way, if a person performs positive deeds with justice, love, peace, balance, compassion, self-respect, and prudence, then such karma spreads unity, harmony, peace, and happiness in the society and leads the society towards equitable development.

The decision of karma to be moral or immoral is left to the conscience of the person. The conscience of a person is considered to be its real decider.

It has been said that importance should be given to every person, and his/her wisdom, personal opinion, and self-determination are important.

It is also believed that the conscience of every normal person gives him a feeling of happiness when his deeds are moral and right and of sorrow when they are immoral.

Human instincts make him understand the difference between morality and immorality on his own. In the book *Gita*, which is the proponent of karma theory, it is said that the nature of karma is realised through feelings and outcomes.

Important points related to the Karma theory

- The origin of this idea is from the Upanishads. It has also been propounded by the Samkhya philosophy.
- The credit for making it clearly explained and popular in practice goes to the *Bhagavad Gita* (BC 3100).
- Its founder and first proponent is the great Indian *Kaal Purush* Shri Krishna, whose epic presence enriched Indian philosophy and social work around 5000 years ago.
- A detailed description of this is found in Patanjali's *Yoga Sutras*, Buddhist texts, and many other Indian texts.
- It has been so popular and important in India that all philosophies and religious sects have adopted it in some form and have also defined it according to their own.
- It is also called Karma Yoga.
- These functions are the causal principle.
- It talks about the self-reliance of a person and being the creator of their life.

On the basis of the *falprakruti* (result-based), it was divided into two parts: *Kamya Karma* (desired) and *Nishkam Karma* (selfless) (Vedvyas chap. 2. 40).

They are also divided into *Kayik* (somatic), *Vachik* (speech), and *Mansik* (mental work). Four types of deeds are considered through actions we do ourselves.

Through actions that others take on our instructions.
Through words.
Through thoughts. (Vedvyas, Chapter 5, Verse 11.)

Infants, innocent young children, and animals' karma do not fall under the principle because they are unable to distinguish between right and wrong. This principle favours human conscience and freedom of choice. It also talks about equality and the importance of all.

Several forms of karma are also classified, such as

> *Karma*: Work done by a person,
> *Akrama*: Nishkama Karma without any expectation or desire for fruit/result, and
> *Vikarma:* the deeds that a person must do, but he leaves them due to any attachment, greed, laziness, or corrupt/unethical deeds that are caused by excessive greed or desire (Vedvyas chap. 4. 16).

The Life Arrangements of Three Rinas (Debts), Three Purusharths, and Three Ashrams

Creating a synergy between the individual's personal life and self-development while harmonising the order and balance of society has always been a subject of the struggle for humanity. When we try to realise and give importance to one, injustice starts with the other. Socialism, nationalism, liberalism, and capitalism are all frequently based on this uncertainty. Subjects like sociology, political science, economics, jurisprudence, and ethics also get confused on the question of what should be accomplished. Are people for the country and society, or is the country and society for the people? If more freedom is given to the individual, social systems have to be limited. Which creates a state of chaos. At the same time, if you create social order and discipline too much, then the freedom of one's life starts to get hampered.

At the place of conflict between the opposing demands of the individual and society, a life system was developed in India. It is able to establish a beautiful co-ordination at the place of conflict between the opposing demands of the individual and society.

At this time, the social system was tied to these solid principles. These are the principles that have not only been seen in Indian society for a long time but have also been highly successful in their times. These three principles, when combined, provided a model for Indian life.

These are different principles, but together they form a smooth and beautiful social system in which the goals, duties, and tasks for different periods of life are given as per their requirements. The most unique thing is that those who will be the exception or want to do something for themselves other than this, were given freedom of choice and a place in it.

Three Ashrams

Human life requires constant self-discipline and self-learning. Sigmund Freud has given Psychosexual Development Theory in the context of different steps of life. In his theory, life is divided into five steps. This theory puts life from zero to fifteen years of life in the first four stages, and the rest of life in one phase (McLeod, 2019; Fisher, S. & Greenberg, 1996; Freud, 1905). This seems a little preposterous because keeping a life span after adolescence in just one phase is not doing complete justice to it. The complexity of life also develops and changes in other stages of age.

Erikson's Stages of Psychosocial Development Theory looks at life in eight steps in more detail, but it focuses more on the individual's emotional conflicts and their selection (McLeod, 2018).

In India, the developmental task theory was brought into practice in the Ashram system as a social experiment. The Ashram system is mentioned in Sanskrit literature and in all the ancient social contexts of India. In the Upanishads, the first mention of the ashram system is found. Only three ashrams (*Brahmcharya, Grihasth,* and *Vanprasth*) are mentioned in the early *Upanishads*, such as the *Chandogyopanishad.* Then, in the last Upanishads and during the *Ramayana* period, another ashram was supplemented, which was a *sanyas ashram*, as required and for some exceptions (Kaane, 2014).

But basically, these three *ashrams* were classified according to the three dimensions and times of life. Let there be no incompleteness in an individual's life; let the quality of life be fulfilled and he should get all the possibilities of success at the physical and individual level. Therefore, three goals were considered for life, which was called *Purushartha. These are Dharm, Artha,* and *Kama.*

In the course of time, another goal was added to it, which was not at all compulsory for all people, but left to their free will. This was called *Purushartha Moksha,* which was a complete spiritual achievement of the individual. To achieve this, a final *ashram* was also added, which is called the *Sannyas Ashram*. Earlier, *Vanaprastha* and *Sannyas* were considered to be the same.

In Vanaprastha, the person kept in touch with his family and also worked for social welfare. But in the *Sannyas Ashram*, the person completely disengaged from society and family tried to walk the path of liberation by becoming self-oriented.

In the Vedic and Upanishad era, complete detachment from society, family, and *sanyas* was not given much importance. Because symbiosis was considered better for human life, but exceptions and the choices of the individual should also be respected, therefore, *Sannyas Ashram* was given importance. The *Mahabharata* text also does not consider *Sannyas Ashram* to be suitable for everyone (Chapter 61 of the Shanti Parva, verses 1-14).

The period of life in which all four *Purusharth* could be attained was called "*Ashram*". According to *Bhrigu Rishi*, "The purpose of the ashram system was to give order to the life of a man so that he could develop his life properly." (Manu Smriti, 6.88, 2020). In order to give importance to the selection of a person, three types of alternatives were given, which are called *Ashram Samuchya, Ashram Vikalpa,* and *Bagh.*

Ashram Samuchya: Complete all the ashrams accordingly.

Ashram Vikalpa: If the person wants to complete all the four ashrams, he can skip any one or two ashrams as per his wish. For example, if someone wants to leave the sannyas ashram, he can leave.

Adopt one ashram entirely in your life, such as Gruhast Ashram.

The word "ashram" is derived from the Sanskrit word "labour", which means "to try" or "to labour". P.H. Prabhu has provided two interpretations. (1) Work Location and (2) Work-related activities (Prabhu, 2019: 83).

Under this, a person rests for some time at all levels (*ashrams*) and then enters the next level. Here, rest means no relaxation, but preparing for the next level (*ashram*). An *ashram* is also a place for preparation and planning for the next phase of life. At that time, assuming the average or full life of man was a hundred years, all the *ashrams* were divided into a span of twenty-five years each. But this age division was not so rigid; it could change depending on the capacity and life circumstances of the person. It was completely dependent on the person.

Brahmacharya Ashram

This *ashram* was considered to be the period in a person's life when they received education and training in their field of interest. This period was also to learn discipline and duties in life. In this ashram, a person was required to acquire skills and practice them even after being away from home.

Self-discipline and observance of rules also required learning the art of restraint and patience. It remains until age 25 to 30 years of age. Most of it was completed in 25 years, and it entered the next *ashram*, the *Grihasth Ashram.*

Those who used to get education in this ashram period were called *Vidyasnatak,* and those who proved to be good in self-discipline were called *Vrat Snatak.* Those who had proficiency in knowledge, skills, and self-discipline were called Vidhya Vrat Snatak. All three types of practices were conducted in this ashram—

- Living in an academic environment.
- To be in lively contact with society.
- To be in solitude for study, thinking, and meditation.

During this *ashram* period, the goal was set that the person would be able to set the direction of his whole life, understand his duties and three debts, and achieve life goals to prepare himself.

Gruhast Aashram

This *ashram* has been given the highest importance and appreciation in ancient literature. This *ashram* is considered the basis of society because a person discharges his family and social responsibilities in this *ashram*. "*Arth*" and "*Kama Purusharth*" are attained in this ashram. This has been considered the basic, necessary, and natural desire of man. In the *Gita*, Shri Krishna said that those "karmas" which are not opposed to "Dharma" (religion) are superior to "Kama" and human attachment to "Artha" and "Kama" is natural.

According to the *Mahabharata*, the importance of *Grihasth Asram* is equal to the combined importance of the remaining three *ashrams*, because only in this *ashram* can some work be done for the gods, ancestors, and guests (*Mahabharata* 12.12.18, 2020).

In the *Grihasth Ashram*, a person selects his spouse, marries, and runs the household. Hence, it is called the *Grihasth Ashram*, but at its core, the purpose of this *ashram* is not just to get married.

In this *ashram*, a person has to give meaning to their lives by being socially productive and useful. This middle phase of a person's life is also considered the most effective period of their life. Everything he learned at *Brahmacharya Ashram* was put into practice.

The main functions of this *ashram* are as follows:

- To be independent and to be the protector of others.
- Earning wealth, power, and fame.
- Creating a place in society.
- Performing duties for society and the family.
- To achieve prosperity and happiness, as well as to fulfil one's desires.
- Obtaining a "kama" companion and giving birth.
- The dominance of productive and creative life.

Vanaprastha and Sannyas

The age for *Vanaprastha* is estimated to be after the age of 50. It is left to the discretion of the person when he considers himself ready for this stage of life. Roughly all the ancient literature says that when a person sees himself again and is detached, then he is ready for *Vanaprastha*.

According to the *Mahabharata*, when the householder becomes old, his children also have children. That is, when the child is able to handle all the responsibilities of the householder, then if the person wishes, he should take *Vanaprastha* with his wife or alone.

In this way, the children used to get privacy and freedom in their lives. The family was also free from problems and stress arising from the generation gap. Being a veteran, there was an effort to keep the person free from attachment, unnecessary stress, and workload.

In this *ashram*, a person used to live a life of sacrifice, restraint, self-examination, self-study, self-reliance, and purity. In this, the person kept trying to do for the welfare of society by staying away from materialism.

He used to take advantage of his life experience, studies, and thinking in public service. *Vanaprasthi* was actually a social servant. He was considered free from family obligations during the maturity of his life.

This is a vacation period free from the chaos of everyday life and it was left to him to dedicate that time. It also enabled him to seek peace, which is, in any case, the most pressing need in his life at the moment.

Generally, the options that "*Vanaprasthi*" used to choose these options are:

- To work for society and the public welfare.
- to impart their experience and knowledge through teaching in society and *gurukuls*.
- self-study and writing.
- Pilgrimage, excursions, and living in nature.
- Strive for spiritual growth.
- It is a religious practice as well as a form of meditation.
- Thinking and contemplating in solitude.
- If you are interested in learning an art, you can do so.

In the *Vanaprastha* phase, when the interest in spirituality increased, one could choose the *Sannyas Ashram*. This used to be a time of complete spiritual practice and a path to attaining the supreme truth of life. In the *Sannyas Ashram*, a person was separated from the world and was trying to achieve self-development.

Purusharth

Abraham Maslow gave the idea of "A Theory of Human Motivation: Hierarchy of Needs" in 1943. It is considered one of the important theories of human developmental psychology. It talks about the progressively increasing order of the human mind, its development and life requirements (McLeod, 2020; Maslow, 1943; Maslow, 1954).

According to this, the order of one's psychological desires and needs after the completion of one moves towards the other. In Indian literature, this type of theory is given a more elaborate dimension as *purushartha.*

Indian theory speaks of the needs of the whole society along with the individual and coordinates the wishes of both. The *Purushartha* theory or doctrine sets the natural desire of man as its goal at different stages of human life. While the four *purusharthas* are mentioned, the fourth *purushartha*, "*Moksha*", is considered rare and not compulsory for all people because it is related to spiritual supremacy.

The other three *purusharthas* have been called "*Triverga*". These three efforts are called *dharma, artha* and *kam*. *Purușhartha* refers to attaining human goals and desires. Its literal meaning is "*Purush + artha,*" which means something that gives meaning to a man's life. Something that makes the person or their lives meaningful. Here, "*Purusha*" is not referring to a particular gender but rather to a thoughtful, awakened person. Whereas the word "*arth*" is used here as a *lakshya*, or purpose, or life goals. Hence, *purushartha* is what gives purpose to a person. The attainment of *Purusharthas* gives a person the meaning and completeness of his life so that he does not experience incompleteness in himself. *Purushartha* also advises the individual on how to become involved in society.The theory of human progress and society is called "*Purushartha*". The idea behind this theory is that the natural goal of human life is to achieve happiness.

Spiritual attainment is the highest form of happiness and contentment, but it is necessary to first motivate and regularise it to attain its natural pleasures. Because ultimately, spiritual progress can also be attained by a very happy and satisfied person.

Dharma Purusharth

The other two are achieved as a result of this, and they are given significance. It is called Dharma Purushartha, but here the word Dharma does not mean the word "religion" in English. Religion is used in many meanings and types in Hindi. The context in which religion is mentioned here is clear from this verse, "*Dharayateitidharmaha,*" which should be attained in religion. To attain what is to be attained. In the *Mahabharata,* persistence in *karma* and qualities like generosity, truth, charity, and kindness have been called "*Dharniya Dharma*".

Even in the *Mahabharata*, it has been written, explaining the religion that "*Dharaṇad Dharmamityahu: Dharmo Dhariyate Praja*" means to attain what is to attain. Something which is followed by society is *dharma* (Vedvyas, Vanaparva 208.9, 33.53, Shantiparva 162.5, 259.16, 2020).

There are three types of *Viveka* (conscience), and *Nirnaya Buddhi* (intelligence of doing the right thing).

- *Regular or daily dharma*: The virtue of carrying out one's daily duties and actions correctly.
- *Vishishtha Dhrama*: The ability to make the right decisions and actions in extraordinary circumstances and occasions.
- *Aapada Dharma*: Flexibility, patience, prudence, and calmness during adverse or tense situations.

In the context of *purushartha*, *Dharma* means acquiring or holding the conscience or morals of good and evil.

Duties that a person considers to be *manan* (deep reflection): Thoughtfully doing good things can be called *dharma*, as can acting responsibly towards one's family, society, environment, and nation of birth.

"*Dharm Purusharth*" has been seen as the duty and work from which the fabric of the life of society and human beings has been woven together. In "*Dharma Purushartha*", understanding, discretion, and knowledge are adopted as practices in life.

This is the first goal of life because if a person acquires knowledge and wisdom and adopts it in life, then the other goals are easy to attain for him. At *Brahmacharya Ashram*, *Dharma* (knowledge, wisdom, and understanding) is achieved based on the principle that lays the foundation of life to earn *Artha* (wealth) and *Kama* (desires). Indian society values the happiness and prosperity of a person, but the happiness of one should not become sorrow for someone else, so *dharma* (conscience or wisdom) was made the criterion.

Through religion, the happiness of the family, society, and nation has been ensured, along with the happiness of the individual. Also, when a person receives pure and innocent pleasures, they are free from guilt and regret.

For example, if wealth and possessions or *karma* are obtained through unrighteous (immoral) ways, it becomes a burden on the conscience of the person. He remains fearful, or he may have to face apprehensions or problems in life.

Tri Debt

Ancient Indian society has been giving more importance to humanism than individualism. As a result, it has proudly declared "*Svasmaswalpamsamajayasarvasva*," which translates as "small for self and all for society". That is why the tri-debt principle has gained so much importance in the life of society and the individual. The tri-debt theory is so old that it is like the ideal principle of the Indian way of life; no one can be its exponent, but the entire culture can be credited for its origin and development. *Panch* Debt (five debts) is also mentioned in a few places, but at its root, these are only three debts. In addition to the *Dev* debt, *Rishi* debt, and *Pitra* debt, the *Atithi* debt and *Jeeva* debt are also included in the five debts, which is basically an extension of these three. As a theory, it is also believed that the duties performed to repay these debts are also called "*tapa*" or "*yagya*".

The actual meaning of *Yagya* is to sacrifice for someone else. An Indian person considers his life to be meaningful or successful only if he is able to pay off these three debts as much as possible during his lifetime. The meaning of these debts is that every person who has got this precious life or whatever he has received spontaneously in life is due to the hard work of earlier generations, great learned people, and nature's blessings. Whatever he has got in his life and inheritance, it is the duty of the person to show gratitude and respect towards it. The most important thing is that he should carry this forward in life and add the next generation on his behalf.

Pitra Debt

For all the biological information related to the body's DNA and the characteristics associated with it (name, surname, wealth, heritage, history etc.), people are indebted to their earlier generations. Science also agrees that the physical and mental characteristics that an individual acquires through inheritance make up a large part of his personality. To feel gratitude for all this is the aim and the principle of *pitra* debt. Due to the previous generation, only the existence of the present generation has become possible. *Pitra* debt can be repaid by honouring the chain of life and by moving it forward to the next generation. It is also about respecting human biological desires and needs. The basic rule of life and existence is that not only human beings, but every organism and even every cell in nature, has this biological goal of life. Whatever possesses it, by giving it to the next cell, considers his life to be complete. Then, in a sense, it does not die and its existence in the form of a new cell remains. No life should become the last part of the chain. Therefore, in order to be free from *pitra* debt, importance has been given to procuring children.

The idea behind *pitra* debt is that individuals and human society are adding a good sense to procure or birth-giving, which can change the perspective of life. There are two ways to repay ancestral debt: fulfilling their duties as their offspring and completing the works left by them, and giving birth to and nurturing a child.

And second, to conserve and enhance the lives of other creatures of nature. The thought that "our lives depend on others" should be brought into life. The first condition of maintaining a good human life is to save the environment, respect every living being and be aware of our duties towards the environment.

Human life is also not possible if the animals, flora, and fauna do not exist, so give them respect as our ancestors and take care of them because our existence is due to them. There are many ways to repay the *pitra* debt. It may be watering the plants, feeding the ants, birds, or animals. The other way of paying off the pitra-debt is by serving every organism.

Developing Debt

Resources such as clean air, water, sunlight, fire, flora and fauna, etc., are all divine and necessary for human life. To protect them and not misuse them is a way to repay dev-debt (divine debt). To perform duties that are in favour of all, i.e. nature, the environment, the earth and its inhabitants, which includes all life, including plants, animals and humans.

To work for the well-being of one's family, society, nation, and the entire world, sacrificing when necessary. Willing to give is also a way to repay the debt. Human life is not meaningful unless some good deeds and duties are performed selflessly for the world around them.The world becomes a good place by helping and doing good for each other, which is the principle of development debt. There are many ways to help others, including doing physical labour for someone, helping them in an emotional way, or helping them financially. These are also ways of repaying *dev* debt.

Rishi Debt

One of the reasons for humans' dynamic development, as well as a significant difference between them and animals, is that when animals begin to learn, they learn and practice the same things in every generation at the same pace level.

They have not developed the ability to pass on the incidents they have seen, the experience they have gathered, and things they have thought by writing them down or by any other medium to the next generation.

They can teach their offspring life skills and fundamental ways to live and survive, but they can not deliver the detailed information and knowledge gained to the next generation by the means of communication or books. Whereas humans are prosperous and in the abundance of the knowledge, information, and skills provided to them by their previous generations, they have actually gained so much. We have not only been prosperous but have developed so much.

Therefore, *rishi* debt means that if a person has learned anything from anywhere or anyone, or has gained any kind of skill or knowledge, it is a debt on him. If he has received the gift of knowledge, it is his utmost duty to try to pass on the knowledge as much as possible to someone else. Rishi debt means carrying forward or adding to the chain of knowledge and being grateful for the fact that they acquired it. At the same time, he should make sure that the knowledge he has acquired should not remain unknown, as well as that people should not be unaware of it. It should move forward. Everyone should get a chance to be proud of their knowledge and the fact that they spread it.

Through the medium of the principle of tri debt, a person does not only fulfil his duties but also gets a feeling of pride by doing things that might seem ordinary but are actually done to live the principle of tri debt. At the same time, this theory constantly inspires him to do well in life. Hence, it leads society towards the healthy maintenance of sustainable social development.

Based on such policies and social theories, a unique structure was developed in India. This structure was based on decentralised governance and power at social and economic levels. Therefore, India was able to form a democratic self-reliant unit at the village level. This can be seen as the first experiment in democracy at the grassroots level.

The dynamic India has been making new models and theories of its development according to demands and necessities.

Rural communities have existed in the agrarian society in India since ancient times. It is not only mentioned in the Rig-Veda, which was written in 1200 BC, but the existence of gram sabha (village council) and the role of eminent people in it is seen in practice around 600 BC also. These village councils served as a conduit for raising local issues with higher- ups (Jha, 2017).

The policies of rural administration and development of Chanakya (Maurya period, 283 BCE) are quite notable and are considered to be the basis of present-day panchayats and village self-reliance models.

Decades ago, while giving his views on the rural environment of India, Gandhiji said, "The independence of India should mean the freedom of the whole of India, and this freedom must start from the bottom up." Only then will each village become a republic, so each village should be self-sufficient and capable. Society will be a parameter whose apex will depend on its base.

He wrote in his book, "*Mere Sapno Ka Bharat*," that "Every village should have all the qualities of a republic. All the powers of the executive, legislature, and judiciary should be with the Panchayat along with independence, decentralization, and self-governance. The decision should be made by consensus or in the public interest, not by counting votes" (Gandhi, 2014).

The village will manage at its level the responsibility of basic amenities for the people, like food, clothes, housing etc., and the accountability of the people's representatives elected by the people will be ensured.

The concept of rural self-governance was the main focus of Gandhi's thought. We should understand the concept of Gram Swaraj in the context of his two main principles—truth and non-violence. Gram Swaraj is a specific principle propounded by Gandhiji and later carried forward by Acharya Vinoba Bhave through the Bhoodan movement.

According to Gandhiji, the word "*swaraj*" means "a continuous effort towards independence and self-reliance," which defines self-government in the true sense. The true meaning of "Gram Swaraj," according to Gandhiji, is to be self-confident in one's own production for one's own use, education, and economic prosperity.Gandhiji conceived of Swaraj in the context of a sacred concept whose fundamental elements are self-discipline and self-restraint.

Trusteeship: In 1903, when Mahatma Gandhi was in South Africa, he propounded the principle of trusteeship. At the core of Gandhiji's theory of trusteeship is the idea that the real owner of capital is not the owner but the whole society.

The owner is only the custodian of that property. Gandhiji believed that the wealth that industrialists possessed was passed down to them in the form of a legacy. He also said that due to capitalism, unemployment has increased all over the world and the importance of labour has decreased. Unemployment has weakened the smallest unit of society. If the rich do not voluntarily give up their wealth and the power derived from it and do not make ordinary people partners in their interests, then surely one day there will be a violent and bloody revolution like the ones that have happened in many countries in the past. He believed the solution to all these problems lay in the principle of trusteeship.

In the principle of trusteeship, the person who accumulates wealth more than he needs has the right to use the property only for the fulfilment of his needs. The remaining property should be managed by him as a trustee and spent on social welfare.

Industrialists and high-income people should limit their needs; only then can the remaining income be spent on the needy. This principle was termed impractical by a large section of intellectuals as a Utopia. Many people criticised his concept of trusteeship, but Gandhiji believed in his principle. Therefore, he started meetings with industrialists and rich people to explain the trusteeship concept and was successful to a great extent in persuading them.

Hundreds of industrialists who agreed with the idea of trusteeship established charitable trusts and foundations and established dozens of educational institutions, hospitals etc.

Among many industrialists who followed the idea of trusteeship, Jamnalal Bajaj was one who adopted a simple lifestyle along with his family. Jamsedji Tata, on the other hand, started using trusteeship in practice even before 1903. The question arises whether in modern India, where big industrialists not only display their luxury spending but also publicise it using the media.

Can trusteeship be considered relevant in such a situation? Presently, these industrialists have become corporate industrialists and engage in corporate social responsibility expenditure to get exemption from corporate tax. Today, there are many industrialists in India who are happy to establish a charitable foundation and trust for their industry and spend a large part of their wealth on social development activities like educational development, rural health, development of indigenous sports and public welfare work. It is necessary to give a live example to show the relevance.

The name of Azim Premji, an Indian IT industrialist and founder of Wipro, is notable here. He donated half of his assets worth Rs. 53 thousand crore to the Azim Premji Foundation. This foundation is mainly doing important work to build the teaching capacity of school teachers in 6 states and one Union territory in India.

In the age of the luxuriant show of the West, industrialists are competing to display their richness. In such a situation, approximately 5 per cent of the country's industrialists are voluntarily using the trusteeship idea in practice successfully for social service, indicating that this principle can be considered practical and relevant in modern India.

REFERENCES

Fisher, S., Greenberg, R.P. (1996). *Freud Scientifically Reappraised: Testing the Theories and Therapy.* New York: Wiley.

Freud, S. (1905). Three essays on the theory of sexuality. *Standard Edition 7*: 123- 246.

Jha, A.K. (2017). *Gram Vikas or Samaj*. Delhi: National Book Trust.

Kane, P.V. (2014). *Dharmshastra ka Itihas.* Lucknow: Uttar Pradesh Hindi Sansthan.

Manu, M. (2020). *Manu Smriti.* New Delhi: Prabhat Prakashan.

Maslow, A.H. (1954). *Motivation and Personality*. New York: Harper and Row.

________. (1943). A theory of human motivation. *Psychological Review, 50*(4), 370-96.

McLeod, S.A. (2019, July 18). *Psychosexual stages*. Simply Psychology. https:/ /www.simplypsychology.org/psychosexual.html.

________. (2018, May 3). *Erik Erikson's Stages of Psychosocial Development.* Simply Psychology. https://www.simplypsychology.org/Erik-ErErikson, E. H. (1950). Childhood and Society. New York: Norton.ikson.html

________. (2020, March 20). *Maslow's Hierarchy of Needs*. Simply Psychology. https://www.simplypsychology.org/maslow.html

Prabhu, P.H. (2019). *Hindu Social Organization: A Study of the Socio-Psychological and Ideological Foundations.* New Delhi: Sage Publication.

Vedvyas. (2018). *Shrimadbhagavad Gita*. Gorakhpur: Geeta Press.

________. (2020). *Mahabharata*. Gorakhpur: Geeta Press.

2

Relevance of Spirituality and Religious Methods for Social Case Works Practice

for Mental Health Support in Major Religions

Bhuvaneshwari Poonam Kunwar Rathore

Introduction

Spirituality and religion is the belief system of the person. Psychiatry or mental health are pure scientific concepts. Generally, we divide the study methods into three parts: Arts, Science and Commerce. If we are to keep religion and spirituality into one method, that method would be Arts. Science and Arts are in two completely opposite directions or dimensions that are not similar in any way but surprisingly mental health is a field where these two polar opposites meet. During the course of Psychoanalysis we study the thoughts, emotions, conscious and subconscious mind of the person and try to untangle layers in any of the above-mentioned dimensions and try to get to the bottom of the thoughts causing such tangles.

Whereas, spirituality and religion helps a person to develop trust and thoughts, Religion and Spirituality are important pillars of the foundation of thought and basis of any further study into it. While working on psychiatry of the person, ignoring this major part could lead to a vacuum in the treatment plan.

Every person has his own unique system of faith and belief whose foundation is already put during their childhood. During their childhood, their mind and emotions are taken shape. Each incident and memory adds a new and unique colour to the canvas of their inner self. Even if the person has been raised in an atheist family, Atheism itself represents a belief. They believe in being atheist but do believe. In psychiatric practice, what is important is how strong the belief is, not what the belief is into.

If the person was religious during childhood and turned Atheist due to any circumstances, this change of belief must have left a mark on their conscience. This change may become an integral part of their psychological condition which should not be neglected during the course of therapy. The first step of psychotherapy is in winning the trust of the client and understanding their beliefs and further work accordingly. Similar cultural background and language between the client and therapist is the basic rule of counselling.

Since time immemorial, every invention has come from the necessity of mankind; hence it is the mother of all inventions. When the man discovered the use of fire and stone, started living in a community and created units of family, this social behaviour leads him towards some beliefs. The primitive man was scared of every element, thing, incidents and creature that was beyond his control. He was Fearful of the unknown. To win over the fear of the uncontrolled unknown, he chose to have faith in the Unknown superpower.

He may now go to sleep fearlessly by believing that this utmost powerful unknown Superpower is his saviour. An unknown that is omnipresent, infinite which controls everything. This thought process and trust gave an immense power to mankind which then evolved into a belief system. Anthropologists and historians believe that during the course of evolution, things the man did not require any more started to extinct gradually such as tail and fur etc.

The faith in the unknown remained important for his inner self, which later evolved into a system over the millenniums. A spiritual revolution has followed by every social, industrial and scientific revolutions around the world. The Faith of revering nature slowly progressed into rituals, philosophy and eventually meditation. As a result, spiritual beliefs and their system became an integral part of man's life and consciousness.

The symptoms of any physical illness are quite evident which makes it easier for the person to understand the problem and decide whether to go to a physician or an orthopedic surgeon etc. But in the case of a mental illness, it becomes very difficult for them to understand what actually happening to them. They cannot able to find out the cause of the problem.

Many common disorders including depression, panic attacks, anxiety etc. are very confusing to the persons who are suffering; they struggle to understand what is happening to them. For instance, there is no real reason to be so frightened during a panic attack. Just a feeling of emptiness during the depression and feeling sad without something having gone wrong in reality. Losing interest in things and laying low is the symptoms that occur generally. The sudden occurrence of such feelings draws the man towards his religious and spiritual faith. To fight the unknown cause and its circumstances, he uses his inner faith as a natural instinct.

He grew up listening and believing in the infinite might of God which also becomes the greatest assurance at that time for him/her. His/her prayers and the place of faith becomes the ultimate comfort zone where he/she can accept his fear and believes that he/she is surrounded by sorrows. As a matter of fact, the principle of acceptance is one of the founding principles of psychotherapy. Since he/she is in need of a quick support, this gives him/her a chance to accept and surrender without the fear of being judged. It also liberates him/her from the pressure of having to look like a happy and successful person and not to spoil the happy image in society as well as friends and family.

This surrender, acceptance and the ability to say it all to god and to go in his/her shade gives quick support and stability of thoughts as well frees him/her from worries, and at times also frees him/her from mental illnesses. It certainly not too difficult to observe that many mental health cases, especially during the beginning (and not too complex) gets cured and the person does not even realize that it was a psychological disorder. It is not an exaggeration to say that spirituality has stopped mental disorders from emerging on a massive scale through its methods of faith, acceptance, surrender and assurance. The same methods also become the foundation of counselling and psychotherapies. Going to spiritual people to seek help after not feeling well on the psychological level is a common practice or at least is seen as the first choice. The problem is that they are hesitant to go to mental health experts because they are afraid of being tagged as mental health patients, which is seen as taboo in society. The need is to see the psychological illnesses just as normally as we see the physical illnesses. There is a huge lack of public awareness in this regard.

A person going through mental health problems is afraid of being laughed at. They struggle a lot to present themselves as normal beings. They lack the courage of speaking/accepting normally about it as they do with other physical health conditions. The truth is, from a normal person to someone with a psychiatric disorder, every individual's mental well-being needs efforts and care. Every kind of individual struggles and keeps trying to maintain the balance within themselves in one way or another. Everyone needs help and support in keeping that balance within themselves at one point of time or another.

All the religions of the world have understood this significant need of the human mind through its long experience. Hence, they all developed several methods on their levels of working on the mind and consciousness of the human being. Since psychiatry was not so developed in those times, this responsibility was being carried by religion. To the extent that if any religion fails in making a person feel safe or in helping his *Mann* (mind) to be happy and in becoming a better person, it comes into doubt and even starts losing its identity.

Besides creating a social structure, the major/ basic/fundamental role of religion has been to keep the people's confidence high and to help them prosper on moral and spiritual levels. Religion started to understand the human mind as well develop methods accordingly even several centuries before when Psychiatry started its deep study on it. These methods can be seen regularly practiced worldwide in many ways, in many cultures and groups of people, but there is a need to put more effort into researching and studying so psychiatry can benefit from it.

Main characteristics of good mental health are not having any mental illnesses, the positive development of the person and their inner self and having the courage to fight any circumstances in life. It also includes keeping one self-calm and not losing control in adverse situations, acceptance towards their mistakes and responsibilities and being productive for themselves and the world. Spirituality has an important role in all these conditions of mental health.

Segment and Jin Charcot mentioned religion as one of the many reasons for neurosis. Some old psychologists have also mentioned that religion can be a cause of increasing mental health problems but modern psychiatry and new researches have shown that spirituality and religion are huge support systems for the mind of a faithful person.

In fact, when those psychiatrists were linking religion with mental problems, England as well as entire Europe was under strictly institutionalized religion, that too in the hands of a few. Just like the political system the religious system too has many forms and types. A state can be democratic or under dictatorship, similarly, religion also has two main types based on its practice which are individual and institutionalism.

When religion works for the people, it helps enhance as well as gives importance to their self-conscience, self-discipline, individual uniqueness and freedom. It shows the welfare and individualistic side of it. At the same time when people and society are for an institutional form of religion, it creates a lot of problems since it is very strict and rigid and there is no room for a mistake. Heavy laws and rules of conduct make the human mind suffocated. Hence, both the means and the purity of the medium going in the wrong direction. When the system becomes more important than the person in a religion, it becomes a cause of mental health disorder. It is not for the people anymore whereas they become mere means for religion. As far as religion awakens the person's conscience and self-confidence, it is favourable to the human mind but also becomes the enemy of mental health, if it controls the person too much, makes him feel guilty or self-hatred.

The role of religion is to show the person the right path and to help him attain a righteous conscience. It also should not make him feel buried under the weight of the guilt of wrong doing. Constantly telling them about their mistakes and making them feel inferior due to their small mistakes would lead the human mind towards mental suppression. This is the system that was in practice during the times of Marx and Freud and that is why they called the religion as opium and cause of psychiatric problems respectively. During their times they witnessed a system where the people were for the religion, not religion for people.

Perhaps, that is the reason why they call a human being as 'AMRITASYA PUTRAHA', in India which means purity or divinity's child, which also protects their pride and self-esteem/confidence. This is one of the reasons why the number of people suffering from mental health problems in India is less as compared to the West besides the fact that the availability of such services is seemingly less.

There is a need to use and experiment with the individualistic methods of religion in psychiatry. One of the most important mental health therapies in Ayurveda is SATTVAVAJAY, which is also mentioned in *Charaka Samhita*. It mentions the use of spirituality as a practice based on the interest and faith of the person. A right lifestyle is developed with a suitable day-to-day routine and behaviours in this therapy which enables the person to come out of the mental health problems.

According to Sir Watt, to make the psychiatric practices more effective, there is a need to reconnect religion with spirituality. The American College of Medical Education calls upon special sessions to discuss how religion and spirituality can be used to help enhance psychiatry. World Psychiatric Association has dedicated an entire session to 'religion and psychiatry'. A psychiatric research in Australia revealed that the majority of clients wanted their therapists to use their spiritual beliefs and faiths as a part of the treatment. The Royal College of Psychiatry of London has a group of specialists to work on spiritual psychiatry. University of New Mexico psychiatry's research professor has conducted research on 226 clients with excessive drinking habits/alcoholism and found out how spiritual psychiatry was more helpful for them to quit drinking.[1]

Some of the Major Religious and Spiritual Paths and their Mental Health Practices

Jainism

Leading a person towards the highest level of consciousness is the main aim of Jainism. It emphasizes making a person disciplined, sacrificing and morally righteous. In this religious branch of India, many principles and methods have been given to keep good mental health and also to treat mental illnesses. These theories and practices can be divided into three parts—To attain inner peace, self-disciplined life, and knowledge.

1. **Attainment of knowledge and self-awareness:** Self-study (to read inspirational texts and literature and discussions) .To attend groups of spiritual discourse, to meet spiritual people, to attempt to find answers to one's questions and by going to temples for a change of atmosphere.
2. **Self-Discipline:** To follow the highest virtue of *Ahimsa* (non-violence) which leads to positivity and self-pride in life. To follow a disciplined day-to-day life this leads to an active and aware lifestyle. To eat a balanced diet and have a balanced routine which then leads towards an organized life. To follow the doctrine of *Anuvrata,* which is a compilation of small day-to-day rules of life like righteousness, not being greedy, self-control etc. which leads to a self-determined and stable life.
3. **Attainment of inner peace:** To follow the ritualistic chanting, to practice *Kayotsarga* meditation for relaxation and removing stress and anxiety. Preksha meditation for concentration and stability practices. Other meditations like *Antardhyan, Anupeksha, Dirghapeksha, Laishya, Bahyavratas* and *Antarik vrata* are very useful for attainment of inner peace.

Buddhism

Buddhism was born out of the upheaval of the inner conscious of the human mind. Hence, it is also known as the most psychological religion in the world. Its founder Gautam Buddha went on a journey to find answers to the complexities of the human mind and its sorrows. The outcome of this journey of discoveries is what we call Buddhism today.

Buddha talks directly about the complexities, psychological disorders and sorrows of the human mind and how to get rid of them at the same time. Perhaps that was the reason why it was seen as a great spiritual revolution born in India that changed the world rapidly. It is 2500 years old and is believed to be followed by approximately 10 per cent of the world's population. He talks about liberating the common fears of the human mind like death, diseases, old age and sorrows. He emphasized making a person self-reliable and efficient. The Buddha theory is knitted around balance and spontaneity. According to him, sorrow is the ultimate truth of life which transcends into a series of sorrows. The first step is acceptance of sorrow and then making an effort to liberate oneself from it by bringing a balance into all aspects of life.

The model of sorrow and its liberation has been mentioned as 4 noble truths:

- *Sorrow*: Sorrow is prevalent in the world.
- *Community*: is the cause of Sorrow.
- *Control/Moderation*: Prevention of sorrow.
- *Path*: Eight Paths towards prevention.

The Eightfold path is balanced view, balanced intention, balanced speech, balanced action, balanced livelihood, balanced effort, balanced mindfulness and balanced concentration. If the person is able to bring balance amongst these subjects, he can get liberated from all disorders and sorrows.

Buddhism developed a lot of branches in which Zen and Tao are purely concentrated on psychological practices. Besides that, the *Vipassana* method has proven very effective in treating psychological disorders like depression, anxiety etc.

Zen Buddhism has greatly influenced the mental health field through the development of Dialectical Behavioural Therapy, an approach developed by Marsha Linehan. DBT is a skill-heavy approach to treatment that teaches emotion regulation and tolerance to high-risk clients such as those with a borderline personality disorder. DBT describes the foundations of mindfulness using two broad categories of 'What' and 'How'. 'What' includes observing, describing, and participating, while 'how' includes non-judgemental, one-mindful, and effective.

In his book *Naikan: grace, gratitude and the Japanese art of self-reflection*, Greg Krech gives the list of elements contrasting features of a traditional approach therapy with *Naikan* based methodologies.

Sikhism

The thought of Sikhism, founded by Guru Nanak Dev, emphasizes inspiring the person to become humble, helpful, engaged in service to mankind and brave. Hence, Sikhism is believed to be a religion most involved in service towards the people, also giving it a unique identity. According to its main principle, ego and arrogance are the roots of many psychological disorders. They are of the opinion to work on the human mind through service and religious practices.

Giving up ego and pride and bringing humility in life is at the core of Sikhism. The ego plays an important role in our relationship it affects our professional, personal and social life. People tide with ego becomes easy prey to mental illnesses. Sikhism teaches us how to keep the ego away and improve our mental health by bringing humility and compassion into one's life. Keeping a materialistic perspective in life makes us find faults in others but ignore our own. According to the *Gurubani* humility is a formidable weapon that can be used by a person to kill the ego within himself as well as stubbornness, anger, arrogance, resentment and jealousy. According to Sikhism someone who follows these principles in the right way can experience the inner joy which leads to healthy mental health.[2]

Islam

Islam is an Abrahamic monotheistic religion teaching that Muhammad is a messenger of God. It is the world's second largest religion with 1.9 billion followers or 24.9 per cent of the world's population, known as Muslims. Muslims make up a majority of the population in 51 countries.

Many practices are found in Islamic traditions; Sufism is an important thought where the focus is on treating mental illnesses through music and meditation. Prayers are also considered to be a form of meditation and a way to connect to God. This keeps them away from much mental illness. Prayers are a form of meditation and remembrance that connects one to the almighty which controls everything.[3]

The holy book of Islam Qur'an describes the *nafs* or self, as operating out of one of three states: *nafs al-ammara* (commanding self); *nafs al-lawwama*—accusatory self; and nafs *al-mutmainna* (peaceful self). Psychology in Islam is used in everyday practices but under different guises, such as spiritualism.

Mental Health Practices

Ramzan: It is a holy month of fasting which brings discipline in daily life which ultimately has a positive effect on mental health.

Zakat: It is an obligation of donating a certain part of one's annual income for philanthropic purposes. Since giving is a great characteristic in a personality, it brings inner joy and peace to the giver which again leads to good mental health.

Aroma Therapy: Aroma therapy is used a lot in the Islamic tradition is useful in treating mental illnesses.

Zoroastrianism

Zoroastrianism is one of the world's oldest continuously practiced religions, based on the teachings of Iranian speaking prophet Zoroaster. This religion is known for its many specialties one of which is Ushta. This is a condition in which the body, mind and spirit are in a state of wellness. Achieving the state of Ushta is the main goal of this religion. Zoroastrianism mentions many practices for the mental, physical and spiritual development of a human being. Under the sect of Haoma healing through mantras is mentioned. It is believed that this approach removes the imbalance from a person's mind, body and soul and cures them naturally. The mantras are those ancient prayers that are believed to be the power of the universe in this religion. Keeping oneself healthy through the practice of haoma plants is considered to be a strong method. This religion is a way of life that connects the spiritual rules with the values of nature resulting in the holistic development of one's life.[4]

Christianity

Christianity is one of the world's largest religion based on the life and teachings of a great teacher and healer Jesus Christ. It is an Abrahamic monotheistic religion followed by more than 2.4 billion people spread across 157 countries of the world. Bible the holy book of Christianity propagated among its followers to care for others for their health and well-being and to be spiritually, physically and emotionally contained.[5]

Verses of Bible about mental illness

Do not be anxious about anything, but in everything by prayer and supplication with thanks giving let your requests be made known to God. And the peace of God, which surpasses all understanding, will guard your hearts and your minds in Christ Jesus (Philippians 4:6-7).

For God gave us a spirit, not of fear but of power and love and self-control (2 Timothy 1:7).

Fear not, for I am with you; be not dismayed, for I am your God; I will strengthen you, I will help you, I will uphold you with my righteous right hand (Isaiah 41:10).

Mental Health Practices [6]

Rosary: A string of beads used to count those parts of the prayer repeatedly in mind that makes the person feel good. It is a way to help the person concentrate and keep away from distraction. Also, repeatedly chanting a positive thought in mind helps the person maintain positivity in life.

Confession: Confession or reconciliation is a Christian tradition where a person in search of divine forgiveness, acknowledges his sinfulness publically or in private in front of the church priest who is considered as the representative of God. This results in freeing the person from guilt and releases him from the sorrow of carrying it in his mind for a long time. This works as a counselling session and results in giving the seeker mental peace.

Thanks Giving: It is an annual Christian tradition where people show their gratitude towards the different aspects of life. It is a festival to connect with friends and family and to be grateful for the small pleasures and things in life. It is a way to live in the moment and feel blissful mentally.

Healing through prayers: It is a tradition in the Christian faith where divine intervention is possible through prayers for healing. One such example is the sect of Christian Science where the practitioner, through prayers and singings tries to heal a person suffering from physical and mental illness.

Judaism

Judaism is an Abrahamic ethnic religion that represents religious and cultural traditions and civilization of the Jewish people. This monotheistic religion was founded around the 18th century BC and is followed by 15 million people spread across the world, while Israel is the only country with a Jewish majority. Judaism has many traditions related to mental health. One of the tradition known as '*Mi Shebeirach*' (prayer for healing), the followers pray for an '*r'fuah shleimah*' (a complete recovery), which includes both '*r'fuat hanefesh ur'fuat haguf,*' meaning healing of the soul and the body. Indeed, Judaism acknowledges a distinction between mental and physical health, Judaism very much accepts the difference between mental and physical health, but their tradition considers them on an equal footing, believing that both a healthy body and a healthy mind are essential for a human being to be complete. Another tradition known as Shabbat is observed from a few minutes before sunset on Friday evening until the appearance of three stars in the sky on Saturday night. Shabbat is considered an important day when Jews exercise their freedom from the routine labour of everyday life. It provides an opportunity to reflect on the spiritual aspects of life and spend time with the family.

Hinduism

Hinduism is one of the oldest religions of the world. It is also known as Sanatan Dharma. It has 1.2 billion followers covering almost 15-16 per cent of the world population is the world's third-largest religion.

Some of the most elaborated and ancient work done in the field of psychiatry is seen in Hinduism. One of the important subjects of Vedas, which are considered as the greatest texts of Hindus, is psyche and psychological well-being. They talked about insanity and psychosis 3400 years ago and mentioned about yoga, prayer and meditation as its treatment.

The most significant text of Hindu philosophy—The Upanishads—has mind, psyche, conscious, ego, self, intelligence and blissful state of mind as its main subjects.

In the course of time, it was further elaborated in the practices of yoga and Ayurveda.

For Hindus, one asks for the blessings of treatment of '*Aadhi*' (Mental Illness) before '*Vyadhi*' (Physical Illness) during the common Hindu prayers. Mental wellness was always held more important than physical well-being.

The common way to greet each other since time and beyond in Hindus is by asking how the other person's *mann* (emotional status) is, since it is the most important part of a person's well-being. The founding text of Ayurveda is *Charak Samhita* was written around 2nd BC. The creator of the epic '*Charaka*' mentions in the *shloka* that *mann* and the body are both the reasons of sorrow and bliss.

शरीरं सत्वसंज्ञंच व्याधीनामश्रयो मतः |
तथा संखातां, यागे स्तु, सखांनां, करणं समः || (1/55 च.स.)

According to *Charak* the body and the mind are not too far apart. Rather they reflect each other, therefore, physical illness in the course of time may turn into a mental illness and *vice versa*. It is the symptoms seen first makes us decide whether the illness is physical or psychological.

Geeta which is the song of the Lord and a pure spiritual text, talks about the origins of mental disorders as well as how to treat them from root. It talks about the management of the emotions. Emotions like anger, delusion and loss of memory etc. are a chain of disorders and *The Geeta* emphasizes on breaking it.

ध्यायतो विषयान्पुसः संगस्तबेपूज्याते।
संगातसजायते् कामः कामातक्रोधो भिजायते।।
क्रोधाद्भवति समाहेः सम्मोहात्स्मति विभम्रः।
स्मृति भ्रंशाद बुद्धिनाशो बुद्धिनाशात्प्रणश्यति।। 2/62-63 (म.गी.)

Thinking too much about any object leads to attachment. For example, attachment leads to desire and from desire comes anger. From anger comes delusion, and delusion leads to loss of memory, from loss of memory comes destruction of intellect and once the intellect is destroyed, the person is destroyed.

Further, *Bhagavad Gita* mentions of diet, life style and atmosphere responsible to provide an order in which the mental illness grows from types of personalities, their imbalances, control over the brain and *mann*, growth of mental illness, to a person's mental deviations and distraction of understanding.

According to *rishi* (sage) *Charak,* not having what is desired and confronting what one does not desire is the root of mental disorders.

Suppressing emotions, such as anger. grief, fear, excitement, sorrow, jealousy, hatred, results in the growth of mental health problems.

There are several methods and practices for mental health. However, some major theories, practices and concepts have been mentioned here. The methods developed and practiced for mental health are divided into three models.

Different forms of Mental Health Practices in Hinduism[7]

***Yuktivyapasrya* (Rational Therapy):** Based on fundamental principles of Ayurveda,viz. *Pancha Mahabhoota*, *tridosa*, *samanya* and *vishesha* etc. The therapy is further subdivided into internal or external cleansing and the use of calming herbs.

***Satvavajaya* (Psychotherapy):** *Sattvavajaya* is aimed at the control of the mind. It plays a significant role in the maintenance of a harmonious state between these three important factors—intellect, memory and patience. In this, by making spiritual and right changes in his lifestyle, routine and environment, good mental health is ensured. *Charak* was the propounder of this theory and therapy. His definition gives a lot of scope for expansion of *Sattvavajaya* '*punahahitebhyo mano nigrah*'. The word *mano nigrah* means control of mind which can be both subjective and objective.

***Daivayaparsya* (Spiritual or Faith Therapy):** It is a faith-based treatment derived from spiritual practices. In *Ashtanga Hridyam*, an important text of Ayurveda, *Vaagbhatta* also talks about the use of spiritual practices according to one's belief for his healing and this is called *Ishvara puja* therapy in which an individual is made to feel mentally happy through rituals (*Ishwar pooja chikitsa* 5/50,51).

Following concepts, methods and practices are mentioned in spiritual text of Hinduism for mental health practices.

Triguna

This is the method of testing personality and measuring its imbalance and bringing it back into balance. In this theory, there are three dimensions of personality in which *Rajas* is considered as the factor of mental and physical activity and *Tamas* is considered as the factor of stability and passivity. *Sattva* refers to their correct balance and the qualities that arise from it.

Combination of different forms of these three results in creating 16 types of personalities. They are also known as sixteen mental constitutions.

The rule of *satva pariksha* (investigation for mental state) has been made for counselling and has three modes for it—*Pravarsatv, Madhyamsatv, Avarsatv*.

Antahkarana Chatustaya: Like the Freudian theory of id, ego and superego, but in a little more detail, the mind and consçiousness of a person have been divided into four parts known as *Antahkaran Chatustya* in Vedant which are *mann* (mind), *buddhi* (intellect), *chitta* (conscience) and *Ahankar* (ego). These can be understood as the layers of a person's self, when these layers are unbalanced, there are many practices to balance them.

Bhoot chikitsa: In Ayurveda, therapies related to mental health are called *Bhoot chikitsa*. In this method naturopathy, psycho shock therapy and belief method etc. are used. At its core is also the use of spiritual beliefs.

Sadavrata: *Sadvarata* is an attempt to make the individual feel good at the level of mind through positive mental and physical discipline in the individual's daily routine. It involves a positive thought process as a part of the lifestyle. It is an effort to prevent and avoid mental health problems in life on a daily basis.

Seva: *Seva* in Hinduism is selflessly serving the living beings and feeling good through completing small tasks. With this, a person is able to experience self-esteem and is freed from the feeling of low self-concept.

Yoga: The basic purpose of the practice of yoga is that the person attains the highest state of consciousness and the highest spiritual state. To achieve this, yoga practices helps individual through creating a balance between the individual's mind, intellect, ego, consciousness and body and keep them healthy. The sages, pioneers of yoga believed that only a physically and mentally healthy person can experience spirituality well, so they developed many methods and practices for sound mental and physical health through research and practices.

There are 8 steps of yoga, they gave importance to the mental health before the physical health, so the steps directly related to physical practice is the *asanas*, which come at number three in this sequence, the first two are mental exercises and the later five also.

(29th sutra of Pad 2 of *Yoga darshan*). There are eight stages of Yoga:

Yama

- *Ahimsa*—Principle of Non-violence.
- *Satya*—Principle of truthfulness.
- *Asteya*—Principle of non-stealing.
- *Brahmacharya*—Continence/celibacy.
- *Aparigrah*—Principle of non-holding or non-possessiveness.

Niyam

- *Shoucha*—Purity.
- *Santosh*—Contentment.
- *Tapa*—Endurance.
- *Swadhyaya*—Self Study.
- *Ishwar Pranidhan*—Dedication.

Asana (Yoga postures/positions)—A stable and comfortable posture that helps attain mental equilibrium.

Pranayam (Breath Control)—Extension and control of breath and different breathing exercise.

Pratyahara (withdrawal of Senses)—A mental preparation to increase the power of the mind.

Dharna (concentration on the object)—Concentration of mind on one object and its field.

Dhyaan (meditation)—Withdrawing the mind from all external objects and experiencing the calm of emptiness.

Samadhi (salvation)—State of super bliss, joy and merging individual consciousness into universal consciousness.

There are many types of meditation according to the personality; it is very effective on both healthy person and person with disorders. In *Pranayama*, both *Sagarbha* and *Nirgarbha* are practiced along with breathing. In *Nirgarbha*, breathing exercises are done without any thought and in *Sagarbha*, a positive thought is selected and repeated again and again synchronized with the breathing. This method is still used prominently in almost all the therapies related to modern mental health.

Guru Shishya Parampara: An important tradition among Hindus in India took birth several centuries ago. and is still practiced in the same way. It is present in all Asian religions. It is a tradition where a very learned teacher with wisdom and spirituality is chosen as a *guru* who is always willing to help his disciples and everyone who needs help in any aspect of life. They are not only spiritual teachers but play the role of a mentor and life coach. A person can talk his heart out with his *guru* and feels free from emotions like guilt, grief, sorrow, anger, sadness. This was an attempt to make personal counsellors available to every person in a way since experts for mental health service and counselling were not available.

Mala and Japa: The use of rosary and chanting is popular in almost all the religions of the world. It has been practiced in India since ages. *Mala* is a type of tool which is used for concentration. It is an attempt to break the negative and unwanted chain of thoughts and keep positive thought in mind. It is a way to train the brain so that it can keep the concentration of thoughts in the desired direction and be free from unnecessary thoughts. The explanation has been given for the mantra '*mannattrayate iti mantrah*' which means bringing one particular mantra or thought in mind repeatedly and freeing it from the vicious cycle of undesired thoughts, whereas *trayte* means to protect, in other words protecting ones sanity and restoring their peace of mind.

Yog Nindra: Through this, the body and mind are directed to be calm and relaxed respectively. This is called the sleep of *yogi's*, it is the state between sleeping and waking or dream and awakening. It is a dialogue with the person's semi-consciousness. This method was invented to stabilize and calm the anxious and disturbed mind and body when they are restless. It is one of the classic and important practices of yoga.

Naad or use of music: The use of music in India for mental disorders is quite old. It started with the singing of Vedic hymns. Out of the four Vedas, the main theme of the Samaveda is singing. and the mantras are actually chanted and not just spoken. Music and sound were considered so important that the *Naad* (The sound) was given the name of Brahma. The first form of God and the first manifestation of the universe took place in the form of sound; this is the idea of the Hindu religion. So much work was done on classical music and on ragas and many instruments were invented. Music is used to both relax and stimulate the nervous system. With the right use of music, the person's mental state can also be brought into a rhythm. Various ragas are used to treat insomnia, anxiety, depression and stress such as *raga Lalit* and *Kedar*.

Certain ragas are used at different times of the day like *raga Bhervi* in the morning, *raga todi* in the afternoon, *Jai-Jayawanti raga* in the evening, similarly to deal with mental disorders like depression *Vihaag* and *Madhuvanti raga* is used and *Sohni raga* is used to treat insomnia. There are also rules for singing mantras and *richas* (*Vedic* rhymes) because singing them voluntarily does not get the full effect of their rhythm, their higher and lower pitches are fixed. If music becomes a regular part of every person's life, then it becomes a regular exercise to maintain good mental health. Therefore, the Mantra and Prayer that are performed regularly are recited with rhythm and singing. The hymns of mantras have been prepared in such a way that whether a person is melodious or not, whether he has good vocals or not, the person can sing them. It also suggests that music and singing should be a part of his regular life.

Conclusion

Here, it is not being advocated for only going to spiritual people or spiritual places for mental health problems. However, the essence of the research here is that everyone related to the mental health fields like social worker, psychiatrists, psychologists, counsellors, therapists etc. should consider using spirituality and religious methods in treating a person based on their faith and beliefs. What could also be considered is that each and every religion in the world has unique ways of their own to deal with mental health problems and have a long line of practices based on their experiences with humanity.

NOTES

1. Spirituality and mental health. (2008, October 1). Retrieved April 15, 2021, from https://www.ncbi.nlm.nih.gov/pmc/articles/PMC2755140/
2. Singh, K.A.L.A. (2007, December 12). The Sikh spiritual model of counselling. Retrieved March 1, 2020, from https://onlinelibrary.wiley.com/ doi/abs/10.1002/shi.331
3. Samah, F. (2018). The Qu'ran and Mental Health. *The Psychologist, 31*(June), 5-6 Retrieved from https://thepsychologist.bps.org.uk/volume-31/june-2018/quran-and-mental-health
4. Eduljee, K.E. (n.d.). Zoroastrian Healing Concepts. Retrieved February 17, 2021, from http://www.heritageinstitute.com/zoroastrianism/healing/index.htm
5. Christianity. (n.d.). Retrieved March 23, 2021, from https:// en.wikipedia.org/wiki/Christianity

6. Biblical Help and Hope for People with Mental Illness: Idea #38. (2015, October 16). Retrieved January 10, 2021, fro(via openbible.info)— https://get.bible/blog/post/biblical-help-and-hope-for-people-with-mental-illness-idea-38
7. Poonam Kunwar Rathore, B. (2021). Evidence of Ancient Indian Work in Mental Health and its use for Modern social work practice. In *Indian Social Work* (First south Asia edition, Vol. 1, pp. 118-136). Oxon, UK: Routledge.

REFERENCES

Biblical Help and Hope for People with Mental Illness: Idea #38. (2015, October 16). Retrieved January 10, 2021, from https://get.bible/blog/post/biblical-help- and-hope-for-people-with-mental-illness-idea-38

Brahmananda, T. (2019). *Charak Samhita* (Tisstreshni ed., Vol. adhyay 11). New Delhi, India: Chaukhamba Publishing House.

Brahmananda, T. (2019). *Charak Samhita* (vimanadhyay , Vol. adhyay 08). New Delhi, India: Chaukhamba Publishing House.

Christianity. (n.d.). Retrieved March 23, 2021, from https://en.wikipedia.org/wiki/Christianity.

Eduljee, K. E. (n.d.). *Zoroastrian Healing Concepts*. Retrieved February 17, 2021, from http://www.heritageinstitute.com/zoroastrianism/healing/index.htm

Poonam Kunwar Rathore, B. (2021). Evidence of Ancient Indian Work in Mental Health and its use for Modern social work practice. In *Indian Social Work*, in Dash, B.M. *et al.* (eds.), pp. 118-136. Oxon, UK: Routledge.

Spirituality and mental health. (2008, October 1). Retrieved April 15, 2021, from https://www.ncbi.nlm.nih.gov/pmc/articles/PMC2755140/

Singh, K.A.L.A. (2007, December 12). *The Sikh spiritual model of counselling*. Retrieved March 1, 2020, from https://onlinelibrary.wiley.com/doi/abs/10.1002/shi.331

Samah, F. (2018). The Qu'ran and Mental Health. *The Psychologist.., 31*(June), 5-6 Retrieved from https://thepsychologist.bps.org.uk/volume-31/june-2018/quran-and-mental-health

Sabry, W.M., & Vohra, A. (2013). Role of Islam in the management of Psychiatric disorders. *Indian Journal of Psychiatry, 55 (Suppl 2)* (January), 205-214. https://doi.org/10.4103/0019-5545.105534

Tripathi, Brahmanand (2019). *Charak Samhita*, Chapter: Tisstreshni Aadhayay 11, p. 244, Public. Chaukhamba Publishing House.

_______, (2019), *Charak Samhita*, Chapter: Vimanadhyay 8, p. 770, Public. Chaukhamba Publishing House.

3
Aurobindo's Integrated Model for Social Case Work Practice

Mithilesh Kumar and *Rajan Prakash*

Introduction

The achievement of humans is their consciousness, and this very consciousness makes humans different from other species. Shri Aurobindo understood this at a young age. He was prominently known for leading the Indian freedom struggle, exploring Indian consciousness, and giving a new direction in philosophy and spirituality. Born on August 15, 1872 in Calcutta, his father, Dr. Krishnadhan Ghosh, wanted to get his higher education and an important government position, so he sent him to England at 7. He was the only one to pass the ICS examination at age 18 in 1890 (Ulrich, 2010). Proficient in many languages, including English, German, French, Greek, and Italian, he established an ashram at Pondicherry where he wrote extensive commentaries on the Vedas, Upanishads, and original texts on yoga practice. He has had a profound influence on philosophy worldwide, and today, followers of his practice are in all countries.

Shri Aurobindo believed in the existence of the soul and held that one who has a soul could touch the souls of others. He passed away on December 5, 1950, but his ideas in philosophy and spirituality are still guiding and showing the path to humanity (Heehs, 2008). With a delighted mind, affection towards all, and an intense feeling of compassion, he touched the hearts of all. His views on integrated philosophy and, more particularly, on integral yoga are relevant for social casework practice.

This chapter will shed light on Aurobindo's Integrated Model for Social Casework Practice. To do so, it will examine Yoga and Aurobindo's integral Yoga; the latter is part of Aurobindo's integrated philosophy.

Besides, it will describe the *sadhana* as Integral Yoga, based on some tools: aspiration, equanimity, faith, the Guru, meditation, peace, personal effort, the psychic being, silence, sincerity, surrender, and work. This model of social casework practiced through integral Yoga is essential for the fullest self-development of the individual.

Yoga and Maharishi Aurobindo

Yoga is a fundamental science. It is divided into various branches, like *Kriya Yoga*, *RajaYoga* and *HathaYoga.* It is a science through which human consciousness merges with universal consciousness. Yoga strikes a balance between these two bodies. It is considered a journey in *Kundalini* Yoga, where the seeker starts the journey from his *Muladhara Chakra* and reaches the *Sahasrar Chakra. On* this journey, the seeker, while practising various siddhis, gets absorbed into *Brahma.*This process of yoga is also the prohibition of the mind, in which the mind of the person becomes completely neutral. That is why Patanjali, in his treatise, considered Yoga a prohibition of *Chittavrittis* (Naikar, 2002).

A person's mind keeps wandering through many types of choices, and the person runs after them. A yogi commands the same mind through his practice. They use their body parts as required and voluntarily. When a yogi reaches this stage, he is entirely free from the miseries of the world. In this sense, yoga is a scientific method to convert the feeling of a sedentary life into an active form (Gupta, 2018). When a yogi attains the state of *Sthitipragya* through the practice of yoga, he is entirely free from the tribulations of material life.

Shri Aurobindo's Integral Yoga could make human life meaningful on a practical level. The ancient tradition of Yoga has been two-polar; at one pole, it is considered completely Maya, or fleeting, and at the second pole, the whole world is considered cosmic. In this way, yogis follow two paths. One view considers the whole life as mortal and unreal, and the other as *Brahma*. However, one of the drawbacks of these views is their practicality and their weaker hold on ordinary people. Maharshi Aurobindo tried to establish yoga at a practical level to transform humanity. He did not reject the idealistic aspect of worldly things but stressed the need to change humans' lives. That is why the yoga of Maharishi Aurobindo is called Integrated Yoga. Individual problems can be diagnosed psychologically, socially, and spiritually using the integrated yoga philosophy relevant to a social worker. The problems in any society are essential incompatibilities in societal elements, and their diagnosis must be made at the same level. The tools below are an aid in that process.

Sadhana

The practice of any method of yoga is called *sadhana*. A yogi who practices *sadhana* is called a seeker. A suitable seeker keeps expanding his consciousness continuously. His consciousness is the light for him. Maharishi Aurobindo stressed the need to abandon narrow-mindedness and ignorance for the seeker. Ignorance nourishes the ego. Narrowness comes with distorted illusions like ego, because of which Yogi's expansion of consciousness is not possible.

This situation makes the yogi deviate from the path of yoga and indulge in *bhoga*. Shri Aurobindo believed that yoga transforms the seeker's life entirely, and this act of transformation opens the door to liveliness and self-reliance (Chaudhuri, 2018). The seeker walks on the path free from attachment, and until a person is free from attachment, he remains trapped in the cycle of various miseries of life and happiness. According to Aurobindo, the main goal of integrated yoga is to develop inner wisdom within the seeker. When the inner wisdom of a seeker is developed, it is completely transformed. As a result, the spiritual practice of a seeker is strengthened, and he is successful in doing better work for his society. Maharishi Aurobindo talks about the first phase of spiritual practice for the seeker and believes that it remains empty as the seeker progresses towards perfection in his spiritual practice. Seen in this way, Maharishi Aurobindo paves the way for integrated yoga practice to develop a person's personality.If every person in the society incorporates the integrated yoga system into their lives, the entire society will be successful in realising the divine.Therefore, in integrated yoga practice, individual social workers should take the initiative in spiritual and social work.

Aids in Sadhana

When a seeker does spiritual practice, he has to follow specific rules and principles. Different yogis have established different rules and principles according to their practice. For example, Maharishi Patanjali established *Yama*, *Niyam*, *Asana*, *Pranayama*, *Pratyahara*, *Meditation*, and *Samadhi* in Yoga. Maharishi Aurobindo also discussed various types of aids as part of his integrated yoga philosophy, referred to as the tool of *sadhana* (Chaudhuri, 2018).These are aspiration, equanimity, faith, peace, Guru, meditation, personal effort, mental state, truth, and surrender.

Aspiration

Maharishi Aurobindo feels the need for aspiration for the seeker. He believes that when aspiration is inside a seeker for divinity or self-realisation, he starts on the path of Yoga. As long as the mind of a seeker is engaged in the consumption of material substances, he cannot walk on the path of Yoga (Feuerstein, 2003). It is necessary that by eliminating the desires of the material world, he should aspire to realise divine consciousness. This makes the seeker attain supreme knowledge and become absorbed in ecstasy. As the aspiration of the seeker strengthens in practice, so too does the sensitivity and receptiveness of his life. In this way, the entire life of the seeker starts to transform. He ignores the things that obstruct his path and is engrossed in the process of yoga while smoothly doing his work. The practitioner's initial practice consists of aspiration, but this aspiration then ceases. When the seeker completes the expansion of his consciousness, he sees the whole universe. This aspiration may arise from the attainment of stimulation at both internal and external levels. When the practice unveils the illusion of Maya in the physical world, the person becomes anxious to know himself and understand life's purpose. To start on the path of yoga, one has to know the impermanence of life from the inside. And when a person realises this impermanence, he gets an aspiration for self-realisation.

Equanimity

Maharishi Aurobindo stressed the need for equanimity for the seeker. Equanimity is a mental state in which the seeker keeps the same sentiment through grief or happiness, profit or loss, life or death. He is neither bothered when adversity comes nor rejoices in favourable circumstances. In this way, the seeker remains unaffected by external things and maintains control over its existence. This is a state of ultimate knowledge and achievement that helps the seeker to move towards self-realisation. In the state of equanimity, the seeker's mind becomes wholly stable, and the life energy inside him becomes the guiding element (White, 1972). As a result of this, equanimity helps the seeker attain self-realisation. If a social worker uses the aggregated sum of these ideas by Aurobindo for the development of harmony within a person, the problems of his life are eliminated from the root, and a person becomes able to bear responsibilities in his life without getting distracted.

Faith

Maharishi Aurobindo considers faith to be an essential value for a seeker. He considers it a belief beyond thought or logic. However, he opposes blind faith. According to him, blind faith is meaningless, held by a person without any evidence, and there is a possibility of deviation.

In contrast, faith is based on evidence, experience, and knowledge. A seeker having firm faith succeeds in his practice. A seeker feels mentally, emotionally, and physically connected to his surroundings when in faith (Rao, 1989). It is attained when both his heart and brain simultaneously become absorbed in self-realisation. The ego becomes absent in the seeker, and he becomes entirely devoted to both his *Guru* and *sadhana*. Faith is a psychological condition in which the seeker dissolves the existence of himself in the ultimate truth.

Guru

The seeker needs a teacher at the time of yoga, fully proficient in the respective practice. The Guru knows the various stages that occur during spiritual practice and the experiences that the seeker has. In yoga, the seeker has different experiences at different stages, and sometimes the seeker gets scared due to an unexpected experience. In such a situation, the presence of a competent Guru plays a significant role in guiding the seeker. And it is only then that he succeeds in self-realisation (Raina, 2002). The Guru's personality is like the Sun, showing light for the development of the entire personality of the seeker. So, a seeker must find a good Guru and start the journey of self-realisation. A seeker's devotion is the most important factor in his search for a guru; if the seeker does not devote his life and is not receptive to the symbol of knowledge, he will not be able to find a good Guru.

Meditation

Meditation, in general, is a tool by which the seeker attains a wide variety of *siddhis*. In the process of self-realisation, the seeker has to meditate. This meditation starts with *Dhyana* and reaches *Samadhi*. *Dhyana* is a mental state in which a seeker focuses on something inside or outside (Cook & Cottone, 2015). Slowly, the same force becomes dominant when meditation is practiced. When meditation is slowly practiced, it takes the form of a *Samadhi*. In the states of *Dhyana* and meditation, the seeker gets to know himself, but in the state of Samadhi, the seeker becomes altogether in tune with the ultimate truth, and he is also free from the miseries of the cycle of life. The Samadhi is called *Ritambhara* or *Moksha*. In the Vigyan Bhairava system, Shiva mentions 112 perceptions of Parvati, and by practice, the seeker can reach enlightenment. It is through these 112 perceptions that the process of meditation is carried out. Apart from this, no other routes have been developed so far. Different yogis develop one of these 112 paths to realise the ultimate essence.

Peace

Maharishi Aurobindo considers peace in *sadhana* important for the seeker as it is necessary for both a mental and physical state. Peace is necessary for the seeker where he practices. There should be no turmoil in the seeker's mind (Merchant, 2004). This is also necessary when the seeker's life is filled with the turmoil of thoughts, making him feel prohibited from going to Samadhi. Only when the seeker is free of desires does he or she find deep peace in life.When one desires, they have to face anger or fear resulting from fulfilling the desire. And in this state, the life of the seeker is disturbed. In such a situation, the seeker must be free from unnecessary desires.

Personal Effort

Personal efforts have an important place in the integrated yoga philosophy of Maharishi Aurobindo. A seeker cannot walk on the path of self-realisation if he is not self-trying and his spiritual practice cannot be completed. This is a process that cannot be forced. If forced, it can have dire consequences. Therefore, the seeker has to make personal efforts continuously (Aurobindo, 1993). In this personal endeavour, one must continually strive for peace and joy while holding values like truth, non-violence, *asteya, aparigraha, brahmacharya*. The seeker has to be freed from hindering emotions like anger, jealousy, slander, and untruth. In this way, personal efforts are essential in providing completeness to the life of the seeker. For this, the seeker has to be continuously engaged in the process of contemplation and spiritual thinking.

Silence

Aurobindo explains the need for silence to the seeker. He believes that there should not be too much talk on the part of the yogi. When a yogi talks, in most forms, the centre of his talk is outward. He deviates from his inner centre in such a situation. The main focus of the seeker is his conscience. When he is silent, he is close to his inner self and gets oriented towards things outside when speaking. Another reason behind the silence is that many external conflicts arise due to talk. If a seeker uses silence, then gradually his thoughts become calm and he starts moving towards his self-centeredness (Shah, 1992). The process of silence provides peace. It makes the peace-making process successful. However, silence is a state of being verbally and mentally controlled, and it starts with silence. Many seekers only gradually go through silence and a situation when they get to know themselves.

Truth

Maharishi Aurobindo considers truth to be an indispensable element for the seeker under integrated yoga. Truth means complete surrender to self-realisation (Sturgess, 2015). When a seeker has complete devotion to the divine life and is free from personal gain, it becomes true allegiance to its goal. It can be said that the complete surrender of "I" for self-realisation is an important goal for the seeker. The seeker does not become what he wants; instead, he becomes one who has ultimate power or divine life. Boasting does not provide meaningful results in yoga. Living life should be completely natural, and this has much relevance to social life, to living life with the whole truth.

Surrender

As in Integrated yoga, the ego and the desire disappear, so a much more natural feeling comes inside the seeker. Surrender is possible only when the seeker maintains true faith in self-realisation. For this, he must experience spirituality in his thoughts, experiences, and actions and try to live them. It can be accepted that the seeker cannot be entirely devoted to the initial phase of self-realisation. However, if the seeker keeps practising, he will gradually become successful at it. When a seeker proceeds to realise the Supreme Brahma, he has to devote himself (Aurobindo, 1993).In devoting oneself, the seeker has to be free from all kinds of egoism and desires. If there is no surrender of ideas, compromise can never be a part of an intense experience. To be a part of a more in-depth experience, the seeker has to open the soul beyond thought, and unwavering faith must be kept in the ultimate power.

Work

"Work" means Karma Yoga. It is a lifelong process in which the seeker never abandons the work of life nor overindulges in it. He is not bound by those things of life even while taking full participation in all life processes. He only witnesses life, and he keeps doing all his actions with the same witnessing sentiment. The seeker does not have any personal interest in this path of *Karma*. Bliss is the goal for the seeker, and he meditates on doing his daily deeds with full enthusiasm (Mulla & Krishnan, 2006). In this way, the seeker can balance the dimensions of life, both internal and external, and *Kamini*, *Kanchan* and *Keerthi*, found in any external environment, do not obstruct any work of life. Maharishi Aurobindo believes that a seeker does not need to do meditation and self-realisation alone, but he can also be successful in doing all his life functions while practising to attain the ultimate realisation. In this context, the integrated yoga philosophy of Maharishi Aurobindo is consistent with the yoga philosophy of the Gita. Lord Krishna preaches to Arjuna that a yogi gets up, sits, eats, drinks, and performs all his deeds. Just as a person engaged in practical life does Karma, a yogi does not abandon the ultimate goal of self-realisation. Like, a lotus blooming in water is completely different from water. When a person lives his practical life doing his karmic duties, he is free from the duality of success and failure, and he keeps on moving towards being conscious of his self-realisation. This process paves the way for an excellent possibility of social leadership within him, and he fulfils that responsibility with full enthusiasm.

Relevance of Aurobindo's Philosophy in Social Case Work Practice

Social casework, considered one of the methods of social work, uses various theories to alleviate the problems of the individual. Practiced both individually and through the organisation, the basic assumption guiding this helping process is the sense of humanity, and this very humanity is the essence of Aurobindo's thought. He described it as:

> "*The greatest service to humanity, the surest foundation for its true progress, happiness and perfection is to prepare or find the way by which the individual and the collective man can transcend the ego and live in its true self, no longer bound to ignorance, incapacity, disharmony and sorrow. It is by the pursuit of the eternal and not by living bound in the slow collective evolution of Nature that we can best assure even that evolutionary, collective, altruistic aim our modern thought and idealism have set before us. But it is in itself a secondary aim; to find, know and possess the Divine existence, consciousness and nature and to live in it for the Divine is our true aim and the one perfection to which we must aspire* (Aurobindo, 1999, pp 359)."

Aurobindo's integral Yoga seeks to realise this essence not only for service users but also for social workers. The ultimate aim of integral yoga is to make one aware of the immediate, superficial hindrances and to recognise and realise the ultimate state of humanity, the divine.

Conclusion

Though yoga in Indian society is a much older concept, Shri Aurobindo's contribution lies in his significant discovery of a scientific method of yoga that can be used to improve human life. The practicality of life lies in diagnosing problems encountered in life, and the Integrated Yoga of Shri Aurobindo sheds much light on it. Sri Aurobindo's Yoga's basic tenets emphasise the individual and bring a positive change to society's problems.

Aurobindo uses the middle path to set a human welfare objective to shape life with practical skills, dedication, creativity, and balance through his integrated yoga philosophy. Thus, the individual social worker can use the consolidated sum of Maharishi Aurobindo's aids to sadhana in making today's complex society spiritual and straightforward.

REFERENCES

Aurobindo, S. (1999). *The Synthesis of Yoga: Volumes 23 and 24. The Complete Works of Sri Aurobindo.* Pondicherry: Shree Aurobindo Ashram Trust.

Aurobindo, S. (1993). *The Integral Yoga: Sri Aurobindo's teaching and method of practice*. USA: Lotus Press.

Chaudhuri, H. (2018). *Integral Yoga: The concept of harmonious and creative living*. London: Routledge.

Cook-Cottone, C.P. (2015). *Mindfulness and Yoga for self-regulation: A primer for mental health professionals*. New York: Springer Publishing Company.

Feuerstein, G. (2003). *The deeper dimension of Yoga: Theory and Practice.* Shambhala Publications.

Gupta, A.K. (2018). "What Yoga Can Do to Us", *Journal of Applied Science and Research*, *6*(5), 1-10.

Heehs, P. (2008). *The Lives of Sri Aurobindo*. USA: Columbia University Press. Merchant, V.V. (2004). "The Global Future, Sri Aurobindo and Peace". *International Journal of Humanities and Peace*, *20*(1), 3.

Mulla, Z.R., & Krishnan, V.R. (2006). Karma Yoga: A conceptualization and validation of the Indian philosophy of work. *Journal of Indian Psychology*, *24*(1/2), 26-43.

Naikar, C.S. (2002). *Patanjali of Yoga Sutras*. New Delhi: Sahitya Akademi.

Raina, M.K. (2002). "Guru-shishya relationship in Indian culture: The possibility of a creative, resilient framework". *Psychology and Developing Societies*, *14*(1), 167-198.

Rao, K.S. (1989). "Sri Aurobindo on the Types of Shraddha (Faith) in the 'Gita'." *Journal of South Asian Literature*, *24*(1), 168-178.

Shah, I. (1992). *Seeker After Truth: A Handbook.* UK: Octagon Press Ltd. Sturgess, S. (2015). *The Supreme Art and Science of Raja and Kriya Yoga: The Ultimate Path to Self-Realisation*. London: Singing Dragon.

Ulrich, E.T. (2010). "Poetic Influences on the Development of Aurobindo's Spiritual and Nationalistic Convictions." *International Journal of Hindu Studies*, *14*(1), 121-146.

White, D. (1972). "The Yoga of Knowledge in the Gītā according to Sri Aurobindo". *International Philosophical Quarterly*, *12*(2), 243-250.

4

Indigenous Social Group Work Practice

Shivani D. Mishra

Introduction

Indigenous-based educational programmes are missing from the Indian curriculum, and the social work programme is no exception. Manifestations of Western Eurocentric perspectives are seen and taught in the social work curriculum. The hegemonic process in education describes colonisation ruling over the culture, economy, and education, with a minor emphasis on cultural competence in the social work training programme. Thus, it gave birth to the "decolonisation" of social work education, as colonisation has influenced social work educators' perspectives. In addition to this, several professional social work associations at the national and international levels hardly emphasise decolonisation or indigenous knowledge; they are more directive and thus not an effective driver for change.

The social work profession emerged in the Western world, particularly in the United States of America and the United Kingdom, at the turn of the twentieth century. For many of these countries, Western social welfare systems were introduced through the colonial empires of the nineteenth and twentieth centuries. The expansion of Western social work to non-Western countries occurred in the middle of the 20th century (Asamoah & Nortey, 1987; Kendall, 1995; Midgley, 1981, cited in Kreitzer, 2004: 8). With the increase in technological knowledge, modernisation, and neo-liberal economic policies, social work is now re-evaluating its role in the international arena of global interdependence (Hokenstad and Midgley, 1997). The contemporary globalisation phenomenon has influenced and challenged the social work profession; other historical conjunctures, such as colonisation and modernization, have also had an impact on social welfare and social work education in non-Western nations.

A review of historical narratives of social work in India reveals that post-Independence social work education was impacted by Western social work information, theories, and techniques. They imported Western expertise with the idea that Western social work knowledge was universal. Such efforts in India's education system bolstered the colonial regime. Prior to independence, India founded the first school of social work in 1936, 10 years after formal accreditation of social work study in Western nations, India was a colonial power at the time. Thus, Western social work expertise is believed to have been introduced into the social work curriculum. However, even in following years, the curriculum remained unchanged, and it did not take into account Indian literature, views, or social reform events.

Presently, many social work institutions use the same curriculum without giving it a single thought about its relevance to the Indian context. Western expertise is at the forefront in Indian schools due to the "angilistic" approach in the social work curriculum. Indian expertise and cultural competency, on the other hand, were pushed backwards. As a result, numerous educators in India at the time were oriented towards this model. As a result, Indian social work educators did not take many attempts to build social work curriculum based on the Indian context, theory, and practice.

The incorporation of Western philosophy into the social work curriculum has distanced social work educators and students from local traditions, cultures, and place-based education. As a result, indigenisation of social work education and practice in India is required. According to Dash (2018a), attempts were made to reject irrelevant and outdated information imposed on India by Eurocentric and American-centric researchers who strove to make it more relevant and suitable to Indian contexts while decolonising the social work curriculum. The underlying goal of researching Indian indigenous practices is to empower social work academics, practitioners, and policymakers to break free from their "culture of silence" (Freire, 1997) and proclaim indigenous knowledge and practice. Such endeavours can contribute in the creation of new knowledge (Kreitzer).

Discovering '*Myself*'

My experience of studying a colonised syllabus has encouraged me to write this article. The word "epistemicide", coined by Santos (2016), came to my mind; he suggests that we kill the students' voice in a curriculum that is meant for their development due to the dominant epistemology of universities. We do not consider the students' predicament. We do not try to understand how they would cope in a colonised-centred environment where there is no space for them to share their ideas and no opportunity for them to grow.

A few concerns inspire me to share my thoughts on indigenous and decolonisation of social work education. The first reason I recalled the days when I was a social work student was that I often questioned my teachers as to why we were following a curriculum that we could not relate to our culture and did not allow us to express our ideas. As a student, I struggled through my conflict and could not cope with Western philosophy and its hegemony. Despite this challenge, I used Euro-centric thinking and promoted Western philosophy in my teaching practice.

I stance with what Mignolo (2009) calls "epistemic disobedience," resisting the notion of knowledge and knowledge production as a neutral enterprise in social work practice, research, and education (p. 160). My association with local thinkers and readings of ancient works of literature challenged my assumptions about Western hegemony. This practice allowed me to contribute to the creation of new knowledge about indigenous social work practice.

The second reason is the concept of 'revolutionary cultural action' (Freire, 1997). He posits that the more radical the person is, the more fully they enter into reality so that, knowing it better, they can better transform it (p. 21). It is time to transform social work education in India and social work educators' responsibilities are more to prepare future social work practitioners.

By writing this article, I am not advocating that if cultural practices are taught and adopted in social work education alone, we can prepare better social work practitioners. I am suggesting that the indigenous base of social work education or indigenization of social work education in India demands cultural competence on the part of professionals (Jaswal and Pandya, 2015: 145). Thus, "the wisdom of indigenous culture can be used to supplement and complement the Western conception" (Tsang, 1998: 178).

The third reason is the principle of self-determination. It is one of the significant factors that encouraged me to strengthen my identity and contribute to writing down my thoughts on indigenous social work education.

This chapter addresses my critical reflection on the need for the decolonisation of social work education in India. There is a dire need for the *Bharatiyakaran* [Indianisation] of social work, which aims to give a new perspective and new direction to social work education in the Indian context through redesigning and redefining the curriculum by bringing about a synergy between Indian wisdom and international standards of social work education (Dash, 2020: 394).

The discussion unfolds into three sections. First, I narrate the significance of indigenisation in social work education; secondly, I examine the historical analysis of the recognition of group work in social work practice in the colonial era. Lastly, I will present the indigenous models of group work practice in India.

Indigenisation in Social Work Education: Literature Review

The valorisation of indigenous knowledge and increasing body of scholarly work found in several countries that experienced colonisation and its impact on a forthcoming generation. I reviewed a variety of literature on indigenous or decolonized social work education and practice.

The term 'indigenisation' needs to be defined to understand its significance in education and the reason for contextualisation. *Random House Dictionary* of the English Language (1969) defines indigenous as "originating in and characterising a particular region or country". The *Oxford Dictionary* (1968) defines it as "native knowledge belonging naturally to the soil." Thus, it is developing local ideas, perspectives, regional experiences, and indigenous innovations in Third World countries (Dash, 2017). Recently, a movement to *Bharatiyakaran*/Indianisation of social work education has emerged, with the goal of indigenizing social work education in India (Dash, 2020).

In social work practice, the term indigenisation is defined by Desai (1997: 151) as "adopting universal concepts and theories to the country's or local situation". Such indigenous knowledge forms an essential link between indigenous social work practice and indigenous social work education. Thus, there is a need for "paradigmatic shifts in social work theory, education, research, and practice" (Gray *et al.*, 2013: 7).

Supporting indigenous education is an international endeavour that helps to establish Indigenous models and practice in education. Discourse observed in several countries like:

Australia (Dittefled, 2020, Rowe & Baldry, 2015).
The Torres Strait Islands (Nakata, 2002).
New Zealand (Royal, 2007, Smith, 2012).
Canada (Battiste, 2002; Kanu, 2011).
Africa (Dei, 2011b; Adefarakan, 2011).
The United States (Brayboy & Maughan, 2009; Deloria & Wildcat, 2002, Crampton 2015).

Hawai'i (Meyer, 2001; Goodyear Kaopua, 2013; Tibbetts, Kahakalau, & Johnson, 2007).
Alaska (Barnhardt & Kawagley, 2010; Kawagley, 1995).

All the authors lambasted the Western models adopted in education. A single point of criticism is that the social work curriculum must be relevant to the Indian context (Gore, 1965; Dasgupta, 1968; Banerjee, 1972; Desai, 1985; Siddique, 1987; Kulkarni, 1993; Desai, 2004; Saldanh, 2008; Dash, 2020; Bodhi, 2021; Dash, 2017).

Notably, it can be precisely indicated that indigenous knowledge certainly creates a new, balanced centre and a new vantage point from which to analyse Eurocentric education and its pedagogies, "new perceptions" and open up "new possibilities" in education (Battiste, 2002: 5, Brayboy & Maughan, 2009: 18).

Social Group Work: A Historical Account

The historical foundation of social group work enables us to understand the influence of colonisation on social work education. In the twentieth century, the profession of social work arose in the Western world, primarily in the United States of America and the United Kingdom (Kreitzer, 2004: 8).

In America, the Federal Council of Christ Church was instrumental in developing group discussion and educational methods used in club and recreational work with youth. Lindeman (1921) and Follet (1918) carried out the conceptualisation of group work through club groups where ideas were generated and nurtured. They travelled around the country preaching the new gospel and training leaders for group work, and they published books on group discussion methods, community resolution, intergroup conflict, and intergroup relations.

The philosophical influences such as the ethics of Judeo-Christian religion, the YMCA, YWCA, Scouting, and the Settlement House Movement's charitable and humanitarian efforts impacted the development of social group work. Furthermore, social group work was also influenced by progressive education as it developed in Europe.

In 1923, the School of Applied Social Sciences offered a group service course at Western Reserve University. The group work method is called "democratic group action", where the individual will have space and place to grow. Kaiser (1930) was a proponent of group work theory and practice and made an effort to recognise social group work as a method in a social work programme. The convergence of several trends during the period between the 1920s and 1930s led to the development of group work as a method of social work and field education.

Group work was introduced in the social work curriculum in 1935 at the National Conference of Social Work. Experts at the conference identified group work as a process, a field, and a set of techniques to enable educators to recognise group work as a method in social work. The critical discourse on group work was presented by Coyle (1930) and Newsletter (1938). They are essential contributors who have explained group work as a helping method, a process, a technique, educational, and a field of practice. Coyle (1947: 146-47 and 165) termed group work as a mode of social action and a way to achieve social goals. This conference led to the establishment of the American Association for the Study of Group Work in 1936. In the early 1950s, the group work method was distinctively introduced in Great Britain, the USA, Canada, and several other parts of the world, including India. The saddest part was that the Indian social work educators accepted western philosophy in the social work curriculum.

Tracing Indian History on Social Group Work

Mehta (1987) suggests that

> "There is evidence of the group approach being used in charity, imparting religious education through the oral tradition, mobilising the people for the freedom struggle against the British, social reform, and more recently in typically indigenous welfare strategies such as the Sarvodaya and Bhoodan movements."

India has a long tradition of social work and social welfare. Group work found its roots in India in the nineteenth century, but we never systematically incorporated it into our syllabus. As it is not an Indian syllabus, it is hardly found in infield practice. When they are placed in agency settings, social work students practice group work by undertaking recreational, educational, and cultural activities (Verma, 1986).

> "Generally speaking, there is in India no 'setting' that can be termed as a 'group work setting', though the techniques and understanding of group work processes are definitely used when working with groups of individuals, whether in a family, an institution, or a community" (Joseph 1997: 119).

If we look at Indian ancient literature, there is a high amount of group work literature written by non-social work educators. However, there is a paucity of writing as per the Indian context by social work educators. Nonetheless, group work theory and practice are rooted in "social reform, social responsibility, democratic ideals, and social action, as well as social relatedness and human attachment" (Lee, 1991: 3).

The philosophy of welfare is deep-rooted in Indian culture and traditions. Indigenous knowledge is rooted in and affiliated with the occupancy of and relationship with the land and is inseparable from a place and local contexts (Shahjahan, 2005 cited in Khan, 2019).

Group work was an indigenous practice in India before independence. The social modes and movements are the best examples of group work practice in India. The indigenous forerunner, Narayan Malhar Joshi, in the year 1911, established an organisation called the Social Service League, an agency of the Servants of India Society, established by Gopal Krishna Gokhale in 1905, a series of lectures were given on social welfare services and social problems in India. Several social work practitioners working in welfare agencies were part of this training-based lecture programme. Over here, the methods of social work are profoundly accepted, especially group work.

A thought-provoking article by Nanavaty in which he discusses democratic values and contends that the roots of dysfunctionality are not to be found only in the individual, but could very well be found embedded in the social situation. He was convinced that the ideal social condition must be democratic, whatever other characteristics such a situation might exhibit. He argued that "voluntary participation with social groups gives an immense opportunity to the participants... to grasp the understanding of democratic methods" (cited in Joseph, 1997). Furthermore, Kaikobad's (1961: 3) also mentions that

> "group work is an effective educational tool, not only to bring about individual change but to help groups to come together for a social purpose which would help 'develop respect and a reasonable attitude not only towards one's cultural heritage but also towards that of others.' develop respect and a reasonable attitude not only towards one's cultural heritage but also towards that of others."

When Western values are taught as a part of the curriculum, it would be too hard for future social work practitioners to put things into practice in the field. The dissonance between western values and Indian values woefully impacts the mind, restricting us from executing the practice and connecting with real-life experience. Students cannot write narrative records of their work as they find conflict among themselves to utilise the body of knowledge acquired in classrooms and the background observed in the field.

In the following section, I demonstrate an indigenous model of group work practice and project that the integration enables future social work practitioners to link with real-life experience. An attempt is not to replace or demean the existing model of group work practice but to suggest alternative needs in social work education.

Indigenous Models of Group Work Practice in India: Scientific Aspects

The indigenous model demonstrated scientific and professional knowledge and every profession concerned with epistemology, ontology, axiology, and methodology. Table 4.1 indicates:

Table 4.1: Indigenous Framework

Social Work Philosophical Approaches	Hegemonic Construction	Indigenous Knowledge
Ontology: Theory of Being	The colonised reality promoted the inter-connectedness of physical and spiritual worlds by imposing its religious practice, language, and cultural practices.	It is rooted in one's own cultural practise that governs one's life. Reality is shaped by the values inherent in social institutions, namely family, economic, and political. Swadrushti (Dash, 2020).
Epistemology: Theory of Knowing	An imposed Christian value was to address the challenges of local problems.	Origins in Ancient literature *Bhagavad Gita*, Upanishads and thoughts of social reformer Swami Vivekanand, Vinoba Bhave, Nanaji Deshmukh, and Dattapant Thengadi. They are ingenious theorists embedded in the Indic thought stream.
Axiology: Values	Values of Social Work and Social Work are provided by associations of social workers that are based on Eurocentric ideas.	Dharmic Values promote individual to flourish human life. *Vasudhaiva Kutumbakam* inculcates values among us from "loftiest Vedantic thought".
Methodology: Theory of Doing	The voice of the colonized approach has been honoured and privileged. Voices of colonized people were incorporated into the curriculum and field practice.	Indian social reformers and the lives of indigenous people are abundant with resources and practice modules for social work practitioners. Several social reformers worked for social justice through innovative group therapy and approaches through ingenious ways and processes.

Indigenous ontology, epistemology, and axiology have the potential to lead to social change and are means for social, cultural, and political awareness. It enables us to understand localised knowledge that is rooted in our culture and social movements.

The social revolutionary movements such as Sarvodaya, Chipko, Bhoodan, Antyodaya, and Satyasodhak Samaj, and gurukuls, ashram shala, are an example of the social group work practice in India. All these movements were found during the colonial period of India.

Indigenous Group Work Practice in India: Few Examples

Prabhat Pheri

'Prabhat' in Prabhat Pheri stands for "morning time," which is normally a time past 4 a.m. during the early morning. And Pheri stands for "walking around". So, during Prabhat Pheri, some people would gather early in the morning and would take a round of their surroundings. It is an Indian ethnic way of promoting and building a sense of unity amongst the people.

The same Prabhat Pheri was used as a strategy during the Indian freedom movement. In 1857, the very first freedom struggle for independence began in Meerut. Immediately after that, the freedom movement began across the country. Before independence and for nearly 15 years, the Prabhat Pheri has been organised. The broader aim of the Prabhat Pheri was to instil energy among the youth to participate with vigour in the freedom movement. The elderly, youth, people from different religions, and different classes were part of the Prabhat Pheri. Prabhat Pheri was a medium where people were given the chance to express their views and opinions.

Historically, Prabhat Pheri has been used as a social service programme to raise awareness about social issues.

Ganeshotsav

Keshav Gangadhar Tilak, an Independence Activist, arranged two festivals that took place over caste and creed, intending to encourage the ordinary man. *Ganeshotsav* and *Shivaji Utsav* started in 1894 for national awakening. *Shivaji Utsav* began in 1894 at Fort Raigad and its popularity reached Japan. *Ganeshotsav* achieved national significance in 1896. He soon began to be considered as unquestioned Maharashtra's leader and in 1893, was awarded the title "*Lokamanya*". *Ganeshotsav* is seen as the practice of "social inclusion", too. Because people from different religions, regions, and caste fraternities come together to celebrate this festival, one could witness that from the artisans who create the idols to the craftsmen who do the decorations, to the presidents of *Ganeshotsav pandals*, belong to some other religions. *Ganeshotsav* in Pune is an all-encompassing festival," says historian Pandurang Balkawade. He explains how Ganesh Puja is a socio-cultural phenomenon with deep roots in heritage, tradition, and politics.

Conclusion

Social group work, a primary method of social work, creates the knowledge production about the nature of social problems that guides professionals to move ahead for practice. The fundamental purpose of the social worker is the pursuit of justice and equality and above indigenous models entail the interdependence among the group to achieve common objectives and work towards achieving social goals. Such a process never taps into the social work curriculum; indeed, Euro-centric and Sino-centric thoughts are encouraged and motivated by social work educators.

Indigenous Group work practice strengthens the practice model of social work in India. In the Independence movement, the intergroup experience, purposeful planning, and group goals are the indigenous practices followed in India. Indigenous group work practice enables social workers to understand the social and cultural dimension and become enablers to evolve a democratically developed society.

REFERENCES

Adefarakan, T. (2011). (Re)conceptualizing 'Indigenous' from anti-colonial Black feminist theoretical perspectives: Living and imagining Indigeneity differently. In G.J.S. Dei (ed.), *Indigenous Philosophies and Critical Education* (pp. 34-52). New York, NY: Peter Lang.

Asamoah, Y.W. & Nortey, D.N.A. (1987). Ghana. In J. Dixon (ed.) *Social Welfare in Africa.* Beckenham: Croom Helm Ltd.

Barnhardt, R. & Kawagley, A.O. (2010). *Alaska native education: Views from within.* Fairbanks, A.K.,: *Alaska Native Knowledge Network*, Centre for Cross- cultural Studies, University of Alaska Fairbank.

Battiste, M. (2002). *Indigenous Knowledge and Pedagogy in First Nations Education: A Literature Review with Recommendations*. Ottawa, ON: Report prepared for the National Working Group on Education and the Minister of Indian Affairs Indian and Northern Affairs Canada (INAC).

Banerjee, G. (1972). *Papers in Social Work: An Indian Perspective.* Bombay: Tata Institute of Social Sciences.

Bodhi, S.R. (2021). Tribal and State Policy in India: Revisiting Governing Principle from a Decolonial Social Work Perspective *British Journal of Social Work,* Vol. 50, 2372-2388, Oxford University Press.

Brayboy, B.M.J. & Castagno, A.E. (2009). Self-determination through self-education: Culturally responsive schooling for Indigenous students in the USA. *Teaching Education*, 20, pp. 31-53.

Crampton, A. (2015). Decolonizing Social Work "Best Practices" through a Philosophy of Impermanence, *Journal of Indigenous Development,* 4 (1) pp 1-11.

Dash, B.M. (2017). Revisiting Eight Decades of Social Work Education in India. *Asian Social Work and Policy Review*, 11(1), 66-75.

Dash, B.M. (2020). Indianisation/Bharatiyakaran of Social Work Education: A national Mission towards Indigenizing social work education in India, *Social Dialogue*, 23, 75-77.

Dash, B.M. (2020). Movement towards Indianisation of Social Work Education. In: S.M. S., Baikady R., Sheng-Li C., Sakaguchi, H. (eds.), The Palgrave Handbook of Global Social Work Education. *Palgrave Macmillan, Cham.*, pp. 393-405.

Dasgupta, S. (1968). *Social Work and Social Change: A Case Study in Indian Village Development.* Boston: Extending Horizon Books.

Dei, G.J.S. (2011). Revisiting the question of the 'Indigenous.' In G.J.S. Dei (ed.), *Indigenous Philosophies And Critical Education: A Reader,* pp. 21-33. New York, NY: Peter Lang.

Deloria, V. & Wildcat, D.R. (2001). *Power and Place: Indian Education in America.* Golden, CO: Fulcrum Publishing.

Desai, M. (2004). Methodology of progressive social work education. New Delhi: Rawat Publications.

Desai, M. (1991). Issues concerning the setting up of social work specialisations in India. *International Social Work*, 34(1), pp. 83-95.

Dittfeld, Tanja (2020). Seeing White: Turning the postcolonial lens on social work in Australia Seeing White: Turning the postcolonial lens on social work in Australia/Semantic Scholar (Accessed on August 2020).

Freire, P. (1970) *Pedagogy of the Oppressed.* London: Penguin Books.

Goodyear & Kaopua, N. (2013). *The Seeds We Planted: Portraits of a Native Hawaiian Charter School.* Minneapolis, MN: University of Minnesota Press.

Gore, M. (1965). *Social Work and Social Work Education*. Bombay: Asia Publishing House.

Gray, M., Coates, J., Yellow Bird, M., & Hetherington, T. (Eds.) (2013). *Decolonising Social Work.* London: Ashgate Publishing Company.

Hokenstad, M.C. & Midgley, J. (1997). *Issues in International Social Work* Washington DC: NASW.

Jacob *et al.* (2018). The Gift of Education: How Indigenous Knowledge Can Transform the Future of Public Education, *International Journal of Multicultural Education,* 2 (1), pp.157-185.

Jaswal, S., Pandya, S. (2015) Social Work Education in India Discussion on Indigenisation. *The Indian Journal of Social Work,* Tata Institute of Social Science, Vol. 76, Issue 1.

Joseph, H. (1997) 'Social work with groups: A literature review', *Indian Journal of Social Work,* 58 (2) 195-211.

Khan, M. (2019). "ASocial Work Perspective on Indigenous Knowledge, Anticolonial Thought, and Contemplative Pedagogy: Thoughts on Decolonization and Resistance. Retrieved from https://caos.library.ryerson.ca/index.php/caos/ article/download/1313/ Accessed on December 2020

Kaikobad, N.F. (1961). Practice of Social Work-II: From the Angle of a Social Group Worker. In A.R. Wadia (ed.), *History and Philosophy of Social Work in India* (399-406), Bombay: Allied Publishers.

Kreitzer, L. (2004). *Indigenization of Social Work Education and Practice: A Participatory Action Research Project in Ghana.* Faculty of Social Work, Calgary, Alberta.

Kulkarni, P.D. (1993). The Indigenous base of social work profession in India. *The Indian Journal of Social Work*, 54(4): pp. 555-65.

Kanu, Y. (2011). *Integrating Aboriginal Perspectives into the School Curriculum: Purposes, Possibilities, and Challenges*. Toronto, ON: University of Toronto Press.

Kawagley, A. (1995). *A Yupiaq Worldview: A Pathway to Ecology and Spirit. Prospect Heights*, IL: Waveland Press.

Mehta, V.D. (1987) *Group Work.* In Encyclopaedia of Social Work in India, Vol. 2 (7-21), New Delhi: Ministry of Welfare.

Meyer, M.A. (2001). Our own liberation: Reflections on Hawaiian epistemology. *Contemporary Pacific*, 13(1), pp. 124-148.

Mignolo, W.D. (2009). Epistemic disobedience, independent thought and decolonial freedom. *Theory, Culture & Society*, 26(7-8), pp. 159-181. doi:10.1177/ 0263276409349275

National Collaborating Centre for Aboriginal Health, Reading, C.L., & Wien, F. (2009). *Health Inequalities and Social Determinants of Aboriginal Peoples Health*, 2009.

Nanavati, M. (1949). Social Group Work Technique for Preserving Democratic Values, *The Indian Journal of Social Work*, 9(4), pp.296-302.

Newstetter, W.I. (1935). *What is social group work? Proceedings from the 62nd Meeting of the National Conference on Social Work*, Held in Montreal, Canada, June 9-15, 1935, pp. 291-299 +https://socialwelfare.library.vcu.edu/social-work/social-group-work/

Pickering, Taima (2010). *Decolonisation as a social change framework and its impact on the development of Indigenous-based curricula for Helping Professionals in Mainstream Tertiary Education Organisations,* University of Waikato, Hamilton, New Zeland. Retrieved from https:// www.collectionscanada.gc.ca/obj/thesescanada/vol2/OSUL/T... Accessed on January 2021.

Royal, T.C. (2007). *The Purpose of Education: Perspectives Arising from Matauranga Maori,* Wellington: Ministry of Education. Retrieved from http://www.mkta.co.nz/assets/educationpurposev.4.pd Accessed on December 2020

Rowe, S. & Baldry, E. (2015). *Decolonising Social Work Research: Learning from Critical Indigenous Approaches Australian Social Work Forthcoming* Retrieved from Decolonising Social Work Research: Learning from Critical Indigenous Approaches (researchgate.net) Accessed on January 2021.

Santos, B. (2016). *Epistemologies of the South: Justice against epistemicide.* Routledge. Taylor & Francis Group, New York.

Saldanha, D. (2008). Towards a conceptualisation of social action within social work: teaching social action as a dialogue between theoretical perspectives and between theory and practice. *Indian Journal of Social Work,* 69(2) pp.111-37.

Simone Rowe, Eileen Baldry & Wendy Earles (2015). Decolonising Social Work Research: Learning from Critical Indigenous Approaches, *Australian Social Work,* 68:3, pp. 296-308, DOI: 10.1080/0312407X.2015.102426

Smith, L.T. (2012). *Decolonizing Methodologies: Research and Indigenous Peoples* (2nd ed.). London: Zed Books.

Siddiqui, H.Y (1987). Towards a competency-based education for social work. *Indian Journal of Social Work,* 48(1): pp. 23-32.

Smith, G.H. (2000). Protecting and Respecting Indigenous Knowledge. In M. Battiste (Ed.), *Reclaiming Indigenous Voice and Vision,* Toronto: ON: UBC Press.

Tibbetts, K.A., Kahakalau, K., & Johnson, Z. (2007). Education with Aloha and student assets. *Hûlili: Multidisciplinary Research on Hawaiian Well-Being,* 4(1), pp. 147-181

Tsang, N.M. (1998). Beyond theory and practice integration in social work: Lessons from the West. *International Social Work,* 41(2), pp. 169-180.

Wepa, D. (2005). *Cultural Safety in Aotearoa,* New Zealand. Auckland: Pearson Prentice Hall.

5
Concept of Sewa in Hindu Scriptures

Abhinav Prakash

सर्वे भवन्तु सुखिनः सर्वे सन्तु निरामयाः।
सर्वे भद्राणि पश्यन्तु मा कष्चिद्दुःखभाग्भवते।
ॐ शान्तिः शान्तिः शान्तिः।

May all sentient beings are at peace, may no one suffer from illness,
May all see what is auspicious, may no one suffer-
Om peace, peace, peace.

Concept of Dharma

For Hindus, dharma is the moral order of the universe and a code of living that embodies the fundamental principles of law, religion, and duty that govern all reality.[1] The *Mahabharata* in verse 8.49.50 explains the Dharma through Bhishma:

धारणात् धर्म इत्याहुः धर्मों धारयति प्रजाः।
यः स्यात् धारणसंयुक्तः स धर्म इति निश्चयः।।
dharanat dharma ityahuh dharmom dharayati, prajah |
yah syat, dharanasamyuktah sa dharma iti nizcayah ||

They call it "Dharma", since it is Dharma that upholds people. That which upholds the created universe, supports it and sustains it, without which the universe just falls apart, is called "Dharma". Dharma sustains and maintains the social, moral, political, and economic order. In verse 1.4.14, the *Brihadaranyaka Upanishad* states the importance of Dharma as:

'धर्मः तस्माद्धर्मात् परं नास्त्य् अथो अबलीयान्
बलीयाँसमाशँसते धर्मेण यथा राज्ञैवम्।
यो वै स धर्मः सत्यं वै तत् तस्मात्सत्यं वदन्तमाहुर्
धर्मं वदतीति धर्मं वा वदन्तँ सत्यं वदतीत्य्
एतद्ध्येवैतदुभयं भवति।।
dharmah tasm addharmat param nasty atho abaliyan
baliyasamaśasate dharmena yatha rajjaivama |
yo vai sa dharmah satyam vai tat tasmatsatyam vadantamahur
dharmam vadatiti dharmam va vadant satyam vadatity
etaddhyevaitadubhayam bhavati ||

Nothing is higher than Dharma. The weak overcome the stronger by Dharma, as over a king. Truly, Dharma is the Truth (*Satya*); therefore, when a man speaks the Truth, they say, "He speaks the Dharma," and if he speaks Dharma, they say, "He speaks the Truth!" Kanāda's *Vaiśesika Sūtra* in verse (1.1.2) begins with a statement saying that its ostensible purpose is to explain *dharma*, specifies that *dharma* is that which ensures the attainment of prosperity (*abhyudaya*) as well as the highest good (*nihœreyasa*) 'यतो अभ्युदय निरू श्रेयस सिद्धिः स्ः धर्म्ः।' ('*yato, abhyudaya, ni, śreyasa, siddhi's, dharm|*') *Bhagavad Gita* in Chapter 3 Verse 35 asks one to perform one's natural prescribed duty, though tinged with faults, rather than perform another's prescribed duty, though perfectly. In fact, it is preferable to die in the discharge of one's duty, than to follow the path of another, which is fraught with danger.

श्रेयान्स्वधर्मो विगुणः परधर्मात्स्वनुश्ठितात्।
स्वधर्मे निधनं श्रेयः परधर्मो भयावहः।।
śreyansvadharmo, viguna, paradharmatsvanuśthitat |
svadharme, nidhanam, zreya, paradharmo, bhayavaha ||

Mahabharata further in verse 12.64.21 gives primacy the dharma of the king and announce it as the most important dharma चात्रो धर्मो प्रयादिदेवात् प्रवृत्तः। पश्चात् अन्ये शेषभूताश्च धर्माः। 'catro dharmo prayadidevat pravritah pascat anye śesabhutaśca dharmah'. The Supreme God first created the code of righteousness for rulers (*raja dharma*) and then incorporated other codes of righteousness into it. The Bṛhadāraṇyaka Upaniśad seeks to define Dharma by linking it with "Truth".

स नैव व्यभवत् तच्छ्रेयो रूपमत्यसृजत धर्मम्।
तदेतत्क्षत्रस्य क्षत्रं यद्धर्मस्तस्माद्धर्मात् परं नास्त्यथो
अबलीयान् बलीया समाश सते धर्मेण यथा राज्ञैवम्।
यो वै स धर्मः सत्यं वै तत् तस्मात्सत्यं वदन्तमाहुर्धर्मं वदतीति धर्मं
वा वदन्त सत्यं वदतीत्यतेद्धयेवैतदुभयं भवति।1.4.14।
sa, naiva, vyabhavat, tacchreyo, rupamatyasrjata, dharmamd
tadetatksatrasya, ksatram, yaddharmastasmaddharmst, param, nastyatho,
abalIyan, baliya, samaza, sate, dharmena, yatha, rajjaivamd
yo vai, sa dharmah satyam vai tat tasmatsatyam vadantamahurdharmam vadatiti dharmam
va vadanta satyam vadatityetaddhyevaitadubhayam bhavati |1.4.14|

He projected that excellent form of "righteousness" (Dharma). This righteousness is the controller of the kshatriya. Therefore, there is nothing higher than that. So, even a weak man hopes to defeat a stronger man through righteousness, as one contends with the king. That Righteousness is verily truth. As a result, they say of someone speaking the truth, "he speaks of righteousness," or of someone speaking of righteousness, "he speaks of truth," because both are the same [1].

[1] Translation from Swami Mādhavānanda of the Ramakrishna Math.

According to Mahabharat (3.9.30), righteousness bestows both wealth and happiness.In fact, everything can be acquired through righteousness. This entire universe sustains itself on the foundation of righteousness. धर्मादर्थः प्रभवति धर्मात्प्रभवते सुखम्। धर्मेण लभते सर्वं धर्मसारमिदं जगत्।। (dharmadartha, prabhavati, dharmatprabhavate, sukhamd dharmena labhate sarvam dharmasaramidam jagat ||).

It also says in verse 13.111.17 धर्म एको मनुष्याणां सहायः पारलौकिकः (*dharma, eko, manu syanam, sahaya, paralaukika*). Dharma is the only companion of man after death, in the other worlds and in verse 12.101.10 'प्रभवार्थाय भूतानां धर्मप्रवचनं कृतम्। यः स्यात्प्रभवसंयुक्तः स धर्म इति निष्चयः'(prabhavarthaya, bhutanam, dharmapravacanam, kṛtam ya, syatprabhavasamyukta, sa, dharma, iti, niścaya |).

Dharma has been preached solely for the upliftment of embodied souls (*jīvas*) A doctrine which has the capacity to bring about all-round progress is befitingly called Dharma. Vagbhat in Sutrasthan, Ashtanghruday सुखं न विना धर्मात् तस्मात् धर्मपरो भवेत्। (sukham, na, vina, dharmat, tasmat, dharmaparo, bhavet) Happiness (and bliss, that is, a superlative spiritual state which is far above and beyond happiness) cannot be acquired without becoming righteous; hence one should be devoutly righteous. is defined by Yogavashishth as "*sukhasya mulam dharma*". Dharma is the root of happiness. The *Gita* says in verse 2.40, and "*svalpam api asya dharmasya trayato mahato bhayat*" that even a small amount of righteousness protects one from great danger.Ramayan in verse 7.49 says Dharma restrains the enemy (unrighteousness) and, in accordance with the law, protects the subjects. The sustainer (dhaaran) is the name given to this form of Dharma.

धारणवद्विदिशाम चैव धर्मेनारज्जायाप्रजा।
तस्माद्धारणमित्यक्तु स धर्म इति निश्चयः। ।
dharanavdivdisam caiva dharmenarajjayanpraja |
tasmaddharanamityuktam sa dharma iti nizcaya ||

Dharma ensures victory.'यतो धर्मस्ततो जयः' 'yato dharmastato jaya' (Mahabharata 13.167.41). Dharma changes according to the situation and context of an individual. The *Mahabharata* clarifies that Dharma takes into account the personal condition of the individual. Some of the verses are mentioned here, explaining dharma in difficult circumstances.

'क्षुधा निर्णुदति प्रज्ञां धर्मबुद्धिं व्यपोहति।
क्षुधापरिगतज्ञानो धृतिं त्यजति चौव हि।।'
'ksudha nirnudati prajjam dharmabuddhim vyapohati |
ksudhaparigatajjano dhrtim tyajati caiva hi ||

Poverty and hunger cause deterioration of an individual's intellect and faith in *Dharma* as well. Hunger destroys an individual's knowledge as well as his confidence. Thus, it is said that an ignorant society that is poverty-stricken and hungry has no association whatsoever with *Moksha* (Ashwamedha parva, Adhyaya 90, Shloka 91).

यथा यथैव जीवेद्धि तत्कर्तव्यमहलेया।
जीवितं मरणाछ्रेयो जीवन् धर्ममवाप्नुयात्।।
yatha yathaiva jiveddhi tatkartavyamahelaya |
jivitam maranacchreyo jivan dharmamavapnuyat ||

If you have to survive, leave no stone unturned. Being alive is always preferable to death, because we can only follow Dharma when we are alive (Shanti parva, Adhyaya 141, Shloka 65).

यस्यैव बलमोजश्च स धर्मस्य प्रभुर्नरः।
yasyaiva, balamojazca sa dharmasya, prabhurnarah |

He who has power and *Tej* (Radiance) becomes capable of abiding by *Dharma* (Mahabharat, Shanti Parva, Adhyaya 152, Shloka 18).

धर्मार्थकाममोक्षाख्यं य इछेच्छ्रेय आत्मनः ।
एकमेव हरेस्तत्र कारणं पादसेवनम् ।।
hạrmarthakamamoksakhyam ya icchecchreya atmanah |
ekameva harestatra karanam padasevanam ||

Accomplishing the four basic pursuits of life, namely *Dharma, Artha*, *Kama,* and *Moksha,* ensures the well-being of mankind. The only way to achieve these goals is to serve Shrihari's (God's) holy feet (Shrimadbhagwat, Skandha 4, Adhyaya 8, Shloka 41).

यस्य धर्मो हि धर्मार्थं क्लेशभाङ्न स पण्डितः ।
न स धर्मस्य वेदार्थं सूर्यस्यान्धः प्रभामिव ।।
yasya dharmo hi dharmartham kleśabhagna sa panditah |
na sa dharmasya vedartham suryasyandhah prabhamiva |

He who performs *Dharmacharan* merely as an obligation in *Dharma* (without understanding its principles) is not a wise man and is the one who becomes unhappy. Just as a blind person does not understand what is meant by the Sun's radiance, so does a person who performs *Dharmacharan* merely as an obligation, not understand the meaning of *Dharma* (Vanaparva, Adhyaya 34, Shloka 23).

Hinduism regards the poor as part of God and regards them as '*Daridra Naraayana*' (those among whom God is present) to reflect the feeling and who should be served with respect and love (Nadkami, 2007). The well known Saint Narsi Mehta reflects the same in his famous song "*Vaishnav jan to taine kahiye je peer parayi jaane re*". He calls that one a true Vaishnava (devotee of Lord Vishnu) who empathises with the suffering of others, and who relieves others' pain with humility. The following are some of the important qualities listed in various scriptures:[1]

1. *Ahimsa* (*nonviolence*): Founded on the concepts of man and reincarnation.
2. *Samyam* (*mind and sense control*): Considered essential for any form of morality.
3. *Tolerance*: For differing beliefs, points of view, religious traditions, and people.
4. *Hospitality*: Exemplifying generosity and the value of service.
5. *Compassion*: Based on atman concepts, the ability to feel for others as we do for ourselves.

6. *Protection*: Providing shelter to others, particularly the less fortunate.
7. *Respect*: Respect for all living beings; respect for the sanctity of life.
8. *Wisdom*: Knowledge is contrasted with ignorance; the ability to distinguish between what is right and wrong.
9. *Austerity*: In addition to theoretical knowledge, austerity entails practical wisdom and discipline.
10. *Celibacy*: One of the four ashrams; important for spiritual life.
11. *Honesty*: In order to avoid self-deception, relationships must be built on trust.
12. *Cleanliness* encompasses both external hygiene and internal purity.
13. *Charity*: A person is considered to be in the quality of goodness when charity is given out of duty, without expectation of return, at the proper time and place, and to a deserving person.

These virtues guide the ordinary Hindu to live a life in harmony with society and nature to ensure the lowest negative environmental impact. Hinduism as a religion has promoted the idea of natural and social harmony. It also promoted the concept of simple living for each individual to ensure less pressure on resources. Within Hinduism, wealth is regarded as a beneficial and positive value, just like love and morality—if pursued within limits.[2]

The idea of universal prosperity and health has always been promoted by the Upanishads. This shows the concern of Hinduism as a religion for the care of all. It also echoed the moral values of a highly principled individual to not differentiate between people like mind and others but promote the concept of वसुधैव कुटुंबकं (vasudhaiva, kutumbakam—The whole world is a family), considering the whole world as a family.

अयं निजः परोवेति गणना लघु चेतसाम ।
उदार चरितानां तु वसुधैव कुटुम्बकम ।।
(पञ्चतन्त्रम, पंचम तंत्र, "अपरीक्षितकारकम्")
ayam nijah paroveti ganana laghu cetasama |
udara caritanam tu vasudhaiva kutumbakama ||
(pañcatantrama, pancama, tantra, "apariksitakarakam").

The statement implies that each person has a responsibility to take care of others, as it is supposed to be done in a family. The oldest manifestations of environmental concern are the Vedic hymns to the earth, the Prithvisukta in Atharvaveda – माताभूमिः पुत्रोहम पृथिव्याः (matabhumih putrohama pṛthivyah) claiming that the earth is our mother which speaks in volume regarding allegiance of Hindus towards nature. The Vedas also urged everyone to make a vow for the sake humanity's well-being मनुष्याणां निधिपो भूवास।। आपत धर्म गृह्यमन्त्र।। (manusyanam nidhipo bhuvasa| apata dharma grhyamantra ||) Bhartruhari Niti Shatkam emphasise the importance of social service, where individual needs to be socially responsible 'एते सत्पुरुषाः परार्था घटकाः स्वार्थं परित्याज्य ये, सामान्या तु परार्थं उद्यता भृतः स्वार्था अविरोधेना ये तेमी मानवा राक्षसाः परहितं स्वार्थया निघ्नन्ति ये, ये तु घ्नन्ति निरथर्कम परहितम ते के ना जानीमहे'। ('ete satpurusah parartha ghatakah svartham parityajya ye samanya tu parartham udyata bhrtah svartha avirodhena ye temi manava raksasah parahitam svarthaya nighnanti ye, ye tu ghnanti nirarthakama parahitama te ke na janimahe'|)

Those are the noblest people who, giving up self-interest, bring about the good of others. Those who undertake a business for the sake of others, not inconsistent with their own good, are the common lot. Those who harm the welfare of others for their own selfish interests are demons in human form. We do not know what to call those who harm others' welfare for no reason at all. Ramcharit Manas in Verse-41 of Uttarkand states that "परहित सरिस धरम नहिं भाई। पर पीड़ा सम नहिं अधमाई।। ("parahita sarisa dharama nahim bhai | para pidh sama nahim adhamai ||") There is nothing more important than taking care of others, while the biggest sin is giving pain to others. *Ramcharit Manas*, in verse 2.173 of Ayodhya Kand, the king was warned to look after people who harm others and care for only filling their own stomachs; they can even deceive the god.

सब विधि सोचिअ पर अपकारी। निज तनु पोसक निरदय भारी।
सोचनीय सबहीं विधि सोई। जो न छाड़ि छलु हरि जन होई।
saba vidhi socia para apakari | nija tanu posaka niradaya bhari |
socaniya sabahim vidhi soi | jo na,chadi chalu hari jana hoi |

Skand Purana explains in detail in chapter 12 shloka 49-51 regarding the importance of people who help others and how lowly are those who do not help others. 'Those who render help to others in accordance with their capacity are blessed ones. They should be known to be very pure and protectors of the world.' "Those who endeavour only to (fill in) their belly should be known as destined to suffer." There is no doubt about this. Hence, O (friends) of auspicious rites, this should be divided by me. You give the Devas whatever you like or dislike. The Thirukkural (72) states that "Those who are destitute of love appropriate all they have to themselves, but those who possess love consider even their bones as belonging to others (Murugesan 2012)."

Concept of Dana

Rigveda in verse 1:29:4 mentions that giver should be awake and non-givers should sleep.

ससन्तु त्या अरातयो बोधन्तु शूर रातयः।
आ तू न इन्द्र शंसय गोश्वश्वेशु शुभ्रिशु सहस्रेशु तुवीमघ।।
sasantu tya aratayo bodhantu śura ratayah |
a tu na indra śamsaya gosvaśvesu śubhrisu sahasresu tuvimagha ||

May the invisible "non-givers" sleep; that the givers are awake; oh you who are brave, make us special among the rays of light, the vital energies, and the thousands of good auspices, Opulent Indra'. *Brihadaranyaka Upanishad* in its verse 5.2.3 recognizes only three virtues as the most important one. 'तदेतत्त्रयँ शिक्षेद् दमं दानं दयामिति' ('tadetattraya śiksed damam danam dayamiti') self-restraint, charity, and compassion for all life forms. Self-restraint is about living a simple life, while charity and compassion are about the behaviour of an individual towards other living forms of the earth. Another Sanskrit verse defines *Daan* (Charity), truth and knowledge as the jewels of an individual, as the cardinal values for a Hindu. हस्तस्य भूषणं दानं, सत्यम कण्ठस्य भूषणं । श्रोत्रस्य भूषणं शास्त्रं, भूषणे किं प्रयोजनं ।। (hastasya bhusanama danam satyama kanthasya bhusanam| zrotrasya bhusanam zastram bhusane kim prayojanam ||).

Chanakya Niti in Chapter 17, Verse 12 echoes the same that Daan is the golden bangle of hand "दानेन पाणिर्न तु कङ्कणेन" ("anena panirna tu kagkanena"). While in Chapter 10, Verse 7, it mentions that the absence of the virtue of *Daan* (charity) makes a human comparable to animals and a burden on the earth. येशां न विद्या न तपो न दानं, ज्ञानं न शीलं न गुणो न धर्मः। ते मर्त्यलोके भुवि भारभूता, मनुष्यरूपेण मृगाश्चरन्ति। (yesam na vidya na tapo na danam jjanam na śilam na guno na dharmah | te martyaloke bhuvi bharabhuta manusyarupena mrgazcaranti |).

Hindu religious texts are full of stories glorifying the virtue of *Daan* (charity). Three such stories that stand out from others are given below:

Story of Raja Shivi from Mahabharat (*Mahabharat, Vana Parva*)[3]

There was once a very kind and generous king called Shibi. One day, he was sitting on his palace terrace when a dove flew straight into his lap and lay trembling there. "Grant me refuge!" pleaded the dove to the king. "Fear not, little dove, for I will protect you," said the king. Then a hawk arrived, in pursuit of the dove. "Give me my dinner," said the hawk to the king. "I cannot allow you to eat this dove," said King Shibi, "for I have granted him protection." "Then what am I supposed to eat?" asked the hawk. "I am starving and will surely die if I do not get a meal soon". 'And my family will starve too if I cannot bring this dove to them.' The king offered the hawk all kinds of alternative foods, but the hawk refused, saying "I only eat fresh meat." "Then have some of my flesh," said the king. The courtiers cried out in alarm. "Bring some scales!" commanded the king, and they brought out a huge set of scales and placed them in the centre of the terrace. On one side of the scales, the king placed the dove, which was still trembling with fear. Then King Shibi took his sword and began slicing pieces of flesh off his own thighs and placing them on the other side of the scales, aiming to equal the weight of the dove. But however much flesh he added to the scales, he could not equal the bird's weight. It was very strange. Despite the wailing of his courtiers and the extraordinary pain of his open wound, the king kept slicing. Eventually, unable to equal the dove's weight, the king climbed up onto the scales, declaring to the hawk: "Eat me! Spare the dove!" At that moment, the birds transformed. The dove revealed himself as the god Agni, god of the fire. The hawk revealed himself as the king of the gods, Indra. "We came to test the extent of your goodness," Indra declared, "and we are more than satisfied!" Indra healed the king's wounds, and the two gods disappeared, leaving all the humans astounded by the events.

Story of Poor Brahmin and Mongoose (Mahabharata, Anugita Parva)[4]

There once lived a very poor man in a small village. He had his wife, son, and daughter-in-law living with him. They lived a hand-to-mouth existence. But because the entire family was inclined spiritually, none of them bothered about their poverty. Unfortunately, a great famine struck the kingdom. The poor family, which already had very little food, now starves almost daily. Unable to bear the suffering of his family, the old man went out and, with great difficulty, got some rice for the family. His wife and daughter-in-law cooked the food and divided it into four parts, one for each one of them. Much to the surprise of everyone, as they were about to eat the food, someone knocked on their door. Surprised, the old man opened the door. Outside, he saw a weary traveller looking almost half dead from hunger and fatigue. The old man immediately brought the man inside. After allowing the man to wash, the old man spoke to the man. Sir!"

The old man said "You look hungry." The weary traveller sadly nodded his head. I have been wandering for several days now without any food. The old man, without even the slightest hesitation, offered the traveller his food. You came to my house at the right time. We were about to have our meal. Please have my portion of the food and satisfy yourself! ' Without pausing to think, the traveller seemed to eat the old man's portion of food. The others in the family watched the guest eating, leaving their own food untouched. The traveller, however, did not seem to be satisfied. He looked at the old man guiltily, as if he was still hungry. The old man's wife came forward and offered the guest her portion of the food. The old man looked distraught that his shrivelled wife was handing over her pitiful portion of the food to the traveller. He took her aside and spoke to her. You do not have to do this.... The old man said "He is our guest." I have given him my portion of the food. But you.... His wife smiled. "I am your wife". I have promised to take part in your life through everything. If you are willing to stay hungry to feed a guest, I think it is my duty to do the same.... The traveller ate the second portion of food. Needless to say, the traveller was still hungry. The old man looked unhappy when the son gave the guest his portion of the food. The father shook his head emphatically when the son held up his hands. Father! Mother! You are my parents. You are my world. I have learnt that it is the duty of a child to fulfil the wishes of their parents. You wish to feed the guest and are even willing to give up your portion of food to satisfy his hunger. Now it is my turn to fulfil my parent's desire and make sure our guest is happy. The traveller had the third portion and still looked hungry. The daughter-in-law came forward. Seeing this, the other three came forward, feeling terrible. The old man shook his head. I ca not let you go hungry, my daughter. It is wrong.... The old woman and the son also shook their heads. The daughter-in-law smiled. "Father! The sacrifice that the three of you have made is the greatest sacrifice in the world....Nothing can come close to it. I wish to be a part of this yagna.... Please give my portion of the food to the guest and let us satisfy his hunger. Though the other three tried to talk the daughter-in-law out of the act, she remained adamant and the fourth portion of the food also went to the traveller. The traveller was thoroughly satisfied, and he was about to leave the house. In that instant, the house was ablaze with brilliant light. The Gods, who had come in the guise of the traveller, blessed the entire family. You have performed the greatest yagna in the world. For this, you have attained moksha...Come! '*A mongoose roaming in the house after their moksha fell on the scrap of food which the family had given to the traveller lying on the floor, half of his body which fell on the food, was transformed into gold!*'

Story of Rishi Dadhichi (Skand Puran)

Indra, the King of the Devas, was once driven out of Devaloka by an asura named Vritra. This asura was the recipient of a boon that made him invulnerable to any known weapon. This demon, Vritra, also stole all the water in the world for his own use and that of his demon army. He did this so that all other living beings would die of thirst and hunger, leaving no human or God alive to challenge his place in Heaven. Indra, who had lost all hope of recovering his kingdom, went to seek the aid of Vishnu. Vishnu revealed to Indra that only weapons made from the thunder—containing (called in Sanskrit as *Vajra*) diamond bones of the sage Dadhichi could kill Vritra. Therefore, Indra and the other Devas approached the sage, whom Indra had once beheaded, and asked for his aid in defeating Vritra. Dadhichi acceded to the Devas' request, but said that he wished that he had time to go on a pilgrimage to all the holy rivers before he gave up his life for them. Indra then brought all the water from the holy rivers together at Naimisharanya, thereby allowing the sage to have his wish fulfilled without further loss of time. Dadhichi then went into a deep meditative state and released his life force from his body. The celestial Kamadhenu calf then licked and removed the flesh from his bones, after which the Devas fashioned the Vajrayudha (Thunderbolt) from his spine and made numerous other weapons. This weapon was then used to kill the asura, allowing Indra to reclaim his place as the king of Devaloka and releasing the water for all living beings. Another version of the story exists where Dadhichi is asked to safeguard the weapons of devas, as they were unable to match the arcane arts being employed by the asuras to obtain them. Dadhichi is said to have kept at the task for a very long time and, finally tiring of the job, is said to have dissolved the weapons in sacred water, which he then drank. The devas returned sometime later and asked him to return their weapons so that they might defeat the asuras, headed by Vritra, once and for all. However, Dadhichi told them what he had done and informed them that their weapons were now a part of his bones. Realizing that his bones were the only way by which devas could defeat the asuras, he willingly gave his life in a pit of mystical flames that he summoned with the power of his austerities. Brahma is then said to have fashioned a large number of weapons from Dadhichi's bones, including the Vajrayudha, which was fashioned from his spine. The devas are then said to have defeated the asuras using the weapons thus created.

The *Bhavishya Purāṇ* in verse 5 states: '*dānamekaṁ kalau yuge*' in the age of *Kali*, giving in charity is the means for purification. Lord Krishna himself explains the righteous *Daan* in *Gita*.

दातव्यमिति यद्दानं दीयतेऽनुपकारिणे।
देशे काले च पात्रे च तद्दानं सात्विकं स्मृतम्।।
यत्तु प्रत्युपकारार्थं फलमुद्दिश्य वा पुनः।
दीयते च परिक्लिष्टं तद्दानं राजसं स्मृतम्।।
अदेशकाले यद्दानमपात्रेभ्यश्च दीयते।
असत्कृतमवज्ञातं तत्तामसमुदाहृतम्।।
datavyamiti yaddanam diyateanupakarine |
deze kale ca patre ca taddanam satvikam smrtam ||
yattu pratyupakarartham phalamuddizya va puna |
diyate ca pariklistam taddanam rajasam smrtam ||
adesakale yaddanamapatrebhyasca diyate |
asatkrtamavajjatam tattamasamudahrtam ||

Charity given to a worthy person simply because it is right to give, without consideration of anything in return, at the proper time and in the proper place, is said to be in the mode of goodness. But charity given with reluctance, with the hope of a return or in expectation of a reward, is said to be in the mode of passion. And that charity, which is given at the wrong place and wrong time to unworthy people, without showing respect or with contempt, is held to be of the nature of nescience. Among those things, some are the best, some are middling, and some are inferior. Food, curds, honey, protection, cow, land, gold, horse, and elephant—these nine are said to be the best gifts; learning, house for shelter, domestic paraphernalia, medicines, and these four are said to be mediocre; shoes, swings, carts, umbrellas, vessels, seats, lamps, wood, fruits, and whatever is old and worn out, and all other unspecified objects are said to be inferior. In *Yajurveda* (I. 210-211), it is said that a man's gift of land (capable of yielding a crop or fruits), lamp, wood, garment, water (water reservoir), sesame, ghee, house for travellers, gold, secures endless happiness. *Chanakya Niti* in Chapter 17, Verse 7 mentions that there is no greater *daan* than food and water. 'नान्नोदकसमं दानं'. ("nannodakasamam danam").

Protecting Animals

The concept of the well-being of everyone in Hinduism does not restrict itself to mankind only; it extends to the other creatures of the earth and then to the rivers, mountains, and, at the end, towards taking care of the whole earth. In the Vedas, we find concern for the well-being of birds and animals. श नो अस्त द्विपदे। श चतुश्पदे ऋग्वेद।। (śa no asta dvipade | śa catuspade) Ṛgveda || (7/54/1). The Vedas also talk about taking care of the earth by considering it as a mother. Animals enjoy a special status in Hinduism which is incomparable to other religions. Each god in Hinduism is associated with one or more animals as their vehicles. This is probably the only religion where God has reincarnated in the form of animals; there are many Gods, such as Narsingh, Hanuman, Ganesha, and others, who symbolise the synchronisation of animals and humans. The care and love for animals in Hinduism has propagated vegetarianism in cuisine and various sects within the religion make vegetarianism a must for their followers. Rishi Tiruvalluvar in his *Tirukkural* (251) has asked, "How can one who eats the flesh of others to swell his flesh show compassion?" He further said, "*manuyir ombi arulalvarku illenba tannuyir anjum vinai.*" The wise say that the evils which his soul would dread will never come upon the man who exercises kindness and protects the lives of other creatures (Thirukkural, 244) and that "*Kollan pulalai maruthaanaik kaikoopi Ella uyirum thozhum*"*:* All creatures will join hands together and worship him who has never taken away life nor eaten flesh (Thirukkural, 260). (Murugesan 2012). *Tirukkural* further emphasises vegetarianism by saying, "What is compassion and the lack of it: not killing and killing; it is not virtuous to eat meat obtained by killing (26.254); and all living things will fold their hands and bow to one who refuses meat (26.260). *Yajurveda* in verse 13.47 urges that no person should kill animals helpful to all and that by serving them they should obtain happiness.

इमं मा हिंसीर्द्विपादं पशुं सहस्राक्षो मेधाय चीयमानः ।
मयुं पशुं मेधम् अग्ने जुशस्व तेन चिन्वानस्तन्वो निशीद ।
मयुं ते शुगृछतु यं द्विश्मस्तं ते शुगृछतु ।
imam ma hinsirdvipadam paśum sahasrakso medhaya ciyamanah|
mayum paśum medham agne juśasva tena cinvanastanvo nisida |
mayum te śugṛchatu yam dviśmastam te śugṛchatu |

In verse 10:87:16 of the *Ṛgveda*, the killing of animals and humans is discouraged, as is stealing milk from milch cows.

. यः पौरुषेयेण क्रघविषा समङ्क्ते यो अश्व्येन पशुना यातुधानः ।
यो अघ्न्याया भरति क्षीरमग्ने तेशां शीर्षाणि हरसापि वृश्च ।।
"yah pauru seyena kravisa samagkte yo azvyena pazuna yatudhanah |
yo aghnyaya bharati ksiramagne tesam śirsani harasapi vrsca||"

The fiend who smears himself with the flesh of cattle, with the flesh of horses and of human bodies, who steals the milch cow's milk away, O Agni,—tear off the heads of such with fiery fury.

In Hinduism, a human being needs to be aware of insects, birds, animals, and other fellow human beings as well. A considerate and tolerant individual can lead to the sustenance of society. However, this tolerance should emerge from knowledge, which is considered the most important virtue. The Vedic philosophy, which serves as the foundation of Hinduism, prescribes Dharma, or the righteous duty of each individual, and Karma, or the path of selfless action to be undertaken without expecting any return towards individuals, families, society, nation, and the Universe.[5]

ॐ द्यौः शान्तिरन्तरिक्षं शान्तिः पृथिवी शान्तिरापः
शान्तिरोशधयः शान्तिः ।
वनस्पतयः शान्तिर्विश्वेदेवाः शान्तिर्ब्रह्म शान्तिः
सर्वं शान्तिः शान्तिरेव शान्तिः सा मा शान्तिरेधि ।।
ॐ शान्तिः शान्तिः शान्तिः ।।

om dyauh śantirantariksam śantih prthivi śantirapah
śantirosadhayah śantih|
vanaspatayah śantirviśvedevah śantirbrahma śantih sarvam śantih
śantireva śantih sama śantiredhi || om śantih śantih śantih ||

May peace radiate there in the whole sky as well as in the vast
ethereal space everywhere?
May peace reign all over this earth, in water and in all herbs,
trees and creepers?
May peace flow over the whole universe?
May peace be in the Supreme Being Brahman?
And may there always exist in all peace and peace alone?
Aum peace, peace and peace to us and all beings!
(*Yajurveda Samhita* 36:17)

NOTES

1. https://berkleycenter.georgetown.edu/essays/dharma-hinduism
2. Important Hindu Virtues (Hinduism and Social Work *Manju Kumar in ed.* Origin and Development of Social Work in India).
3. https://berkleycenter.georgetown.edu/essays/hinduism-on-wealth-and-poverty
4. http://www.storyandreligion.div.ed.ac.uk/wp-content/uploads/2015/08/King-Shibi-and-the-Dove.pdf
5. https://www.sacred-texts.com/hin/m14/m14090.htm
6. https://link.springer.com/chapter/10.1007/978-3-319-71849-1_11

REFERENCES

https://berkleycenter.georgetown.edu/essays/dharma-hinduism

Kumar, M. (2010). *Hinduism and Social Work, Origin and Development of Social Work in India,* IGNOU, New Delhi.

https://berkleycenter.georgetown.edu/essays/hinduism-on-wealth-and-poverty

http://www.storyandreligion.div.ed.ac.uk/wp-content/uploads/2015/08/King-Shibi-and-the-Dove.pdf

https://www.sacred-texts.com/hin/m14/m14090.htm https://link.springer.com/chapter/10.1007/978-3-319-71849-1_11

6
Indian Religions and Social Work

Sunil Prasad and *Arul Actovin*

Introduction

The social work profession is a practice-based discipline aimed at identifying, assisting, and caring for individuals who need help. Social Work attempts to determine an individual, group, or community's issue and provides support and care. This support and care are given over the long term through research, direct practice, policy, crisis intervention, and education on behalf of those suffering from poverty or other actual or perceived social injustices and abuses of their civil and human rights (Tsui, 2000). Social work is a profession established to oversee the very broad and complicated structure of public service that society has placed in place. It is a scientific discipline that has an imaginative and artful approach to working with people, groups, and communities that have problems. The social work profession addresses life difficulties and improves the welfare of people by involving them in structures (Popple and Leighninger 2011; International Federation of Social Workers, 2014). The National Association of Social Work (NASW) identifies spirituality and religion as components of cultural diversity (NASW, 2007: 4).

Religion consists of belief systems, principles, codes of conduct, and rituals. It is a way of communicating an individual's spirituality. Preferably, religion offers a spiritual atmosphere (Canda *et al.*, 2019) as well. Religion is defined by Koenig (2008) as "a system of beliefs and practices observed by a community, supported by rituals that acknowledge, worship, communicate with, or approach the sacred, the divine, God, or ultimate truth, reality, or Nirvana". Religion "involves the patterning of spiritual beliefs and practices into social institutions, with community support and traditions maintained over time". Instead of the foregoing, it is hopeful for social workers to consider spirituality and religion as essential in the assessment of clients' problems and the intervention process (Furness & Gilligan, 2010). Respecting spiritual beliefs, values, and religious practices is important in social work assessment and practice with a variety of clients, including younger adults, children, the elderly, and others (Nelson *et al.*, 2006). In India, religion has always played a significant part in all reform movements. The influence of religion is highly apparent, especially in the ongoing search for social and political correctness. It is the purpose of this chapter to give an overview of the inherent philosophy of Indian-originated religions, i.e. Hinduism, Buddhism, Sikhism, and Jainism, and their relationship with the growth of the modern social work profession in India.

Hinduism and Social Work

Hinduism is recognised as one of the oldest religious traditions and philosophical values practiced by India's indigenous people since the Vedic era. Hinduism, originally known as *Sanatana Dharma* (eternal or immortal faith), is more of a "*way of life*" than a philosophy of belief; it is a religion practiced and not only conceptual. Social work is a problem-solving profession that makes a person self-reliant in all respects and empowers one's potential for a happy life (Admin, 2019). Social Work originated with a focus on the "Person-in-Environment" approach. This specific approach is a practice-orientated principle that highlights the significance for social work practitioners of having a sound understanding of human beings in light of the environmental contexts in which they live, behave, and respond to others (Kondrat, 2013). This prepares academically, as a distinct and specialised discipline, workers who are deemed to be qualified social workers. This article reviews the relationship between Hinduism and the social work profession in India and its relevance and implications.

For the sake of humanity, Hinduism spreads for Dharma (righteousness), Bhakti (devotion), and Yoga (discipline). "Karma Theory" denotes that each person is under two forces, i.e. the social atmosphere and the individual's own. The law of Karma, as stated by the Puranas and Vedas, is an ethical law that demands social responsibility. The Vedas provide the highest spiritual awareness as well as a code of conduct and moral principles (Ranganathananda, 2013). The theory of *karma* stands for the law of cause and effect, which applies to human life and action. It is the everlasting confirmation of human liberty. In the theory of *karma*, we think of one's misery because of one's *karma* and usually remain oblivious to our suffering fellow-man, assuming that his/

her pain is due to the unfortunate sufferer's *karma*. Yet *karma* theory says if misery is their *karma*, it is our *karma* to go out and help them. Society will develop into a positive communication medium where we help each other grow. The social climate will begin to help us go higher and higher. Everybody should support others in their ability to reach their full potential (Ranganathananda, 2013). Likewise, social work stands for this theory of *karma*, which only adopts new methods and techniques.

According to Hinduism, the meaning of life is seen as being merged with God, and the virtues of grace and compassion are seen as spiritual and thus advantageous to impart in one. The idea of guided emotional involvement was expounded quite extensively in the *Gita*. The Hindu belief in the divinity of man makes it consistent with the philosophy, and the self-actualization of all human beings allows even the so-called worst offenders to maintain a non-judgmental attitude. Vedic Ontology enshrines the principle of the right of the individual to dignity and self-determination, and the principle of acceptance is the most basic of the various concepts of professional relationships and is central to the Social Work profession (Dash, 2017).

The primary principle in Hinduism is the dignity of individuals, held as a fundamental value of social work. It is from the philosophy of Atman that the belief that one's true nature is determined by its divinity, not by physical and social characteristics, is derived. In Hindu philosophy, *Ahimsa* (nonviolence) is regarded as the highest form of dharma (*Ahimsa Paramo Dharma*) and *ahimsa* practice emphasises the absence of resentment towards or accusing the person of recovery or improvement. Not only does it mean refraining from causing purposeful harm to others, not only pure empathy, but it also requires selflessness, love for goodwill, reconciliation, and harmony. Professional social workers have important values such as hospitality, security, discipline, fairness, and compassion that have many important Hindu ethic values. Charity is also supported by Upanishads such as *Chhandogya*, *Brihadaranyaka*, and *Taitiriya*. The idea of charity is needed to carry out charitable programmes for the well-being of the needy and deprived sections of society, i.e. the elderly, the widowed, the children, the disabled, and the sick. Social workers should cultivate a sense of benevolence towards their clients, responsibly and spiritually, to solve their problems. Charity in Social Work is seen as the basic concept in the field of Social Work. Unlike modern social work, Hindu philosophy claims that human beings can and do change their life's goal through self-actualization.

> "The Hindu philosophy propagates the values of selfless social service, compassion, mutual aid and interdependence, unconditional love for the vulnerable groups and concerns for the community which are considered important in social work education and practice" (Dash, 2017).

Mazumdar (1999) discussed the concepts of Hinduism and its connection to the personal experiences of social work practitioners. She pointed out Hinduism's core values to different field activities that emerge from behind to reinforce the central concerns of the theory of social work and practice. Dash and Nagar (2020) have also discussed the relevance of Hinduism in social work.

In addition, professional social work should accommodate the ideology of Hinduism as a philosophy for modern welfare and developmental issues. The relationship between the person and the social worker requiring support is a vital component of social work practice. In India, the Vedas are known as the most sacred books. Vedic epistemology and ontology may be important tools for solving different social issues that could be integrated into the Indian Social Work field. But unfortunately, the philosophy of Hinduism has not been given importance in social work education.

> "There is no doubt or dispute that professional social work values, principles, ethics, and practices are embedded in Hindu religious texts and scriptures, which have received little recognition and legitimacy in professional discourse. It is heavily weighted toward Hinduism, Hindu Philosophy, and Vedic traditions" (Dash, 2017).

Buddhism and Social Work

Buddhism, rooted in Indian culture, evolved from the 5th century B.C. until being developed by Buddha (Siddhartha Gautama). Buddha is a great human being who has made the greatest contributions to humanity. Lord Buddha did not lose his attempt and launched a remarkable transformation in social mores and notions in ancient India. Through Buddhism it was quickly introduced to Asian countries, and it has become a means of psychological and practical liberation for the oppressed and of economic growth to impoverished people through committed Buddhism. It is sometimes used as a platform that gives voice to the political aspirations of the people, bringing down national governments (King, S.B: 1). Buddha's primary aim was to help people to be free from any kind of human suffering. Social workers assist people within their local communities to live better by helping them find solutions to their problems. Social workers form relationships as mentors, advocates, listeners etc. with individuals. He may be the ideal social worker who, like Buddha, had more humility and wisdom. This dedication is not distinct from Buddhism's spiritual practice but very much believes in the social, cultural, political, and ecological issues of society as an expression of action. This is no longer purely focused on the motivations of charity, benevolence, or moral imperatives (Karma, 2004). The Buddha stated that "there will be only one flavour in his world: the flavour of liberty." There are two positive social changes: a shift in a social situation and personal improvement. Buddha also pointed out that "Cattaro Vanna Samasama", which means "*four castes of human beings are equal*". It means "*human beings are all equal*". This is the society of classlessness that has been established by Buddha to open a free society to all deserving individuals by not creating a distinction between caste and class. The only difference was in seniority of ordination, like monks, nuns, and novices, but the aim and destiny were the same.

Buddha spread the concept of equality among all human beings found in society, irrespective of sex, creed, caste, social order, and importance. Everyone could search for refuge in his monasteries, which welcomed everyone who came to him. The Buddha rejected the differences in sex, age, and caste. Committed Buddhism is part of spiritual practice and social action to tackle legal, cultural, scientific, educational, political, and economic issues. Contrary to the ignominious and brutal past of wars, bloodsheds, massacres, torture, and misery at various rates of human life in the form of family, tribe, culture, religious or ethnic groups, there is also a glorious history of peaceful, harmonious, cooperative, and community-based coexistence between the people's widely diverse religions and regions (Vyas, 1999). In Buddhist viewpoints, social welfare provides the ideals of personal and social well-being, which are not distinct but are two fundamentally interrelated facets of the search for liberation from suffering: "In protecting oneself, one protects others; in protecting others, one protects oneself" (Chon, 2017).

In Buddhism, though there are no words for "rights", it appears that human rights are referred to as specific obligations or commitments set out in the Buddhist precepts (Judy & Kheang, 2003). This advocacy is completely evident in the Universal Vehicle (Mahayana), with its implied meaning in the Individual Vehicle (Hinayana), both in the conduct of the Buddha and in his teachings. This attention in the latter was on self-transformation, the prerequisite of social transformation. Therefore, it is at the very essence of all Buddhist teachings to position universal values on real contemporary issues to create legal, even political, guidance for practice (Kotler, 1996). The Dalai Lama claims that people will attain peace of mind through the self-internal transformation of goodness, love, and compassion, but the world can never attain permanent peace through this harmful practice (Chon, 2017). Maybe the most credible evidence is that "Buddhism originated in India as the philosophical force against social inequality, against degrading rituals, practices, and sacrifices of superstition. It rejected the injustice of the caste system and supported fair rights for all people" (Gail & Richard, 2000).

Phil Henry (2013) focused on three types of Buddhist social work, i.e. recreation, reform, and revisionist models. This Buddhist model of social work seeks to reconcile the concept of Buddhist heritage and contemporary practice (Hanna *et al.*, 2017).

Sikhism and Social Work

Sikhism is one of India's youngest religions, and its originator is Guru Nanak Dev (1469-1531). The Sikhs of the world are known for their hard work and dedication to serving humanity. Wherever they live, they wholeheartedly commit to their services. Everything they won and owned, they won through their perseverance. The effect of the Gurus' teachings can be seen in the Sikhs' lives and conduct (Kohli, 1994).

The Sikh is defined as "any human being who faithfully believes in,

- One immortal being,
- The Ten Gurus, from Guru Nanak to Guru Gobind Singh,
- The Guru Granth Sahib,
- The utterances and teachings of the ten Gurus,
- The baptism bequeathed by the tenth Guru and who does not owe allegiance to any other religion is a Sikh" (Rehat Maryada, Sikh Code of Conduct).

Sikhism has different facets and principles closely linked to social work. It believes in equality, universal brotherhood, and health. It provides a very high status for women and individuals' value and dignity. Sikhism is a way of life that must be followed on a regular basis.The principal value is that of simplicity. There's no supernaturalism or mythology that it relies upon. It is not accepted as true by angels, demons, or spirits in heaven. If all nonviolent means for such resistance are exhausted, Guru Gobind Singh says, the use of the sword is lawful. The Guru created a new spirit among its warrior saints with the creation of the Khalsa. They were ready to combat tyranny. Thus, the tenth Guru set in motion a profound change in the cultural and political system of Punjab's Mughal province by transforming Sikhs into a community of self-governing warriors (Dhavan, 2011). His army was most instructive in never fighting a war for gain, wealth, or personal anger: "The Khalsa was resolved to protect justice and oppose only that which is false" (McLeod, 1997).

The Panjkakars (Panj = five; Kakar = symbols) are the most prominent and unique marks of the Sikhs, particularly the members of the Khalsa brotherhood. The five faith articles are:

- Uncut hair (*Kesh*), a gift of salvation from God;
- Cleanliness, symbolised by a wooden comb (*Kangha*);
- A steel bracelet (*Kara*) represents self-restraint and a link to God;
- A short sword (*Kirpaan*), an emblem of courage and commitment to truth and justice;
- A type of underwear knickers (*Kachhehra*) represents the purity of moral character.

Sikhism places great emphasis on equal rights for all men. Every human being before God is fair and fair. They are all to be handled fairly, valued, and loved. Sikhism is opposed to both ritualism and formalism. According to Guru Amar Das, "All are created from the seed of God. There is the same clay in the whole world; the potter (God) makes many kinds of pots."

Sikhism condemns all types of distinctions that have to be made by gender, race, religion, income, castes, or faith. A total denial of the caste system is a hallmark of Sikh tradition. In reality, Sikhism emerged as a voice of protest against the numerous problems that prevail in contemporary Indian society. The first Guru of Sikhism, Guru Nanak, condemned caste and caste ideology as perverse and rejected the Vedas' authority and Brahmin power.

Guru Amar Das carried out a robust effort to eradicate the barbarous and barbaric custom called Sati. Sikhism accepted these elements and aimed at granting women equal rights in all areas of life, while also fostering the same ideals in professional social work. Sikhism's commitment to empowering women and granting them equal status is in line with social work ideals and values. The Sikh Gurus were concerned about the nature of man as a whole. There has been a holistic approach to social and individual issues that often goes hand in hand with the theory of social work. In Sikhism, the moral concept of ahimsa, which is close to that of the principles of social work such as compassion, devotion, universal brotherhood, equality, and self-respect, must prevail. When these are broken, however, man must resist. Non-violence and speaking the truth are inherent to both social work and Sikhism.

The philosophy behind the "Langar" (the kitchen-*cum*-eating-house of Guru) is similar to the principles of social work, based on the dignity, acceptance, and equality of a person. The social work profession is aimed at helping individuals, families, groups, and communities improve their collective and individual well-being. It helps a person develop their skills and ability to utilise their own and community resources more effectively to solve problems (Payne, 2011). Langar is the shared kitchen room in the Gurdwara where everyone sits together and eats from the shared kitchen, irrespective of caste, gender, race, religion, and sex. It is not just for the person. The Sikhs' community programmes are similar to the idea of group work found in social work. Through Sikhism as well as social work, kindness and empathy can be seen. Over the years, social work has imbibed these techniques, principles, and traditions from different religions, national leaders, and social movements. In India, Sikhism has contributed to the development of social welfare and modern social labour.

Jainism and Social Work

Jainism is 2500 years old and its values have had a significant and profound impact on the culture of India. Self-reliance was an essential component of and ultimate confidence in one's ability to live a good life and solve the universal problem in order to achieve salvation. Jainism believed that every human being could realise absolute knowledge and achieve absolute bliss through intensive human effort (Jaini, P.S., 1998). Jainism was based on the three doctrines of right *faith, right awareness, and right conduct,* which are known as the "three jewels" (Damodaran, 1967). Social work as a discipline plays a crucial role in helping people, organizations, and communities recover their capacity for social functioning and create optimal conditions for achieving their objectives. Social work as a career aims to promote community development in line with the principles of social change and growth, social stability and empowerment, and rural autonomy while upholding the ideals of social justice, human rights, and respect for diversity.

Jainism believes that aggression cannot bring about greater benefit for individuals or society. Jainism teaches that the forms of violence include lying, cheating, taking more than one's fair share, the immoderate pursuit of sensual pleasures, and possessiveness. Many of these include emotions, self-and other mental abuse. As Dale Riepe observes, "The principles of

Jainism, so far as it is humanistic, are naturalistic". The Jain tradition does not rely on any divine surrender or interference to attain moksha. As a human being, he knows happiness is at the heart of his power (Riepe, 1996). The most important contribution Jainism made to the social system was establishing social equality within the society's Varna system. Lord Mahavira succeeded in gathering his large number of followers into a compact social order somewhat different from that of the Brahmanic social order of his day, which was fraught with inequality, bigotry, and inter-caste rivalry. In addition to engaging in religious practice, the Jain Acharyas, true to the ideals of Jain philosophy, made indelible contributions by continuously working for the well-being of mankind—eradicating social evils, reforming social norms, establishing the national culture, and educating the people on the principles of nonviolence, universal peace, and brotherhood.

Jainism has its philosophy, beliefs, and ideals very much in line with the ideas of social work, code of ethics, morality, and theory. Jain monks who engage in strict asceticism and follow less rigorous practices fail to attain equal faith in this lifetime. The Jain code of ethics is taken very seriously. Five vows are followed by chastity (Brahmacharya), non-stealing (*Asteya*), non-violence (*ahimsa* or *ahinsa*), reality (*Satya*), and non-possession or non-possessiveness (*Aparigraha*). Such vows were also observed as principles of social work by skilled social workers. Jain's conviction is that Atma (soul) will lead one to become Parmatma (liberated soul) and that this has to come from inside. No Jiv (life) can offer a different path to redemption, but can only lead the way. Even in social work, the social worker is the guide and philosopher of the client who shows the way and the client's choice is left with the final decision or act. Jainism emphasises the divine freedom and dignity of all life, with a particular focus on non-violence, which is one of the methods advocated in many countries by the Social Work profession.

Jainism encourages compassion for all life, whether human or non-human. Human life is viewed as a special, precious opportunity to achieve salvation and kill someone, no matter what crime he/she may have committed, which is unimaginably abhorrent. This is the only religion that requires the monks and laity to be vegetarian in all its sects and practices. Also, the Jain Monks' great efforts over the centuries to cultivate peace among different population groups are lessons for the social work profession that are required to support people in various problem situations to improve themselves. The importance of Jainism to human life is very important to the field of professional social work. Jainism's ideals, beliefs, and teachings are close to those of the social work profession, and Jainism had a strong association with promoting the social work profession in India. Social work discipline needs to be more inclusive of Jainism beliefs, ideals, and other religious teachings on literature.

Conclusion

The aim of the social work profession is entrenched in a set of core values and is the basis of social work's unique purpose. These core values are social justice, service, *dharma*, *ahimsa*, dignity, the importance of human relationships, integrity, worth of the person, and competence, which are emphasised in Indian religions. These values and principles have been incorporated by social workers throughout the profession's history in India. In Indic philosophy, the concepts of "*Vasudhaiva Kutumbakam*" (the whole world is our family) and "*Sarve Bhavantu Sukhinah*" (let all be happy) are the possible guiding principles that can lead the social work profession in India in the right direction. In the case of the Western model, cultural and religious excuses are offered to explain why the principle of universality is inapplicable to all (Mohammed *et al.*, 2020). Perceptions about the relationship between religion and social work services also differ significantly. While the provision of welfare services has been central to many religions, it is not always evident that service providers have specific standards. Canada has been involved in developing and promoting resources on religious and spiritual problems for social work programmes (Canda, 1989; Canda & Furman, 1999). Social work practitioners who interact with clients impacted by these situations will incorporate faith and spirituality into their assessment and intervention. Bearing this in mind, practitioners should acknowledge that spirituality and religion have the benefit of empowering the individual through connecting him/her to a supreme force, which might, in turn, provide psychological stability and perhaps recovery (Basu, 2011). Helm *et al.* (2000) found that positive health outcomes are associated with increased participation in private religious activities (Helm *et al.*, 2000).

In India, therefore, any attempt to interpret the social, political, and economic environment while ignoring the spiritual and religious foundations of Indian thought would not only be incomplete but also pointless. Swami Vivekananda, one of the courageous saints, developed a theory of action, an outlook on which modern social engineering can rely to its advantage. The social work advocates of indigenization claim that social work must be designed to fit local contexts, which is not something new or special, but an implicit necessity of social work. While it is an implicit necessity in social work, the creation of social and cultural awareness should be beneficial for social workers. Indian social work did not need any imported wisdom about the needed indigenization process because it has itself been a major phase of a developmental effort for social welfare. The business of the social work profession is to care, cure, and change to ensure the betterment of society. The social work profession should look for a change in its approach towards contemporary issues. Social work educators have to play a major role in their different theoretical perspectives. As social workers, we are generally expected to combine social and cultural knowledge and sensitivity with expertise in order to complete a task that is both socially and culturally relevant and effective in providing support. The integrated aspects of social work deal with the welfare of people. The main aims of this are to help people in one or other ways.

From the above discussion about Indian major religions and the social work profession, we find the inherent relationship between religions and social work, i.e. social work practice adopted a set of values and principles which are also found in these Indian-originated religions to ensure they work for the well-being of the clients. Social workers usually work with people to consider the person in their environment and the larger sense of their life, and to identify the interaction between the past, present, and future of the individual. Thus, social workers are likewise expected to understand the religious beliefs and expressions of clients, as they could impact treatment outcomes, given the fact that all human beings are religious. Multicultural diversity is part of religious practices and beliefs. As such, social work professionals need to incorporate skills and knowledge in this area to work effectively with a diverse population, and equally important is the process of incorporating the basic values, ethics, and philosophy of Hinduism, Buddhism, Jainism, and Sikhism into the social work profession in India, which is the key to the indigenization of social work education and practice. Now, it is the time for social work professionals in particular to rethink adding religious content at all levels of practice in the social work profession in India.

REFERENCES

Admin. (2019, March 19). *Hinduism and Social Work.* Retrieved July 31, 2020, from https://article1000.com/hinduism-social-work/

Basu-Zharku, L.O. (2001). *The Influence of Religion on Health Student.* Pulse Online Academic.

Canda, E.R. (1989). Religious content in Social Work education: A comparative approach. *Journal of Social Work Education*, 25, 1, 36-45.

Canda, E.R. & Furman, D.L. (2010). *Spiritual Diversity in Social Work Practice: The Heart of Helping*. New York : Oxford University Press.

Canda, E.R., and Furman, L. (1999). *Spiritual Diversity in Social Work Practice: The Heart of Helping*. New York: The Free Press.

Canda, E.R., Furman, L.D. & Canda, H.J. (2019). *Spiritual diversity in Social Work Practice: The Heart of Helping*. USA : Oxford University Press.

Charles, S.P. & Kenneth Ken'ichi, T. (1998). *The Faces of Buddhism in America*. California: University of California Press.

Chhon, K. (2017). New Models of Buddhist Social Work in Cambodia. *Journal of International Buddhist Studies*, 8(2), 60-87.

Damodaran, K. (1967). *Indian Thought: A Critical Survey*. New York: Asia Publishing House.

Dash, B.M. & Nagar, A. (2020). Relevance of Hinduism in Social Work, in Dash, B.M.; Kumar, M.; Singh, D.P.; & Shukla, S. (edit.), *Indian Social Work*, Routledge, India, pp. 165-172.

Dash, B.M. (2017, September 2). *Relevance of Hinduism in Social Work Education*, New Delhi Times, September 2, retrieved on July 27, 2020 from http:// www. newdelhitimes.com/relevance-of-hinduism-in-social-work-education/-

Dhavan, P. (2011). *When Sparrows Became Hawks: The Making of the Sikh Warrior Tradition, 1699-1799*. New York: Oxford University Press.

Furness, S. & Gilligan, P. (2010). Social work, religion, and belief: Developing a framework for practice. *British Journal of Social Work*, 40(7), 2185-2202.

Gail, P., Karsten, S. & Richard, O. (2000). *The Philosophical Quest: A Cross-Cultural Reader*. Boston: McGraw-Hill.

Hanna, H., Ute, H., Mark, T., Vladimir, T. and Koen, W. (2017). *Buddhist Modernities: Re-inventing Tradition in the Globalizing Modern World*. London: Routledge.

Helm, H.M., Hays, J.C., Flint, E.P., Koenig, H.G., and Blaser, D.G. (2000). Does private religious activity prolong survival? A six-year follow-up study of 3,851 older adults.*The Journals of Gerontology*. Series A, Biological Sciences and Medical Sciences, 55, M400-M405.

Henry, P. (2013). *Adaptation and Developments in Western Buddhism: Socially Engaged Buddhism in the UK*. A&C Black.

International Association of Schools of Social Work & International Federation of Social Workers (IASSW & IFSW). (2014). *The Global Definition of Social Work*. Retrieved from http://ifsw.org/policies/definition-of-social-work/

Jaini, P.S. (1998). The Jaina Path of Purification. Varanasi: Motilal Banarsidass Publishers.

Judy Ledgerwood & Kheang Un. (2003). Global concepts and local meaning: human rights and Buddhism in Cambodia, *Journal of Human Rights*, 2(4), 531-549, DOI: 10.1080/1475483032000137129.

Karma, L.T. (2004). *Buddhist Women and Social Justice: Ideals, Challenges and Achievements*, New York: State University of New York Press.

King, S.B. (2009). *Socially Engaged Buddhism*. Honolulu: University of Hawaii Press.

Koenig, H.G. (2008). *Medicine, Religion, and Health: Where Science and Spirituality Meet*, Philadelphia: Templeton Foundation Press.

Kohli, S.S. (1994). *Real Sikhism*, New Delhi: Harman Publishing House.

Kondrat, M.E. (2013), *Person-in-Environment. Encyclopedia of Social Work*, Oxford: National Association of Social Workers and Oxford University Press.

Kotler, A. (Ed.). (1996). *Engaged Buddhist Reader: Ten Years of Engaged Buddhists*. California: Parallax Press.

Mazumdar, K.S. (1999). Hinduism: A Social Work Perspective. In C. Patel, *Social Work Practice: Religio-Philosophical Foundation*. New Delhi: Rawat Publications.

McLeod, H. (1997). *Sikhism*. London: Penguin Books.

Mohammed, A.A., Uddin, M.S., and Bougangue, B. (2020). Starting the Indigenisation Process of Social Work Practice in Malaysia. Social Work & Society, 18(1).

National Association of Social Workers (2007). *Indicators for the Achievement of the Nasw Standards for Cultural Competence in Social Work Practice*. Place of Publication: NASW.

Nelson-Becker, H., Nakashima, M. and Canda, E.R. (2006). Spirituality in professional helping interventions with older adults. In B. Berkman & S. D'Ambruoso (Eds.), *Oxford Handbook of Social Work in Health and Aging*. New York: Oxford University Press.

Payne, M. (2011). *Humanistic Social Work: Core Principles in Practice*. Chicago: Lyceum Books.

Popple, Philip R., and Leslie L. (2011). *Social Work, Social Welfare and American Society*. Boston: Ally & Bacon.

Ranganathananda, Swami (2000). *Proceedings of the Question-Answer Session: Vivekananda Vedanta Society*, Chicago, 1982. Calcutta: Advaita Ashram, Publication Department.

Riepe, D.M. (1996). *Naturalistic Tradition in Indian Thought*. Varanasi: Motilal Banarsidass Publishers.

Vyas, N.J. (1999). Non Violence and Man-Making Buddhist Philosophy. In C. Patel, *Social Work Practice: Religio-Philosophical Foundations*. New Delhi: Rawat Publications.

7

Core Values of Social Work

"Ashrams" Perspective

Dimple Mishra

Introduction

Values are the general and strong beliefs that one should act, live, behave and respond in a socially acceptable manner. Values build our character as what we should be and how we should perform. It is believed that a child starts learning from his/her parents when he/she takes birth. The parents are the first teachers of their children. Whatsoever is taught to the children in early years of age by their parents, are learnt by them. Therefore, in an early stage of life, the children are taught the values of how and what to speak, how to greet elders etc.

Values unite us through various mediums such as performing rituals; respecting and helping others; obeying the elders; selflessly performing our duties; protecting our environment, animals (extinct and endangered species), and the vulnerable sections of our societies. The value, which is said to be professional, is not a separate entity from societal value. Keeping in mind the societal values, the persons perform their professional obligations. In turn, society dispenses the professionals with supportive legislation, funding, and a delegation of responsibilities for certain societal functions and mechanisms to ensure that these functions and mechanisms are appropriately performed.

Traditionally, only value-based education was imparted among the children both at home and at *Gurukul*. The parents used to send their children to *Gurukul* or *Guru-ashram* for inheriting value-based education. It was like an exile for the *Shishyas* (children) to learn and grasp education during the Vedic period. The role and responsibility of *Gurus* were not only to educate their *Shishyas* (children) but also to make them value-oriented and value-laden person. Values guide us about the correct direction to follow throughout our life. It is believed that the person without values is the person without manners. Therefore, value plays an essential role in our life.

Values of Social Work

The essential and crucial function of the social work profession is to upgrade human prosperity and help meet the fundamental human needs and strengthening of individuals who are defenceless, abused, and living in neediness. A notable and characterizing highlight of social work is the profession's attention to singular prosperity in a social setting and the prosperity of society. Major to social work is regard for the ecological powers that make, add to, and address issues in living.

Social workers advance social equity and social change with and for the benefit of clients. "Clients" is utilized comprehensively to allude to people, families, gatherings, associations, and networks. Social workers are delicate to social and ethnic assorted variety and endeavour to end segregation, persecution, destitution, and different types of social bad form. These exercises might be as immediate practice, network sorting out, management, conference, organization, backing, social and political activity, strategy advancement and execution, instruction, and examination and assessment. Social workers try to improve the limit of individuals to address their own needs. Social workers likewise try to advance the responsiveness of associations, networks, and other social organizations to people's needs and social issues.

The crucial the social work profession is established in a lot of fundamental beliefs and values. These fundamental beliefs and values, grasped by social workers all through the profession's history, are the establishment of social work's interesting reason and point of view. The prominent values laid by the National Association of Social Workers (NASW) are:

- Service,
- Social Justice,
- Dignity and Worth of the Individual,
- Importance of Human Relationships,
- Integrity, and
- Competence.

This constellation of fundamental beliefs reflects what is extraordinary to the social work profession. The guiding principle, and the rules that stream from them, must be adjusted inside the unique situation and multifaceted nature of the human experience.

The Indic esteems are unceasing and general qualities that can be applied in the Indian setting as well as at the worldwide level. In the Indian setting, the social work profession being a spiritual profession, Indic ethics and values are very important for Indic social workers. Social workers manage every person in a mindful and deferential manner. Remembering the client's needs is steady with the qualities, moral rules and guidelines of the profession.

Social Work Values in the Indian Context

There are ample social work values laid in the Indian context. Psychology says that the process of socialization starts from the womb and ends up at the tomb. Socialization is the process of learning to act and behave in a way that is acceptable to society. The process of socialization and values are interrelated. One cannot think of being socialized without values. The values laid in the NASW Code of Ethics were included much later in the Vedic period. Therefore, it would be apt to consider these values as Indian values which are laid in the NASW code of ethics. Giving these values an Indian touch, the founder Director of School of Social Work, Indira Gandhi National Open University (IGNOU), Prof. Gracious Thomas has incorporated six contemporary values in the social work curriculum. Each of these values is defined in the global context which is applicable universally according to the respective countries. Each of them has its own significance in regard to its adherence and applicability in India as well as in other countries. These values are:

1. Hard work,
2. Teachership,
3. Loyalty to the profession,
4. Cultural sensitivity,
5. Patriotism, and
6. Responsibility and commitment.

Dash (2019) has made a significant attempt to bring Indic values into the social work discourses. He has aptly described the Indic values and its importance in Social work education (Dash, 2019). He says,

> "In Indian context, social work profession being a spiritual profession, Indic values are extremely relevant for Indic social workers. Social workers deal with each individual in a very caring and respectful way keeping in mind the client's needs in consistent with the values, ethical guidelines and standards of the profession."

Dharma: Dharma is considered the major unceasing standard of Hinduism. It has likewise alluded to the existing line of Hindu Dharma. The term dharma is a wide and extensive term and it is hard to characterize dharma in a straightforward way with regards to Hinduism. The idea of dharma passes on various implications in various settings. While in Hinduism, alludes to conduct the continuation of life and universe and speaks to obligations, laws, rights, excellencies, lead and so forth. In Buddhism, it speaks about nailing peace and in Jainism; it speaks to the educating of the Tirthankaras. In Sikhism, dharma implies the way of exemplary nature and appropriate way. In *Mahabharata*, Lord Shri Krishna says dharma secures and safeguards all that is made. In *Mahabharata*, dharma suggests love and fondness to everyone just as government assistance of every living being.

Ahimsa: Non-brutality is considered as perhaps the most noteworthy ethicalness in the Indian old customs. Indeed, even the Jains practice the most elevated type of peacefulness as they even would prefer not to hurt or harm even the smallest living being on the planet. It is one of the five anuvratas or promises to be trailed by each Jains before the start of their otherworldly way to finish monkhood. Buddhism likewise engenders peacefulness and its devotees cling to the eight-fold paths of Buddhism. *Ahimsa* is the most noteworthy type of dharma as referenced in *Mahabharata*. While clarifying the significance of dharma to Yudhishthira, Bhishma says, whatever be the outcome gotten by affection, is dharma. '*Ahimsa Paramo Dharma*'—it implies not just shunning purposeful damage to other people, not even simple resistance yet, in addition, incorporates sympathy, pardoning, benevolence, harmony and agreement.

Nishtha: The word '*Nishtha*' signifies total commitment, confidence with trust and certainty to the customers and each individual. Social workers ought to acknowledge the customer as he/she is. The guideline of acknowledgement is an all-around acknowledged rule in social work. In *Bhagavad Gita* likewise, Lord Krishna notices two kinds of *Nishtha*, *Jnana yoga* and *Karma yoga*. The social workers must secure through and profound information on social work hypothesis and practices. They should have profound enthusiasm to gain proficiency with the most recent advancements in the field of social work so they can serve the customers viably towards their fulfilment. *Karma yoga* is likewise significant for social specialists. They should think intensely with devotion.

Upeksha/Upekkha: *Upeksha* is a Sanskrit expression that implies restraint, resilience and furthermore non-connection.Upeksha is the fourth component of the Buddhist Brahmaviravas. Patanjali's *Yoga Sutras* likewise depicts *Upeksha* as a model for getting a healthy lifestyle, expelling bigotry and thinking about it all similarly. The estimation of *upeksha* among the social workers causes them to look at the circumstance comprehensively. It likewise guzzles among the nature of fearlessness to deal with the circumstance effectively. It is additionally a fundamental quality for affinity development among the customers just as partners. It likewise inspires the social workers to work for the bliss of others with a dedicated psyche. Along these lines, *upeksha* is a significant incentive to adequately convey social work intercessions.

Satya: *Satya* is the Sanskrit word for truth. It alludes to honesty in one's activities and conduct. *Satya* is one of the significant incentives for social specialists. They ought to be a lot of legit in their connections with the customers. They ought to avoid beguiling the customers and from lie. This will at last lead to better affinity development just as legitimate recognizable proof and arrangement of the issues of the people. This will likewise advance further confidence in the social workers.

Besides this, there are many more values laid in our Indian epics which are as follows:

***Tyaga* (Renunciation):** *Tyaga* means renunciation. This is the fourth stage of *Ashram* in which the person has supposed to renunciate worldly life and get fully devoted to *Parabrahma.* In Hinduism, it is believed that the entire life of a person is like a pilgrimage. The *karma* which is performed throughout life, adds to the act of being virtuous and in turn completing the pilgrimage. *Tyaga* is one of the most important values of Indic culture. If we see it in the context of *Ashrams*, it is apt defining this value as each phase of *Ashram* describes the way of living through sacrificing things.

"*Naasti vidya samamchakshu, naasti satya samamtapah. Naasti raag samamdukham, naasti tyaga samamsukham*". It means knowledge is the best eye. Truth is the most noteworthy repentance. Attachment is the greatest torment. Renunciation is the most elevated joy.

***Daan* (Donation, Alms):** *Daan* means giving. Every religion has the custom and provision of offering the needful to the poor and the needy. There is a *shloka* in *Ramayan*:

> "*Daridraya Krutam Danam Soonya Limgascha poojanam*
> *Anadha Pretha Samskaram Aswamedha samamviduhu*|"

It means helping the poor with money, doing worship to the *Shiva Lingam* of a dilapidated temple, doing funeral rites to the corpse of an orphan are equal to doing *Aswamedha Yagam*.

Daan is considered as one of the greatest Indian value. In *Mahabharata*, the story of *Karna* is not a hidden fact. Everyone knows him about his inordinate donations. In Hinduism, donations are given to the needy and the poor people even without any specific occasion in order to help them. It is believed that as more you give, the more you will receive. Therefore, *Daan* is estimated as an important value in our Indic value..

***Aadhyaatmikata* (Spirituality):** Spirituality is an expansive idea with space for some points of view. By and large, it incorporates a feeling of association with an option that could be greater than ourselves, and it commonly includes a quest for importance throughout everyday life. All things considered; it is a general human encounter—something that contacts everyone of us. Individuals may depict a profound encounter as holy or extraordinary or basically a profound feeling of being alive and interrelatedness. Some may find that their spiritual life is complicatedly connected to their relationship with a congregation, sanctuary, mosque, or gathering place. Others may implore or discover comfort in an individual relationship with God or a higher force. Still, others look for significance through their associations with nature or workmanship. Like your feeling of direction, your own meaning of spirituality may change for a mind-blowing duration, adjusting to your own encounters and connections.

> "*Manmanabhav mad-bhaktomadyajimaamnamaskuru mam-evaisyasisatyamtepratijaanepriyoasi me.*"

It means always think of Me, become My devotee, worship Me and offer your homage unto Me. Thus, you will come to Me without fail. I promise you this because you are My very dear friend (*Bhagavad Gita*, chapter 18, Text 65).

***Swikaaryata* (Acceptance):** Acceptance means the fact of being received as adequate, valid and suitable. Everyone likes being accepted. It is of two types—Self-acceptance and social acceptance. Self- acceptance means accepting oneself as the way we are. We should always remain in a contented state of mind. Social acceptance means being accepted by others. When society accepts individuals, they are motivated. Whereas if not accepted, they feel depressed, isolated, stressed and in turn, suicidal tendencies enter their minds. Therefore, everyone should be accepted irrespective of their caste, class, creed, religion etc. It is everyone's right to be accepted.

> "*Samudra vasnedeviparvat-stan-manditey, Vishnu-patninamastubhyampaad-sparsh sham-swa me.*"

It means Mother Earth, who has the ocean as clothes, adorned by mountains and forests, and is the Consort of Lord Vishnu; I bow to you to please forgive me for touching you with my feet.

***Aadar* (Respect):** Everybody must respect individual people. This is a fundamental prerequisite of living in the general public. Each individual is unique, with various social and social qualities. Social workers are aware of those distinctions, rewarding every individual with pride and regard and advancing their customers' ability and chance to address their own needs and improve their own circumstances. Social workers must be mindful of their obligations to both individual customers and to society in general and look for answers for their clients that likewise bolster society's more extensive interests. We surely owe an essential degree of with respect to other people. Moreover, suitable Respect must appear to individuals who sway our lives. This incorporates our folks, family members, educators, companions, individual specialists, authority figures, and so on. Perhaps the most ideal methods of indicating admiration to others is tuning in. Tuning in to someone else's perspective is an incredible method of Respect. Generally essential, we should permit an individual to communicate his perspectives regardless of whether we can not help contradicting them. Another significant part of regarding others is strict/ political perspectives. Strict and social convictions of others ought to be given a great deal of thought. Regarding others' Religions is positively an indication of demonstrating full-grown Respect. Everybody must respect the individuals who are in power. Nearly everybody manages individuals in their carries on with that hold authority. In this way, a sound measure of Respect ought to be given to such individuals. Individuals of power can be of different classes. These are chief, cop, strict pioneer, educator, and so forth. Taking everything into account, Respect is a significant part of human socialization. It is surely a valuable worth that must be safeguarded. Deferential conduct is crucial for human endurance.

> "Yasmin deshe na sammano na vritrin cha baandhavah, na cha vidyagamo-apasyati vas-satram na kaaryet". According to *Chanakya Niti* where there is no respect, no employment, and neither friend nor relative, where there is no education and where there is no quality in the people living, houses

should not be build up at such places. Such places should be immediately left off.

***Charitra Nirmana* (Character Formation):** Character formation is that profoundly internalized example of qualities and mentalities and the ensuing activities that are frequently settled in pre-intellectual occasions of life through the common and typical instructive examples that are proper for youthful children. Character formation is a mental idea that alludes to all the ongoing methods of feeling and responding that recognizes one individual from another. Sigmund Freud had a supported enthusiasm for the subject of character development, since it addresses the significant topics that intrigued him: "anatomo—physiological destiny," memory follows, and, all the, for the most part, the job of gaining characteristics, just as the capacity of sublimation concerning the "remaining parts" of the pregenital libido.

> "*Videsheshudhanamvidya, vyasneshudhanammati. Parlokedhanamdharmah, sheelamsarvatravaiy shaman.*"

It means knowledge riches in a foreign land. Intelligence riches in difficult stretches. Righteousness riches in another world. Verily, Good Character riches all over the place and on all occasions.

***Sunyum* (temperance, self-restraint):** Temperance is the goodness that directs our fascination of delights and gives balance in the utilization of things of this world. It guarantees the will's dominance over senses and keeps wants inside the restrictions of what is righteous. Temperance in its advanced use is characterized as balance or wilful self-restraint. It is regularly depicted regarding what an individual deliberately avoids doing. This incorporates limitation from retribution by rehearsing peacefulness and absolution, restriction from pomposity by rehearsing lowliness and humility, restriction from overabundances, for example, excessive extravagance or spending too much by rehearsing judiciousness, and restriction from fury or desiring by rehearsing tranquillity and discretion. Moderation has been portrayed as ethicalness by strict masterminds, scholars, and all the more as of late, clinicians, especially in the positive brain research development. It has a long history in the philosophical and strict idea.

> "*Jeetatmanah-prashantasyaparmaatma-samaahitah-shitoshanasukh-dukheshutathaamaan-apmaanayoh.*"

It means the self-controlled and peaceful person's supreme self is balanced in cold and heat, pleasure and pain, as also in honour and disgrace.

***Daya* (Compassion):** *Daya* (compassion), not at all like a balanced worry for the prosperity of others. This implies the hole among ethical quality and personal circumstance will be littler for the caring individual. Sympathy additionally has the benefit of focusing our consideration towards the enduring of others in a manner that is hard to ignore. Compassion is one of the fundamental beliefs of the Mutual Learning approach. Empathy implies briefly suspending judgment with the goal that you can value others' points of view or circumstances when they are not the same as your own. To be caring you should be truly worried about the other individual or individuals' needs.

> "*Na saadeekshanasaabhiksha, na tad dhyaanam, na tad maunamdaya yatra navidyate.*"

It means without compassion; preparation for a religious ceremony, donation, austerity, concentration and quietness are all void.

***Saadagi* (Simplicity):** Simplicity is valuing the little things throughout everyday life. It is away from the material wants and enthusiastic wants and emphasise on the consent to just "be". Simplicity maintains a strategic distance from squander, shows economy, evades conflicts muddled by covetousness, dread, peer pressure, and a misguided feeling of personality. Gandhiji quoted the concept of simplicity as "Simple Living and High Thinking", which means being away from all the lustrous and alluring desires and focus on the concentrated fruitful things which are helpful in the strong building of society.

***Arjava* (non-hypocrisy):** *Arjava* or non-hypocrisy is the act of being as he/she is. It does not belong to the concept of deceitfulness, bigotry, dishonesty, duplicity, fraud or insincerity. Rather it literally means righteousness, truthfulness, trustworthiness, fairness, frankness and being sincere. This is itself is of the greatest worth of being valued. It is applicable for both the client and the social worker. When the client is trustworthy and narrates a clear picture of his/her situation, then it becomes easy for a social worker to solve his/her problems. And when the social worker depicts the way he/she is, then it becomes reliable for his/her client to believe him/her without having any doubt. Therefore, it is one of the most prominent values considered in all arena.

> "*amanitvamadambhitvamahinsakšhantirarjavamach-aryopasanamshauchamsthairyamatma-vinigrahaÿ.*"

It means humbleness, freedom from hypocrisy, non-violence, forgiveness, simplicity, service of the Guru, cleanliness of the body and mind steadfastness and self-control are some of the values laid in *Bhagavadgita,* Chapter-13, verse-8.

Samarpan **(Dedication):** *Samarpan* means complete devotion. It may be towards a person, family, and community, learning practice or *Parabrahama. Samarpan* is an act of binding oneself to a course of action. It is very much useful and required value of social work. It is seen in our Indian history that social activists like Medha Patkar and Sundarlal Bahuguna was fully dedicated to environmental protection. Therefore, their efforts and dedication towards the initiatives of social concerns bore fruit. Bhartrihari, a famous Sanskrit poet, in his "*Neeti Shatakam*" brings out the importance of human birth as a service with dedication. The shloka is as follows:

> "*Paropakaraya Phalanti Vrukshaha Paropakaraya Vahanti Nadyaha Paropakaraya Charanti Gaavaha Paropakarardha Midam Shareeram.*"

According to Bhartrihari, trees bear fruits for others' sake, rivers flow for others' sake, cows wander for others' sake and the *shareeram* (human body) itself is for others' sake (i.e. the beneficial use for others).

Kshama **(Forgiveness):** *Kshama* can even prompt sentiments of getting, sympathy and empathy for the person who hurt you. Absolution does not mean overlooking or pardoning the damage done to you or making up with the individual who caused the mischief. Absolution brings a sort of harmony that causes you to go on with life. Forgiveness is for our own development and satisfaction. At the point when we clutch hurt, torment, disdain, and outrage it hurts us unquestionably more than it hurts the wrongdoer. Forgiveness liberates us to embrace the here and now. Forgiveness permits us to proceed onward without outrage or scorn or looking for vengeance.

> "*Kshama-balshaktanaam-shaktanaam-bhushnam-Kshama-Kshama- vashikriteloke-kshmaya-kimna-sidhhayati.*"

It means forgiveness is the strength for weak people, forgiveness is the ornament of strong people, forgiveness has tamed this universe, what can not be done with forgiveness?

Ashrams

Ashrams are divided into four parts which is based on the person's Karma and Dharma. Each precept of antiquated India, cut out by the old holy people, depends on logical and sound thinking. Be that as it may, to put them to utilize they should have been socially inserted. Thus, techniques like, the Ashram framework was remembered for the Vedic culture. The normal existence of an Indian was viewed as 100 years. Based on this there were four ashrams of Vedic life:

Sl. No.	Ashram	No. of Years	Role Performance
1.	Brahmacharya	Up to first 25 years	Performing role as student.
2.	Grihastha	Second 25 years (26-50 years)	Performing marriage and household tasks.
3.	Vanaprastha	Third 25 years (51-75 years)	Retirement from household tasks and handing over the authorities to the next generation.
4.	Sannyas	Above 75 years	Complete renunciation from worldly thoughts, desires, responsibilities and surrender to God.

The objective of each stage or *ashram* was to satisfy the standards on which these stages were separated. The phases of *ashram* life infer that an individual takes cover in all four phases of life relying upon his age. These stages delineate the obligations that man needs to rehearse in the course of his life. These four divisions are clarified in antiquated Manu's contents. With such procedure, the then contemporary society additionally planned for holding the social foundations together. Since the beginning man was demonstrated the ways of morals, poise, knowledge, logic, love, empathy and control. He was guided to avoid eagerness, remorselessness, sloth, pride and a few different indecencies.

History of Ashrams

This arrangement of *ashrams* is accepted to be predominant since the fifth century B.C.E. in Hindu society. Be that as it may, history specialists state that these phases of life were constantly seen more as 'standards' than as a typical practice. As indicated by one researcher, even in its very beginnings, after the first *ashram*, a youthful grown-up could pick which of the different *ashrams* he would wish to seek after for an amazing remainder. Today, it is not normal that a Hindu ought to experience the four phases; however, it despite everything remains as a significant "column" of Hindu socio-strict convention.

1. Brahmacharya Ashram

In Brahmacharya Asharam, a person is expected to undergo learning (schooling) to earn *vidya* (education). Brahmacharya is a time of formal training going on until around age 25, during which, the understudy ventures out from the home to remain with a master and accomplish both profound and commonsense information. During this period, he is known as a *Brahmachari* and is set up for his future calling, just as for his family, and social and strict life ahead.

2. *Grihasth Ashram*

In *Grihasth Ashram*, a person is expected to live a married life, earn money and serve his family. This period starts at marriage when one must attempt the duty regarding procuring a living and supporting a family. At this stage, Hinduism underpins the quest for riches (*Artha*) as a need and guilty pleasure in sexual joy (*Kama*), under certain characterized social and grandiose standards. This *ashram* goes on until around the age of 50. As indicated by the Laws of Manu, when an individual's skin wrinkles and his hair greys, he ought to go out into the backwoods. In any case, most Hindus are such a great amount in adoration with this second *ashram* that the *Grihastha* stage endures for ever.

3. Vanaprastha Ashram

In *Vanaprastha Ashram*, a person is supposed to serve society selflessly and earn *Punya* (good deed). The *Vanaprastha* stage starts when an individual's obligation as a householder reaches a conclusion: He has become a grand-dad-mother; his youngsters are grown up and have set up lives of their own. At this age, he ought to deny all physical, material and sexual joys, resign from his social and expert life and leave his home for a backwoods cottage, where he can invest his energy in petitions. He is permitted to take his life partner along, however, keeps in touch with the remainder of the family. This sort of life is to be sure brutal and unfeeling for a matured individual.

4. Sannyas Ashram

In *Sannyas Ashram*, the person leaves the material life and devotes himself to *Moksha* (salvation). At this stage, an individual is completely devoted to God. He is a sannyasi, he has no home, no other connection; he has denied all wants, fears, expectations, obligations, and duties. He is for all intents and purposes converged with God, all his common ties are broken, and his sole concern becomes accomplishing *moksha* or discharge from the hover of birth and passing. (Get the job done it to state, not many Hindus can go up to this phase of turning into a total austere). When he kicks the bucket, the memorial service functions (*Pret-karma*) are performed by his beneficiary.

Values and Ashram: Interconnectedness

The Indic values mentioned above are very directly connected to each and every phase of *Ashram*. All the phases of *Ashram* work the value of *Tyaga* (sacrifice) as *Brahamacharyaashram* teaches us to leave all the worldly desires at the time grasping education whereas *Grihasth Ashram* teaches us to serve the household activities. To serve others is also considered as *Tyaga*. *Vanaprastha ashram* is the phase towards leaving the charge of household activities to the next generation and start devoting oneself to *Parabrahma* and *Sannyas ashram* is the complete renunciation of worldly life and surrendering oneself to *Parabrahma*. "*Daanenbhutanivashibhavanti daanenvairanyapiyaantinaasham, Paropibandhutva-bhupaitidaanerdaaamheesarvevyasananihanti.*" It means "anyone can be bewitched through donation. Enmity is ended up through donation. Enemies become brothers/friends through *daan* and all the calamities are gone by donation." Therefore, helping those who are financially unsound and teaching them the way of earning is considered as part of earning which is the first and foremost value of social work. It is believed that giving donation irrespective of any phase of *Ashram* add our qualities in getting *Moksha* (attainment of bliss). *Aadhyatmikta* (Spirituality) is the recognition of a sense or feeling in which one understands others oneself better and put others in front more than himself/herself. This form of value is performed at *Vanaprastha* and *Sannyasa ashrams* when the person leaves the terrestrial life psychologically and at the time keeps oneself at the stake to help others. We repeat mistakes throughout our life irrespective of any stage of life. The possibilities of committing the mistakes are most often in the first two phases of *ashram*, i.e. *Brahmacharya* and *Grihastha*. *Swikaaryata* (Acceptance) is also a prominent principle of social work. In each phase of the *ashram*, it is necessary to accept whatever teachings are being imparted. It is important indeed to accept self as well as others to perform the activities needed. This is so because respect is shown to others and the activity or the work which is being performed is done cohesively. Giving *Aadar* (Respect) to someone shows the sign of acceptance. As during the first phase of the *ashram*, respect is shown to the Gurus in order to grasp education. *Charitra Nirmana* (Character formation) is the result of respect and acceptance. It is initiated at the very first phase of *Ashram* when the child is born and imparted education. His/her way of behaviour depicts the sign of how his/her character is formed. *Saadagi* (Simplicity) should be maintained throughout each phase of life (*Ashram*) as this provides a sense of satisfaction and set higher goals in life. *Sanyam* (Tolerance) gives us the power of self-control. Through this education, marital life or *moksha* is easy to achieve. Being empathetic and sympathetic are the signs of compassion. The person who understands the pain of others and feels it like its own is the greatest form of value. It is taught in almost all phases of the *ashram*. When a person performs his/her duties being the way he/she is and not as being a hypocrite, learns the real meaning of life and life span. In turn he/she receives bliss. *Samarpan* (Dedication) is a kind of value which is inculcated in *Brahmacharya* for getting actual education, in *Grihastha* for happy household life, in *Vanaprastha* willingly handing over the household charges to the next generation and in *Sannyas* getting *moksha*. *Kshama* (Forgiveness) is the ultimate indication of receiving bliss. A person is considered to be a saint who forgives others and give them a chance to rectify the mistakes done. This kind of value preferably adheres at the time of *Vanaprastha* and *Sannyas ashrams*.

Conclusion

Ashrams are the different phases of life span. The *ashrams* cannot be thought of without the Indic values mentioned above. Values dispense the method of living in a given situation. It is often said that a person thinks according to the values incorporated. It has been written in *Kathopanishad* (*Krishna Yajurveda*), "*Prathame na arjita vidya dwitiye na arjitam dhanam tritiye na arjitam kirtih chaturthe kim karishyati*." It means "who did not acquire knowledge in the first *Brahmacharya ashram*, the second who did not earn money, i.e. *Grihasth Ashram*, did not earn fame in the *Vanaprastha ashram*, what will he do in the fourth *Sannyas ashram*? According to *ashrams*, it becomes essential for a person to perform the duties prescribed in it. The duties/activities can only be performed effectively and efficiently through the incorporation of values mentioned in the above text as values are the guiding factors/principles of a person's life. In Hinduism, values are unlimited. The values described above are very few but are apt in the context defining *ashrams*. These values are even relevant in the context of explaining the Indic perspective of social work. Therefore, values are relevant in defining each phase of the *ashram*.

REFERENCES

Dash, B.M. (2019). Indic Social Work Values, *New Delhi Times*, April, 22, retrieved from https://www.newdelhitimes.com/indicsocialworkvalues/
?fbclid=IwAR3jJfklyaTdOoTXDWMXUM6sveJi-sBRXArVpNFn0RUFRbDmXgMKtIlShfM.

Framarin, C. (2011). The value of nature in Indian (Hindu) traditions. *Religious Studies,* 47(3), 285-300. Retrieved August 6, 2020, from www.jstor.org/stable/23013368.

Goodwin, W. (1955). Ethics and Value in Indian Philosophy. *Philosophy East and West*, 4(4), 321-344. DOI: 10.2307/1396742.

Hiriyanna, M. (1938). The Indian Conception of Values. *Annals of the Bhandarkar Oriental Research Institute*, 19(1), 10-24. Retrieved August 6, 2020, from www.jstor.org/stable/41688382.

National Association of Social Workers. (2008). *The Preamble to the Code of Ethics*. Retrieved May 4, 2008, from http://www.socialworkers.org/pubs/Code/ code.asp.

Srinivas, M. (1993). Changing Values in India Today. *Economic and Political Weekly*, 28(19), 933-938. Retrieved August 6, 2020, from www.jstor.org/stable/4399700.

Thomas, G. (2016). *Social Work: The Value-Based Profession*, Jaipur: Rawat Publications.

http://www.indianculture/home/ethnicity/indianvalues&beliefs.com.

8
Triguna Theory of Personality

Bhuvneshwari Poonam Kunwar Rathore

Introduction

The first step towards treating mental illness is examining your personality. The complete analysis of personality is the basis of every mental health therapy. Although every personality is unique, mental science divides each personality into certain main structures and categories for study; there are several types of examinations and classifications of a personality. The West has enriched the field of mental science by giving a lot of traits and personality theories.

These theories help understand mental science better, but there is still a great need for a universal, more compatible theory to understand modern mental science. One of the major problems with current theories is that they analyse the personality based on a specific symptom, such as physical symptoms or certain behavioural patterns such as likes and dislikes. In other words, they consider these fixed patterns as personality. At the same time, the "whole" personality is a combination of both subtle and gross elements, and at the same time, a personality is an ever-changing construct. It is impossible that a personality is not affected or changed by health incidents, meeting new people, or learning new things in life. It is astonishing that the structure of each personality is different through different aspects and stages of life. With the combination of ordinary incidences (components) in different ways, the ever-changing structure creates a unique personality.

Insufficiencies of Current Practicing Theories

- A fixed set of behaviours.
- Psychological or physiological traits.

- Not very specific.
- It does not count gross and subtle elements.
- It does not treat a person as a whole.
- It does not assess personality imbalance.
- Limited personality types for a diverse range of human personas.
- It does not explain the reasons behind different personality constructs.
- It generally entitles a person to just a good, bad, or average personality.
- It does not possess a universal approach.

For thousands of years, the East experimented and researched to find the greatest possibilities for the development of a human being's personality, and it has created a universal, time-tested, and scientific principle. All we need to do is to understand it and focus more experiments on it. Since the focus of ancient Indian philosophy, spirituality, yoga, and medical science was on the imagination of the whole human being, they were not in favour of studying a person in fragments. They believed that the main field was important, but at the same time, the focus was to work on a person as a whole. That is why the seemingly different principles and content of their subjects are in harmony with each other.

As an important note in the *Charak Samhita*, *Charak* says, studying one subject only can make a student into a doctor, but to become an expert in the true sense, he must have knowledge of all the fields related to human studies, like grammar, literature, law, philosophy, religious studies, ethical studies, logic, physics, zoology, biology, botany, geography, chemistry etc.

> *Ekam shastra madhiyano na vidya chchastrinischiyam*
> *Tasmadwahushrutah shastram vijaniyachhhikitasikah //*
>
> Charak Sanhita 4.7.

Modern science works on the theory of dividing a person into fragments for treatment, which results in the curing of one part and the ailing of the other due to the side effects. Similarly, many times, subjects directly affecting human beings, such as psychology, medical science, philosophy, and spirituality, may contradict each other, hence creating confusion with regard to the treatment and disturbing the idea of considering the personality as a whole. This might be the most developed and best available method of physical science, but in the field of psychology, it is important to understand a person as a whole. Leaving one part or aspect of a personality out of treatment may result in a wrong mental analysis of the person.

Charak writes in the *Charak Samhita* that any physical illness can turn into a mental illness in the course of time, and *vice versa*, just that whichever symptom appears first becomes the basis of diagnosis.

That is why the analysis of personality in the Indian *trigun* system is based on an integrated approach which depends on the person's physical condition, behaviour, likes and dislikes, lifestyle, spiritual condition, eating habits, the way he reacts to things, communication, sleep cycles, thought process etc. There are subtle and gross things that are kept in mind during the analysis.

What is also unique is that this *trigun* experimental system does not only apply to psychiatry in India but also applies to *Aayurveda* and *Siddha* medical sciences, yoga, philosophy, and spiritual development to understand a person's religious conditions and to understand a person's role in his social and family life. Hence, and so this theory is universal. This theory is so prevalent in the east that even someone who is completely unfamiliar with subjects like Ayurveda, Philosophy, and Medical science can casually explain to someone how he is very *satvik* or *tamsik* in nature.

The Structure of a Personality

It is believed in Ayurveda and Siddha medical sciences, yoga, spiritual and meditation-related texts, philosophy, and mental sciences that the characteristics of personality are made up of many layers. Like the onion, which is an entity made of many layers, in the same way; a human also consists of many layers, each layer having an important place in the personality.

Following are the layers:

- *Panchmahabhoot (five elements)—Prithvi (earth), Jal (water), Vaayu (air), Aakash (space), Agni (fire).*
- *Panchkosh (five sheats)—Annmay (gross body), Pranmany (votal air), Manomay (self), Vigyanmay (intellect and knowledge), Anandmay (bliss).*
- *Panchkarmendriya (organs of action)—Vaani (voice), Haath (hands), Per (legs), Guda (anus), Upasth (reproductive organ).*
- *Panchgyanendriya (sense organ)—Kaan (ear), Twacha (skin), Netra (eyes), Jivha (tongue), Nasika (nose).*
- *Panch Pran (five vital life force)—Pran, Apaan, Samaan, Vyaan, Udaan.*
- *Sapt Dhatu (seven types of tissues)—Ras (body fluids), Rakt (blood), Maans (mascular tissues), Med (adipose tissue), Asthi (bony tissue), Majja (bone marrow and nervous tissue), Shukra*

(generative tissue including semen and ovum constituents and stem cells).

- *Antah Karan Chatustya (conscience the inner cause)—Manas (mind), Buddhi (intellact), Chitta (memory), Ahankaar (ego).*
- *Tri Sharir-Sthul (gross material body-body that can be seen), Shukshm (subtle body—this subtle body cannot be seen in your dreams you perform all your actions with this body), Kaaran (causal body—body created by one desire).*
- *Tri Dosha (three fundamental bodily bio elements)—Vatta (all moments in the body is due to properties of vatta), Pitta (pitta represents metabolism, it is the energy principle which uses bile to direct digestion and enhance metabolism), Kapha (watery nourishing elements of the body).*
- *Tri Guna—Sattva, Rajas, Tamas.*

Out of these, *panchkosh, tridosha,* and *antah karan* are related to the person's subtle body. Triguna is the fundamental dimension that creates a personality. *Swabhav,* or fundamental/engrained nature, is a unique word that is used in its advanced meaning while defining personality. It has a broader definition as compared to the English adjective "personality."

To understand it better, nature is not subjected to change, whereas personality is ever changing. Personality can be developed or deteriorated, but nature ca not be developed nor changed. A personality can be made or enhanced by learning, but nature is beyond learning. Shri Aurobindo in "Essasys on the *Geeta*" uses the word "spiritual personality" to further define nature. *Swabhav,* or nature, could also be defined as an essential quality. The external expression of nature is personality.

The swabhaav is created by Triguna and Tridisha, while the personality is created by Triguna and Tridisha. Tridosha is the basis of the physical side of a personality, whereas *triguna* is the basis of the psyche. It is an interesting fact that *Ayurveda* has described the physical dimensions. That is, *tridosha* (*vatta, pitta, kapha*) as imperfections, whereas the psychological dimensions as *gunas* (*sattva*, *rajas*, *tamas*) meaning qualities. At the same time, if one of the *gunas* is present only by itself, it is called a *dosha.* For example, in reference to the psyche, *rajas* alone is mentioned as *rajodosha* and *tamodosha. Sattva,* on the other hand, is a *guna* always since it is a balance between the other two. The Western mindset of dealing with a mental or physical illness is to beat it or fight it. For example, terms like "fighting with depression," "beating cancer" etc.

Whereas, the eastern mindset believes in the principle of curing an illness by finding out the cause of the imbalance in the body and then balancing it. The point is not to fight with or within the body, but to bring it back into harmony. Ancient mental science uses *triverg vishleshan* (tripartite analysis) to bring the body back into harmony.

Tripartite Analysis

Analysis based on physical status	Tridosha	Vatta, Pitta, Kapha
Analysis based on aspects of life	Tri Purusharth	Dharma, Artha, Kaam
Analysis based on Personality	Trigun	Sattva, Rajas, Tamas

Triguna—'*Tri*' stands for three and '*guna*' for qualities, state of mind and attitude. *Ayurvda* calls it as *triguna prakruti.* The trigunas are three dimensions of creation.

- *Sattva*—*Sattva* being goodness, compassion, illumination and positivity.
- *Rajas*—*Rajas* being activity, creativity, passion and impulsivity, potentially good or bad.
- *Tamas*—*Tamas* being the quality of deep thinking, contentedness, solitary, ignorance, rebellious, lethargy.

All matter of *prakruti* (creation) according to *sankhya* philosophy, has these three *gunas,* but in different proportions. The interplay of these *gunas* defines the character of someone or something of nature and determines the progress of life.

The Historical Journey of Triguna

The concept of *trigun* has travelled from *Atharvaveda* to *Upanishad,* from here to *Sankhya Darshan*, then to *Mahabharata,* from *Mahabharata* to *Shrimadbhagavat*, then it went through *Ayurveda* and finally, came to modern psychiatry. Continuous research since ancient times has made it more developed and reliable.

The first reference to yoga is found in the *Rigveda*. *Atharvaveda*, on the other hand, is concerned with a person's psyche and overall well-being. The foundation of *trigun* theory in *Atharvaveda* seems relevant to the discussion above. *Mandukya and Taittariya Upanishad play an important role in studying consciousness and personality with reference to psychiatry.Shwetashwara Upanishad mentions three fundamental qualities of elements, although all other texts has discussed it, the credit of developing it as a scientific principle goes to samkhya darshan which dates back to 3000 BC. Samkhya* and *Geeta* made it popular and widespread, whereas Ayurveda and *Yoga* gave it a practical form through which it started being used in psychiatry.

The ancient text of *Ayurveda* (*Charak Samhita*), which dates from the first to the second century, also uses *triguna* and *tridosh* theory for personality tests. *Samkhya karika* and *Samkhya sutra* texts have been popular since the 3rd century BC. Based on its age, *Trigun* theory can be absolutely called the world's oldest personality analysis theory.

Historical Journey of *Triguna*

Time Period	Books	Glosser, Translator and Author
1500 BCE to 1200 BCE	Nasadiya Sukta Rigveda 10.129 (This hymn is one of the roots of Samkhya)	Kramer/Christian, Larson, Bhattacharya and Potter
1200 BCE to 1000 BCE	Atharv Veda	Pandit Shree Ram Sharma Acharya
800 BCE to 600 BCE	Chandogya Upanishad, Kaushitaki Upanishad	Richard Grabe (1898), Dandekar (1968) Surendranath Gupta (1922)
400 BCE	Mahabharata Book Ashwamed Parv (36-39), Geeta (Ch 14 and 17)	Ved Vyas, Pndt Ram Narayan Shastri
300 BCE	Swethas watra Upanishad 5.23 Essential Qualities	Arthur Keith (1925), Johnston (1937), Ruzsa (2006)
300 BCE	Samkhya Karika and Samkhya Sutra (3.48 to 3.52)	Kapil Muni, James R. Ballantype
200 BCE	Charak Samhita	Charak, Dr. Nishi Arora

The concept of *Triguna* mentioned in various ancient Indian Literatures

Yog Literature	Ayurvedic Literature	Art Literature	Philosophical Literature	Religious Literature
Yog Sutra-Patanjali	Charak Samhita	Naty-Sastra of Bharata	Sankhya Kapilopdesh	Dharma-Shastras
Shiv Sutra and Malini Vijay Oddara Tantra (kashmir shavi jan)	Shushurut Samhita	Kala Tattva Kosh	Mimansa	Valmiki Ramayan

(Contd.)

Yog Literature	Ayurvedic Literature	Art Literature	Philosophical Literature	Religious Literature
Yog Komudi	Ashtaang Sangraham and Ashtaang Hridyam	Kamasutra	Vaisheshika	Mahabharata Geeta
Yoga Bija a hatha Yoga	Sharngadhara Samhita and Bhava Prakash	Rati Shastra	Nirukta	Bhagwat Puran
Yoogacayar bhumi Shastra	Madhava Nidanam	Ashtadhyayi	Nyaya	Yog Vasistha

Samkhya Darshan

Samkhya Darshan is one of the six schools of thought in philosophy. Its founder is Rishi Kapil, who is also mentioned in the *Mahabharata* as a *Samkhya* speaker and a great thinker. The 3rd '*skandha*' of *Shrimad Bhagavad Gita* says he was a son of Rishi 'Kardam' and' Devhuti', who was his mother. The first person who explained the *Samkhya* and *Trigun* theories then created the *Samkhya Sutra Grantha.*

Max Muller has also said something about it being ancient. According to Ruzsa, about 2000 years ago, 'samkhya' became the representative philosophy of Hindu thought in Hindu circles. Creation, destruction, and psyche are the main subjects of *samkhya sutra.*

> *The samkhya sutra discusses eight natures, sixteen disorders, five elements, three gunas, man, the universe, and the Holocaust.*

Kapil does not believe in the theory that God has created the world. He sees the whole creation as an evolution process. He does not believe that worldly problems are the law of God but rather an imbalance in the harmony of natural elements. He has mentioned and categorised 25 *avayav* (particles) of nature. According to him, nature has three qualities that are present in everything in the materialistic world on the basis of the different behaviours of the elements of *sattva, rajas,* and *tamas*. He has categorised the types, diversities, and qualities of personalities based on the *triguna* theory.

Descriptions found in different texts

(1) *Kapil Upadesha:* According to it, "*Prakruti*" is constituted of three *gunas* of *sattva*, *rajas*, and *tamas*. It is imperceptible, not being

apprehended by any organ of knowledge, but it exists externally as it provides the basis and substance for all objects in their casual and effectual conditions.

(2) *Samkhya Sutra*: *Samkhya Sutra* mentioned *Triguna* in Chapter 3 Verses 48 to 52 (*Shruti Bhed* and *Gunaprabhedan*).

(3) *Mahabharata:* In the *Ashwamedh Parv* of *Mahabharata* (verses 36 to 39), it mentioned the qualities of people possessing *sattva, rajas,* and *tamas.*

(4) *Shrimadbhagavad Gita:* In *Guntrayovibhag* of *Shrimadbhagavad Gita Chapter* 14 Verses 5 to 18 and Chapter 17 (*Shraddha Tray Vibhag*) Verses 7 to 14 mentioned *Triguna.*

(5) *Aagam Tantra Grantha:* In *Aagam tantra grantha, tamas is* explained in terms of desire, *rajas* as action, and *sattva* as a source of knowledge.

Rajo Guna: *Rajas* works by giving energy to be active; it provides inspiration and strength to do things. The dominance of *Rajas* makes a personality hard-working, entrepreneurial and successful. A *Rajas* person is always eager for materialistic pleasures, and another quality is a desire for a luxurious lifestyle. He is overtly inclined towards physical and bodily pleasures and delicious and rich food. He is always attracted to new things. Satisfaction on both physical and mental levels is very important to him. He always seeks attention and attracts the attention of the people. A highly pleasurable, luxurious, and opulent lifestyle in India is called "*Rajasi*". Another quality of *Raja's* personality is his ability to live the king's life and always make efforts and work hard to achieve it.

yattu kaamepsunaa karma saahankaarena vaa punah kriyate
bahulaayaasam tadraajasamudaahritam/

Bhagavad Gita 18.24

Translation: Action that is prompted by selfish desire, enacted with pride and full of stress is the nature of passion.

rajo raagaatmakam viddhi trishnaasangasamudbhavam,
tannibadhnaati kaunteya karmasangena dehinam/

Bhagavad Gita 14.7

Translation: O Arjun rajoguna is of the nature of passion. It arises from worldly desires and affections and binds the soul through attachment to furtive actions.

It is *Rajoguna* behind every person's desire and the inspiration to fulfil it. *Rajoguna* is present to a different extent in each person. Someone with higher *rajoguna* in comparison to *tamoguna* or *sattva* is called a *rajasic* person.

The more *Rajas* grows in a person, the more active and greedier he becomes. The excess of *Rajoguna* will start reflecting the negative sides of it. For example, anxiety and unstable communication, feeling restless, not being able to sit still for long, moving constantly and playing with things etc.

The same happens with thoughts; an uncontrollable flow of directionless thoughts goes on in his mind. Lack of decision-making and impatience grow. A mere thought of losing their pleasure can bring them into depression. They start to feel dissatisfied with themselves and their lives. Hence, the growing *rajoguna* takes the person slowly towards frustration, depression, anxiety, and violence.

lobhah pravrittir aarambhah karmanaamashamah sprihaa
rajasyetaani jayante vivriddhe bharatarshabha/
Bhagavad Gita 14.12

Translation: O Arjun when greed restlessness, exertion with great endeavour for furtive activities, agitation of the senses, incessant desire for sensual indulgence, all these arise, the mode of passion predominates.

raagee karmaphalaprepsur lubdho himsaatmako'shuchih
harshashokaanvitah kartaa raajasah parikeertitah/
Bhagavad Gita 18.27

Translation: The performer is considered in the mode of passion when he or she craves the fruits of his or her work, is covetous, violent in nature, impure and moved by joy and sorrow.

Tamo Guna: *Tamas* is the quality that gives rest and slowness. Stability, firmness, and the ability to feel come from *tamas.* It is responsible for sleep, attachment, and the stability of the personality. A person whose *tamas* is higher in comparison to *rajas* and *sattva* is called a *tamsik.*

People with higher *tamas* are slower and rest more lovingly. They can sit for a while. They like to sleep and talk slowly. They do things at a slower pace. Once a thought is struck in their minds, they cannot get rid of it easily. They are deep thinkers. The dominance of *Tamas* makes good thinkers, writers, and artists. They like to do intense, peaceful activities rather than the ones that involve intensity or energy. They are too attached to their bodies but do not react easily. They are usually calm, but when angry, they can be furious. They are overly attached to their loved ones. Overattachment and being whimsical are also qualities of a *tamsik* personality. Their imaginations are very good; they tend to get lost in thoughts, daydream, and are very sacrificing. They take a long time to come out of sorrow, sadness, and fear. If the *tamas* quality is raised to a very high level, the person might develop many imbalances.

tamastwajnaanajam viddhi mohanam sarvadehinaam/
pramaadaalasyanidraabhis tannibadhnaati bhaarata//
Bhagavad Gita 14.8

Translation: O Arjun, tamoguna, which is born of ignorance, is the cause of illusion for the embodied souls. Negligence, laziness, and sleep delude all living beings.

A clear symptom of increased *tamas* is an unprecedented increase in sleep, laziness, and dizziness. The individual develops a procrastination habit. He loses his interest in all things and slowly turns into a lost person with no alertness for him. The world seems to be a dark and depressing place.

Aprakaasho'pravrittishcha pramaado moha eva cha
tamasyetaani jaayante vivriddhe kurunandana/
Bhagavad Gita 14.13

Translation: O Arjun, nescience, inertia, negligence, and delusion are the dominant signs of the mode of ignorance.

ayuktah praakritah stabdhah shatho naishkritiko'lasah vishaadee
deerghasootree cha kartaa taamasa uchyate/
Bhagavad Gita 18.28

Translation: A performer in the mode of ignorance is one who is undisciplined, vulgar, stubborn, deceitful, slothful, despondent, and procrastinating.

yayaa swapnam bhayam shokam vishaadam madameva cha na
vimunchati durmedhaa dhritih saa paartha taamasee/
Bhagavad Gita 18.35

Translation: That unintelligent resolve is said to be a determination in the mode of ignorance, in which one does not give up dreaming, fearing, grieving, despair, and conceit.

Ignorance has been defined as darkness, which is why *tamoguna* has been associated with darkness in a negative connotation. Another effect of *tamoguna* which relates to darkness is the birth of life and nurturing, which happens in darkness as a natural process. The way a seed germinates, a body heals itself during sleep; the growth of life in a mother's womb is an example of *tamoguna* being the source of life force in its limited capacity. Hence, *tamoguna* has also been associated with fierce desire. In comparison with others, a *tamoguni* person is more inclined towards lust and desires. Tamoguna and darkness are inextricably linked to life's growth, sensuality, death, sleep, *nirvana*, meditation, unconsciousness, and meditation.

A *tamoguni* person does not work tied up with rules but goes with his own will. That is why he is rebellious and revolutionary in nature. He has the ability to do things, but is very procrastinating. Despite having consciousness, their lives appear to be careless. Increased *tamoguna* can lead a person towards depression and even suicide. *People in Tamoguna* are prone to depression.

Satoguna: While *Rajoguna* is *karma shakti, Tamoguna* is relaxation, ease, and composure. *Satoguna* is the fine balance between them. *Sattva* is the best of the conditions between the two extremes. *A Sattva guna* person can be entrepreneurial, active, and very peaceful and relaxed too. Harmony between activeness and stability can be seen as a sign of *sattva guna.* Self-control, free from doubt and responsibility for fulfilling the duties are qualities of *satoguna.* A *satoguni* person is happy by nature, is someone who can work hard and can also have the quality of feeling totally relaxed.

pravrittim cha nivrittim cha kaaryaakaarye bhayaabhaye bandham
moksham cha yaa vetti buddhih saa paartha saatwikee/
Bhagavad Gita 18.30

Translation: The intellect is said to be in the nature of goodness. O Parth, when it understands what proper action is and what is improper action, what is duty and what is non-duty, what is to be feared and what is not to be feared, what is binding and what is liberating.

An excess of *sattva guna* in a personality can result in a total balance and control of the senses. Wisdom, selfless love, generosity, spirituality, creativity, and positivity are always present in it.

These qualities are also present in *tamsik* and *rajsic* personalities in a limited capacity and are not constant. People with these qualities have unstable emotional and mental levels. At the same time, because of its balance, *sattva* becomes the source of pleasure and wisdom.

tatra Sattvam nirmalatwaat prakaashakam anaamayam
sukhasangena badhnaati jnaanasangena chaanagha/
Bhagavad Gita 14.6

Translation: Amongst these, sattva guna, the mode of goodness, being purer than the others, is illuminating and full of well-being. Oh sinless one, it binds the soul by instilling a desire for happiness and knowledge.

sarvadwaareshu dehesmin prakaasha upajaayate jnaanam
yadaa tadaa vidyaadvivriddham Sattvamityuta/
Bhagavad Gita 14.11/

Translation: When all the gates of the body are illumined by knowledge, know it to be a manifestation of the mode of goodness. When the mode of passion predominates,

A *satoguni* person is satisfied with himself, his intellect, and his *karma*, just like a scientist with his research or an artist with his art. *Sattva guni* people are not affected by emotions like grief, anger, and sadness for too long. They make successful attempts to get themselves out of it. They are filled with impeccable patience and excitement and are also spiritual.

muktasango'nahamvaadi dhrityutsaahasamanvitah
siddhyasiddhyor nirvikaarah kartaa saatwika uchyate/
Bhagavad Gita 18.26

Translation: The performer is said to be in the mode of goodness when he or she is free from egotism and attachment, endowed with enthusiasm, determination, and equipoise in success and failure.

In short, *sattva guna* helps a person live in harmony and experience optimum happiness, *karma*, and wisdom. All three *gunas* have their own functions and qualities, the absence of any one of which can result in an imbalance in a personality.

Sattvam sukhe sanjayati rajah karmani bhaarata
jnaanamaavritya tu tamah pramaade sanjayatyuta/
Bhagavad Gita 14.9

Translation: Sattva binds one to material happiness; rajas conditions the soul toward action and tamas clouds wisdom and binds one of the delusion.

Sattvam rajastama iti Gunaah prakritisambhavaah
nibadhnanti mahaabaaho dehe dehinamavyayam/
Bhagavad Gita 14.5

Translation: O mighty-armed Arjun, the material energy consists of three *gunas* (modes): *Sattva* (goodness), *Rajas* (passion) and *Tamas* (ignorance). These modes bind the eternal soul to the perished body.

Having been able to describe the qualities and characteristics of all three personalities, one thing is of great importance here: it is very rare to find a person who is completely *tamsik, rajsik,* or *sattvik*. While one quality would be the dominating one, each personality would have the other one in a minimalistic way. The dominance of a *guna* can keep changing depending on a person's life and efforts. Many times, it is seen that two *gunas* can be dominating in a personality.

rajas tamas hchaabhibhooya Sattvam bhavati bhaarata rajah
Sattvam tamaishchaiva tamah Sattvam rajastathaa /
Bhagavad Gita 14.10/

Translation: Sometimes goodness (*sattva*) prevails over passion (*rajas*) and ignorance (*tamas*), O scion of Bharat. Sometimes passion (*rajas*) dominates goodness (*sattva*) and ignorance (*tamas*), and at other times, ignorance (tamas) overcomes goodness (*sattva*) and passion (*rajas*).

The reason why these things are repeatedly mentioned here in this article is that a *tamsik* person will definitely have some *gunas* of *sattva* and it can also be the other way around. While analysing a personality, it is equally important to study this factor as much as the dominance factor.

Fig. 14.1: Tridev—Brahma (*rajas*), Vishnu (*sattva*) and Mahesh (*tamas*)

What is also to be kept in mind is that *tamsik* and *rajsik* personalities should not be considered as bad people or only *sattvik* as good ones. This should always be considered as diversity. To pay respect to these diversities, Hindu texts have given high importance to *tridev* and *trideviyan*.These *tridevs* are said to be the source of *triguna.* The personification and symbolization of qualities and *gunas* of life and nature can be seen clearly in them. The same *gunas* are reflected in *Tridevas* in a masculine and *Trideviya's* in a feminine form, respectively.

Fig. 14.2: Trideviyan Mahasaraswatiji (*sattva*), Mahalaxmiji (*rajas*), Mahakali (*tamas*)

Fig. 14.3: Brahmaji and Saraswatiji

Brahmaji and Saraswatiji:.Creation, according to Hindu belief, is a never-ending process. Brahma's constant action reflects *rajas*. He applies his energy in creating new life and things. *Rajas* are constantly occupied with creation, desire, glory, diversity, and extension.

Brahma's wife is *Mahasaraswati,* who is a symbol of pure knowledge that represents *sattva.* To give Brahma's continuous creation the right direction and goal, he needs *Mahasaraswati*, the symbol of knowledge and perspective, as his wife, although quite opposite in their *gunas,* in the quest to balance each other's *sattva* and *rajas*, wisdom (*Mahasaraswati*) and desire (*Brahma*) mingled with each other for continuous creation.

Brahma's big family is mentioned in which their countless children, including *rishis, munis*, kings, sculpturists etc., engaged with him in the creation. *Rajas Guna gives* importance to teamwork and working together. *Saraswati* is a symbol of pure wisdom, which is always living blissfully in solitude.

She has simply dressed in a quality found in intellectuals (*sattva gunis*). *Being* very modest, she only adorns herself with pearls and "*sfatic*" (crystal), which are a symbol of transparency, and white clothes represent purity. *Sattva guni* people are transparent and very clear in their actions, decisions, and thoughts. They wish to spend more time blissfully in solitude and are detached. *Saraswati* is seen happily playing the *veena* (a musical instrument) in isolation and holding texts in her hands that symbolise knowledge.

Rajsic people are worried, insecure, and stressed about different aspects of life. In religious literature, for example, Brahma is depicted as being concerned and constantly striving to sustain the creation.

Vishnu and Mahalakshmi: Vishnu maintains the stability and continuity of the universe. He maintains stability and stability indicates the "*sattva*" and Vishnu is the symbol of "*sattva*". When not occupied, he seems to be resting over *Sheshnag* (the symbol of infinite time) and whenever he sees imbalance, he incarnates himself and gets immersed in rigorous *karma. Sattva* is the ultimate combination of both action and relaxation. He can remain alone as well as together. To fulfil the needs as well as to control and regulate *the Sattva* needs *of Rajas,* therefore, Mahalakshmi is the companion of Vishnu, who is the source of power, glory, well-being and resources. Mahalakshmi represents *Rajas;* the colour white symbolises *sattva,* black symbolises *tamas,* and the colour of *Rajas* is red. Mahalakshmi wears red clothes, as red is considered the colour that draws attention. The *Rajas gunas give* importance to attention; they wish to seek everyone's attention. *A Rajsik* person likes to remain at the centre of it all. Mahalakshmi is depicted in the centre of Vishnu, Saraswati, Ganesh, Kuber, and Yaksha, and elephants. Mahalakshmi is known for her fickle nature. Both her birthplace and residence in the ocean also indicate instability and volatility. It is considered that *Rajsik* personalities are predominantly volatile and unstable.

Vishnu is known for his lowliness, courteous and decent behaviour. He is also known for his emotional sensitivity. We can discover that devotion, compassion, prudence, fury, sorrow, and humour in appropriate proportion. The equal proportion of all the above qualities is the main indication of *sattva.*

In sacred texts, Shiva and Mahakali: Shiva are mentioned as the main sources of *tamas guna*. Relaxation and calmness are the qualities of *tamas.* One can find *Shiva* either in meditation or in *samadhi* (a state of deep meditation). He remains in the utmost state of relaxation.

Lord Shiva can be found practicing knowledge and contemplation, self-involved, stable and neutral to the universe, enslaved to the world of *karma*. In its ideal form, *tamas* has all such qualities.

Shiva gets furious in extraordinary conditions, but his anger is dire and beyond imagination and control. His love is equally extreme in all ways. It is deep and very obvious. As an example of this extreme love, he roamed around the universe for a long time holding the corpse of his wife

Sati with intense attachment. Tamas forces love, anger, and attachment to be extreme.

Fig. 14.4: Shiva and Mahakali

Tamas gives the ability to observe with stability and sensitivity. It helps create the art of feeling things deeper. *Tamas's* dominated personality's main trait is to minutely observe and accept new ideas and imagination. *Shiva* is considered the ultimate intelligent, learned, and artistic creator.

Both *mahaakali* and *mahakal* are neutral to the outer décor; they can adopt even the hideous and the horrible. *Tamas* is also known for devastation and extermination, as well as recycling and redevelopment. With extinction, he abolishes the cosmos and universe, but he also lays the foundation for revolution, recycling, and new life. *Tamas* is also related to darkness and night (*sattva* for sunrise and sunset, *rajas* for daytime and brightness). *Mahakal* and *mahakali* are symbolically attached to it and are ritually worshipped at night. Life takes birth in the darkness, and *mahakal* and *mahakali* are the sources of the same darkness in *tantra* text. Shiva and Mahakali are treated as the ideal couple and the symbol of the art of lovemaking.

The Shiva and Shati idols are evidence of how *kaama* and life spirit are linked to the *tamas guna.Tamsik* food includes all types of intoxicants and meat-based foods. Here, the observable fact is that all types of drugs like weed, marijuana, and other narcotic substances are palatable to Shiva, and it is even a well-known tradition to sacrifice an animal to Mahakali.

Triguna's Theory Helps in Balancing the Imbalance of Personality

What is unique about *Trigun's* personality theory is that it is different from all other related theories. It does not only describe the types of personality, but it also tries to identify the reasons for such an imbalance and suggests a remedy to balance the *sattva, rajas,* and *tamas.*

For example, if a person is suffering from depression, their *tamoguna* will definitely be at an increased level. If we study the factors affecting the balance, we will come to know that the person's social atmosphere, company, daily routine, incidents in life, food intake, etc. are responsible for increasing *tamoguna.* Therefore, it results in his suffering from loss of interest, hopelessness, grief, idleness, and depression. To balance the imbalance of *triguna,* the individual has to make efforts to increase *sattva* and *rajas* in the body. Therefore, from now onwards, his daily routine, food intake, attire, work etc. should be designed in such a way that his *sattva and rajas* begin to increase. After continuous practice to increase, the individual's *sattva* and *rajas* will begin to enhance and the individual will be free from depression and anxiety gradually.

Here, one factor must be observed: because the individual's *tamo guna* is already at an increased level, he might have a liking towards things that increase *tamo guna.* It is a widely accepted fact that an increased level of *tamo guna* will definitely prompt an individual to do all those things that force him to enhance their *tamo guna.* In such a situation, strategic and sagacious efforts are required to bring him towards *rajo guna* and *sattva guna.* It requires patience and time from the patient's side as well as from the counsellor, because the individual has to be treated from all dimensions.

Physiological and Psychological Parameters: Constructs from Ayurveda and *Shrimadbhagvad Gita*

The constructs that were taken into consideration from Ayurveda (*Tridosha*) to develop the items for the *Trigun* indicate that mostly *Vatta* is affiliated with *Rajasguna, Pitta* is affiliated with *Sattva Guna,* and *Kapha* with *Tamoguna.*

Psychological constructs are derived from the *Shrimadbhagvad Gita, Mahabharat,* and *Samkhya* philosophy. The *Shrimadbhagvad Gita* has clearly explained the psychological components of personality. The checklists are as follows:

1. The body constructs the chest, the calf, the joints, the gait, the veins, and the tendons.
2. Complexion and countenance.

3. Skin texture, wrinkling of the skin, nails, hair texture, forehead, eyes, teeth, and eyebrows.
4. Perspiration and micturition, the odour of the body, mouth, armpits, and sweat.
5. Sexual potency and behaviour.
6. Tremors.
7. Food habits, hunger, appetite, thirst, and digestion.
8. Dietary likings, taste preferences.
9. Liking for coldness, warmth, and tolerance to heat.
10. Allergies and fondness for fragrance and food.
11. Grasping power, memory, intelligence, concentration.
12. Speed of activities and movements, speed of speech.
13. Bowel movements.
14. Immunity to diseases, strength.
15. Duration of sleep and pattern.
16. Various behaviours are exhibited.
17. Command of one's senses and desires.
18. Working style.
19. The pattern of excitement.

Triguna Scale Table for Scaling of Triguna: Bhagavad Gita

Types of Personality

In Ayurveda, Charak and *Shushruta* recognized different types of personalities based on the dominance of the *gunas* in their personality and body.

The first seven kinds of Personality

- People with dominant types *Sattva Guna.*
- People with dominant *Rajas Guna.*
- People with dominant *Tamas Guna.*
- People who have a strong *Sattva-Rajas Guna.*
- People who are dominated by *Sattva-Tamas Guna.*
- People with dominant *Rajas-Tamas Guna.*
- People with balanced gunas or with the *Sattva-Rajas-Tamas guna* combination.

More specifically, 16 types

- 7 types of Sattva: Brahma Sattva, Mahendra Sattva, Varuna Sattva, Kuber Sattva, Gandherva Sattva, Yama Sattva, Rishi Sattva.

- There are six types of Rajas Sattva: Asura Sattva, Rakshas Sattva, Paisaca Sattva, Sarp Sattva, Praita Sattva, Sakuna Sattva.
- Tamas Sattva is classified into three types: Pasava Sattva, Matasya Sattva, and Vanaspatya Sattva.

Very Specific Types

Some literature related to Ayurveda and philosophy also mentions 21 types, 121 types, and 384 types of personalities. Because this theory believes that every person is an original. Hence, the combination of *sattva, rajas,* and *tamas* may be different for each person. Therefore, the *Triguna* theory permits measuring innumerable types of personalities.

Sixteen types of personality based on Ayurveda

1. Brahma	Clarity, integrity, purity, truthfulness, loves towards all. Detached from anger, ego, greed and jealously.
2. Aarsha	Someone who is devout to God, religious and believer, practicing celibacy.
3. Indra	Dominant behaviour, foresightedness.
4. Yamya	A strong believer in karma.
5. Varuna	Fond of aquatic sports and adventure.
6. Kuber	Protector of wealth, possessiveness, relaxed and assertive.
7. Gandharva	Artistic, fond of dancing, singing, performer.
8. Asura	Cruel, dreadful-looking, ruthless, fierce.
9. Rakshasa	Meat eaters, short-tempered, intolerant.
10. Pishacha	Psychopath, Conspirers, Womanizers.
11. Sarpa	Active only when needed, otherwise lazy.
12. Praita	Foodie, greedy, envy.
13. Shakuni	Cunning, Conspiring.
14. Pasava	Excessively indulged in sexual activities.
15. Matsya	Cowardly, restlessness, timid.
16. Vanaspatya	Indulged in eating, lack of intelligence, ignorant, idle.

Summary of *Triguna* Theory

- This theory measures physical traits, psychological traits, and even lifestyle.
- Triguna theory gives a maximum number of personality types.
- Triguna theory encompasses all personality types, from the most rare to the most common.

- This theory not only measures the imbalance of personality but also suggests how to balance it.

REFERENCES

Gerald, J.L. (2011). *Classical Samkhya: An Interpretation of its History and Meaning*, Varanasi: Motilal Banarsidass.

Goyandka, J. (2014). *Shrimadbhagavad Gita*, Gorakhpur: Geeta Press.

Mike Burley. (2012). *Classical Samkhya and Yoga- An Indian Metaphysics of Experience*, London: Routledge.

Rathore, Bhuvneshvari P.K. (2020). *Evidence of Ancient Indian Work on Mental Health and Its use for Modern Social Work Practice*, in Dash, B.M., Kumar, S., Singh, D.P., & Shukla, S. (eds.). *Indian Social Work*, Routledge, India.

Sharma, R. (2005). *108 Upanishad Gyan Kaand*, Mathura: Yug NirmanYojna.

Shastri, A. (2019). *Susruta Samhita of Maharshi Susruta*, Varanasi: Chaukhamba Sanskrit Sansthan.

Tripathi, B. (2012). *Ashtanga Hridyam of Srimad Vagbhata*, Delhi: Chaukhamba Sanskrit Pratishthan.

Tripathi, B. (2019). *Caraka-Samhita as Precepted by the Great Sage Agrega Punarvasu of Agnivesa* (Vol. 1), Varanasi: Chaukhamba Surbharti Prakashan.

Tripathi, R. (2017). *Padharth Vigyan*, Delhi: Chaukhamba Sanskrit Pratishthan.

Vyas, V. (2013). *Mahabharat* (6th Vol.), Gorakhpur: Geeta Press.

9

Hindu World-Views and Social Work Practices

A New Conversation

Chittaranjan Das Adhikary

Introduction

India's society and culture are both ancient and unique. Our spiritual ethos, enshrined in the eternal Vedas, Upanishads, Brahmanas, and Epics, defines the way we live, lending it a distinct uniqueness. The majority of Indians (Hindus) swear by the life purposes given in these sacred texts. They lend meaning to our lives. Hindus are divided as *Chaturvarna*, Lives in four *Ashrams* (Progressive Stages of Life), Follow *Chaturvarga* or four *Purusharthas*. A holistic framework represented by *Brahmanas*, *Kshatriyas*, *Baishya* and *Shudras* provides social integration. Four Progressive stages of Life denote or *ashrams* give organization to the life of an individual. *Purusharthas* allow aligning oneself with purposes that covers society, culture, this world and the other world. *Purushartha* pervades societies, *varnas*, *ashrams* and individuals in each of these. *Purushartha* is a Sanskrit word that can be translated as the "object of human pursuit" or "goals of man." The term is derived from the Sanskrit, *Purusha,* meaning "person," and *artha,* meaning "purpose." This is an important term in Hinduism and relates to the four ideal aims a person should have. The four *purusharthas* are considered to be the following: *dharma* (moral duty), *artha* (economic prosperity), *kama* (love or pleasure) and *moksha* (spiritual liberation). While all four of these aims are classed as being important, *moksha* is considered to be the ultimate goal for any human. After this, dharma takes priority over the others.

In the contemporary age of science and rationality, the advancement in science and technology has expanded the horizons of human knowledge and made life more comfortable and more secure, giving us mastery over nature and replacing belief with knowledge and knowledge-making. Science and spirituality often share a dialectic relationship. One grows at the expense of others. The dialectics are manifest in science claiming the death of spirituality and infinity with the coming of finite knowledge of life-based on empiricism, rationality and logic on the one hand, and spirituality; on the other hand, claiming that science is just but only partial truth, that spirituality and transcendence is higher science. This duality has been subjected to innumerable scrutiny with no unanimity of a resolution. Science has not only made life easy but also presented us with new sets of challenges like crime, violence, disruption and dissent. Science, as well as spirituality, has a single purpose of sustaining life on earth. So in a way both are part of the same Dharma. However, science without spirituality is blind and spirituality without science is lame. Both are complementary to each other which are not the case as of now. The problem lies in the loss of a balance between science and spirituality. The rising number of crimes, corruption, unrest and demoralization almost at every level of the society has triggered a search for new solutions. Science and scientific practices of social work have proved to be inadequate in arresting the quality of life. In this backdrop it is wise to consider whether the old values are enshrined in our ancient texts may be useful in solving the crisis of contemporary problems. When science fails to check such propensities, the ancient scriptures have to be restored to moderating the disastrous power and influence of science. If we get more and more power from science and more and more moderation from the scriptures, their combination will certainly yield a very balanced way of living. Social work as a profession seeks to help and guide people with problems in their lives through care, counselling and protection within a framework of justice, equality and empowerment. Ignoring the sacrosanct principles that guide individual and collective action in India, social work stands a half chance of winning the battle against social evils, both understanding them and eradicating them. If we can creatively incorporate this age-old ethnic wisdom, still held sacred and works in the back of everyday activities, it will also go a long way in reorienting the thrust areas of social work practices, academics and philosophies.

Vedanta

The Indian socio-cultural tradition rests on the teachings of the Vedas, particularly the Vedanta or Upanishads, which is also known as the Jnana Kanda, or living embodiment of revealed truth. The Vedas, taken as a whole, are the main fountainhead of the entire Indian culture. The Veda is the source of other fundamental Hindu scriptures such as Dharmashastras, Itihasas, Puranas, Agamas and Darshanas (Rao, 2004). The Upanishadic thought mostly revolves around issues such as *Brahmana, Atman, Moksha, Samsara, Karma, Upasana*, and Knowledge. They try to answer important philosophical questions like the existence of God, the relationship between man and the universe, and The *Brahman vis-à-vis Jiva-Jagat*. In fact, God has been declared in the Srutis as the being that is to be known only through the Upanishads (The Cultural Heritage of India, Vol. I). The Cardinal Principles of the Upanishad are as follows:

1. The Brahman (God) is all-pervasive.The same divine power pervades everything and everywhere. All this is verily Brahman [*Chandyoga Upanishad*, III, 14.1].
2. Atman and brahman are inseparable. The Brahman resides in all individual consciousness in the Atman. [*Aham Brahmasmi, Brihadarankya Upa*., I, 4.10].
3. The Principle of the Oneness of Humanity. The Vedantic concept is that all human beings, because of their shared spirituality, are members of a single extended family [*Vasudhaiva Kutumbakam, Svetasvetara Upa*., II, 5].
4. Unity of all religions. The truth is one; the wise call it by many names. The *Mundaka Upanishad* talks of all the streams and rivers that arise in different parts of the world but flow into the same ocean.
5. Uncompromising commitment to the truth. *Satyameva Jayate.*
6. Privileges: Physical, mental, and spiritual freedom. The Upanishads call upon the people of the world to become free.
7. Happiness through spiritual enlightenment. There is no such thing as infinite bliss; only the infinite is bliss [*Chandogya Upa.,* VII, 23]
8. The principle of integral humanism. *Jivatma and Paramatma* are an integral part of the same reality. *Brahman resides in all atman.* [*Mundaka Upa*., II, 2.5].
9. The Upanishads emphasise *Karma*. Arise, awake, and do not stop till the goal is reached. The Goal of life is *Atma Jnana* (Self-knowledge).

The smritis is a body of secondary that derives its authority from the Upanishads. It consists primarily of (a) Dharmashastras or Law Code, (b) Epics, (c) Puranas or Chronicles, (d) Agamas or Manuals of Worship, and (e) Darshanas or schools of Philosophy. These kinds of literature expand and clarify the principles of the Upanishads. Among these, the *Bhagavad Gita* deserves a special mention as the source of the Hindu ethos. In the words of Pandit Madan Mohan Malviya, "in all the living languages of the world, there is no book so full of true knowledge and yet as handy as the *Bhagavad Gita*." If the Upanishads talk of unison with the supreme beings, *Bhagavad Gita* shows us the ways of this union through *Karma Yoga, Jnana Yoga, Bhakti Yoga*, and *Raja Yoga*. If the Upanishads mention *Karma*, the *Gita* broadens it to include *Niskama Karma* (desireless action). Now we move on to how these immortal truths and high morals apply to our daily life through the institutions of *Purushartha*, *Varna, Ashram* and *Dharma*.

Purushartha

The term '*Purushartha*' consists of two words, viz. *Purusha* and *Artha*. '*Purusha*' means a person or self. '*Artha*' means the aim or goal of human life. The concept of *Purushartha* basically indicates different values to be realized in human life through human efforts. There are four *Purusharthas*, or aims of life, as propounded by Manu, viz. *Dharma* (virtue), *Artha* (wealth), *Kama* (pleasure), and *Moksha* (liberation). One can find the reference of these *Purusharthas* in various texts of Indian Philosophy. These *Purusharthas* are studied in-depth, from their origin to their first occurrence and also its different interpretations by different thinkers. Today, these *Purusharthas* have taken a new form, and to the ordinary layman, dharma is equated with duty, *artha* with money, *Kama* with pleasure, and *moksha* with death.

To understand the purpose of our life, we get nothing looking from outside as to where the world is heading, but should rather look within, as to what we really aspire and achieve. The things that we aspire should satisfy us and make us feel the fulfilment of the purpose of our life. Our so-called goals are always an end to our small aspirations, never come under the category of satisfying eternally. Modern society has made us blindly follow other people's aspirations and fall into the rat race, and in the end, realize that we have been on a meaningless trip, by then it is too late. So let's pause and try to understand what it is that we want to attain, so that we can fulfil the purpose of life. Let's look within, introspect, and discover. Such fundamental questions are the starting point for self-awareness. The scriptures do not ask us to blindly follow, but only to help us conduct this inquiry. This is called the inquiry into the *Purusharthas* of life. The four *Purusharthas* are:

Dharma

Dharma is the foundation and the first of the four goals. Dharma is a universal law, harmony, truth, duty, wisdom, and the inherent nature of things. It is a process of alignment, whereby one moves steadily, wisely, and with a clear mind in the natural flow of Truth. Dharma refers to moral duties, obligations, and conduct, namely, *Vidhis* (do's) and *Nishedha* (do nots). Dharma is always given the highest importance.

Artha

Artha, the second goal of life for the householder, is the attainment of wealth and material prosperity. It has to do with providing for the hunger, thirst, and safety needs that are inherent in living in a physical body. *Artha* recognises this level of physical or material need, which is not contrary to spiritual life. The efforts or means of realizing this goal must have a righteous and moral basis.

Kama

The *Kama* is the fulfilment of desires, in the world: biological, physical, and material. Without deep, latent desires there would be no incarnation. The *Kama* is the enlivened desire that emerges from those dormant conditionings. Desires must be acknowledged and reasonably fulfilled with mindfulness so as to move towards freedom from them by not adding them to a continuous cycle of fulfilling and escalating. *Artha* and *Kama* are important goals for the growth and progress of society.

Moksha

Moksha means liberation from the web of *Maya*, the cycles of birth and death, and the experiences of bliss. Liberation is not some posthumous state to be attained after death, but is a state to be attained right here in this very life. This is the ultimate goal of human life. Liberation is freedom from a sense of lack, insecurity, and fear. This is possible when a person discovers that he is free from all limitations of time, space, and individuality and that he is really the transcendental reality himself. Scriptures say that Dharma and *Moksha* are like the river bed to *Artha* and *Kama*, which are rivers. If the river is breached and flows out of the river bed, it is a disaster.

Varna Vyavastha

Varna is from the root '*vri*' which means choice according to inherent traits. *Varna* seems to have been the division of the society in the Rigvedic times when there were four classes. These classes were all *Brahmin, Kshatriya, Vaishya*, and *Sudra*. From the Vedic literature, it is found that *Varna* meant the colour of the skin, according to which society was divided into four classes. These classes were based on the distinctions and differences between the white or the Aryans, and the black or Dravidians.

Another viewpoint means accepting a professing identity. In this sense, *Varna* represents the occupational groups into which Hindu society was divided. So we can have at least two interpretations of the concept of *Varna*: First, Varna has been used as the colour of the skin and it means the classification of society on racial differences: second, *Varna* means the division of society on occupational differences. The functional part of each Varna was specially laid down.

There are passages in Vedic literature regarding the *Varnas*. There is a hymn in '*Purusha Sukta*' of the Rigveda which says that the Brahman Varna represents the mouth of the Purusha, or the universal man, the Kshatriya Varna forms his arms, the Vaishya forms his thighs, and the Sudra, his feet. The division into four Varnas is related to the duties assigned to each Varna. Accordingly, each Varna had to pursue a particular vocation. It appears that the original part of the Vedas did not know about the caste system and the caste system, came later on. In Rig Vedic society, there was no restriction on an individual regarding a particular occupation. People belonging to a particular Varna could accept and practice any profession they liked. A Brahmin could take the profession of a physician. Similarly, there were no restrictions regarding food, drinking, or diet among the Varnas. Besides, there were no restrictions on intermarriage between the different classes of the Aryan race. Hence, the Varnas were "open classes". The classes were not watertight compartments. These classes were based on individual traits and not on birth.

Ashram Vyavastha

Ashram Vyavastha is one of the fundamentals of Hindu Social Organization. The old Hindu thinkers took man into account as a social being. The literal meaning of the word "*Ashram*" is "a halting or resting place". As a result, Ashram denotes a halt, a stoppage, or a stage of rest in the journey of life to prepare a man for the next journey. The word "*Ashram*" is derived from the Sanskrit root "*Srama*", which means "to exert oneself." Hence, "*Ashram*" stands to mean (I) the place where exertions are performed and (2) the action of performing such exertions is initiated. In the words of P.H. Prabhu, "The word, therefore, signifies a halt, a stoppage on a stage in the journey of life just for the sake of rest, in a sense, in order to prepare oneself for the further journey". He further says that "The Ashrams then are to be regarded as resting places during one's journey on the way to final liberation, which is the final aim of life" (Prabhu, 1979).

The first stage of life is called *Brahmacharya Ashram*. A boy enters this Ashram through the performance of the Upanayana ceremony. Through this initiation rite, a person is said to be reborn (*Dwija*). The age of initiation into the first stage of life differs from Varna to Varna. The initiation ceremony takes place for a Brahmin at the age of 8, for a Kshatriya at the age of 10 years, and for a Vaishya at the age of 12 years. The Sudra child is not allowed to go through the first stage, as he was traditionally not allowed to have an education. After the initiation rites are over, the education begins at the residence of a teacher (*Gurukula*). The student is required to learn the Vedas, which contain the cultural traditions of the Aryans. His speech and thought must be pure and guarded by the studies of the Vedas. The student acquires knowledge of both *Shastras* and *Shastras, Tattwa* and *Vyavahara, Sidhanta evam Padhati*. The life of the student is regulated in such a manner that there is a balanced development of personality. Strict discipline is required of a student, and he has to lead a hard life. He is required to restrain his senses. Control over the senses also means control over sex desires. The student is also observant of complete celibacy. In this manner, the life of a *Brahmachari* is a life of discipline (Sivananda, 2008). With the completion of the life of studentship, the next stage of life begins, which is called *Grihasth Ashram*, or the life of a householder. This stage starts with his marriage ceremony. Marriage is more of a social obligation as its main purpose is the performance of Dharma and the perpetuation of the family, as well as the continuation of the group through progeny. According to the Ashram system, the Dharma of a householder consists of performing the five Maha Yajnas, or the five great sacrifices. These Maha Yajnas are offered to Brahma and are called Brahma Yajna, Pitri Yajna, Deva Yajna, Bhuta Yajna, and Nara Yajna. The Brahma Yajna is conducted by the recitation of the Vedic Mantras. Pitri Yajna is done by offering *Tarpan*, that is to say, the offering of water and food. This is commonly known as "*Sradha*". Deva Yajna is done by offering burning obligations to the gods. *Bhutas* are satisfied by sacrifice. Nara Yajna is performed by receiving and entering guests at home. Of these five Yajnas, the first three refer to *Deva Rina*, *Rishi Rina*, and *Pitri Rina*. Apart from this, a householder is also supposed to offer food to animals, saints and anybody who happens to pass through, by chance. People belonging to the other three Ashrams depend upon the *Grihastha*, and it is the duty of a householder to satisfy birds, animals, and insects and persons belonging to all the social rungs. The Pancha Maha Yajnas include a wider field of social duties including men and bhutas. This Ashram is mainly meant for the satisfaction of man's material and emotional urges, i.e. 'Artha' and 'Kama'. The Hindu as a householder is expected to fulfil his acquisitive and instinctive urges within the framework of Dharma. The age at which a person enters this Ashram is about 25 years.

Vanaprastha Ashram

It is the third Ashram of life, and an individual is expected to enter this stage at the age of 50. In the Vanaprastha Ashram, a person has to leave his family and the village too. He is expected to hand over all the household responsibilities to his grown-up children, and he must go to the forest. The person must live in the forest to bring under control his senses of enjoyment (*Niyatendriyah*). He has to eat only fruits and vegetables, and he should not touch meat. His clothes must be of deerskin or the bark of a tree. He must practice "*Tapas*" (penance) to purify his body and soul. In this manner, a Vanaprasthi must devote himself to study and meditation. A Vanaprasthi must lead a life of self-control, friendliness, and charity to others. If a person dies during the Vanaprastha Ashram he will attain *Moksha*. Although a Vanaprasthi used to live in the forest and his wife was allowed to live with him, it was for the sake of humanity that they lived together. The presence of the wife is permitted to facilitate the performance of social duties. The affiliations and associations of the householder come to an end.

Sannyasa Ashram

It is the last Ashram of life. After passing through the Vanaprastha Ashram, the person enters the last Ashram, i.e. Sannyasa Ashram at the age of 75 years. In this Ashram, a person breaks off all attachment with the world. At this stage, a person is expected to devote their entire time towards meditation to recognize the subtle nature of the supreme soul and its presence in all organisms, both the highest and lowest.

In this manner, the aim of the Ashram system is to perform the Ashram Dharma. The Ashram Dharma is not only social in its implications, but it emphasizes renunciation of the world in the Vanaprastha and Sannyasa Ashram. The Ashram system is a way of training through which the individual is to attain his end, i.e. *Moksha*.

Dharma

Dharma is the supreme principle of life. It is the major end of human life. The word '*Dharma*' is derived from the Sanskrit root '*Shri*', meaning '*to hold together*, to sustain, to preserve. It holds together the whole universe. It is essential for maintaining the stability of society. According to the *Mahabharata*, Dharma is created for the well-being of all creation. All that is free from doing harm to any created being is essentially Dharma. Thus, Dharma protects all. It is capable of preserving the universe. According to the Bhagavad Gita, "He who protects (follows) dharma is protected in turn by dharma." This is the highest ideal in Hindu philosophy. Thus, dharma is the holder of balance. The basic principle of Dharma is the realisation of the dignity of the human spirit. It is the law of nature that helps man to attain the supreme end of life. Dharma is not a religion. The Sanskrit word 'Dharma' should not be equated with the English word Religion. Religion basically indicates a system of dogmas and a particular way of worshipping. Dharma is a living experience. It is the guiding principle of life, a complete rule of life.

Dharma involves knowledge of reality and the performance of duties. Non-performance of duties produces sins. According to Hindu philosophy, Dharma is a way of life. Hence, 'Dharma' means the righteous way of living. It is intended to provide guidelines for all social actions. It harmonises relations between *Kama* and *Artha*. It is a corrective to social evils. Dharma is the foundation of social structure. 'It enjoins the members of the society to subject themselves to obligations and responsibilities regardless of individual differences. Shastrakara Manu speaks of what is known as '*saptadharmas*' (seven types of Dharmas). They are as follows: (1) Samanya Dharma: consists of general rules and duties which are almost universal in nature. For example, truth, nonviolence, non-stealing, control of senses etc. (2) Raja Dharma: The king's duties and responsibilities. (3) Stree Dharma: concerned with the duties, responsibilities and character of a woman. (4) Dampatya Dharma: Duties of husband and wife towards each other, towards their family, children and the larger society. (5) Varna Dharma: Duties of different Varnas—Brahmins, Kshatriyas, Vyshyas, and Sudras towards each other and society. (6) Ashram Dharma: This refers to the rules relating to different stages or Ashrams in the life of a man, such as Brahmacharya, Grihastha, Vanaprastha, and Sannyasa. (7) Apaddharma: This refers to certain specific rules to be followed by individuals when they are caught in a crisis or highly critical situation. These rules would act as guides and help them to overcome or face the distressing situation without sacrificing the Dharma.

According to the Smritikars, the nature of the Dharma can be better understood only if one knows the sources from which it emerges. Smritikara Gautama, Apastambha, and others have said that the Vedas constitute the main source of the Dharma. Manu, who accepts the superiority of the Vedas, mentions four other sources of Dharma in the second chapter of his Smriti: the Vedas, traditional lore, usages of good men, and what is agreeable to one's self, including desires born out of due deliberation (Kane, 1990).

Contemporary Relevance as Social Work Practice

Social work as a profession seeks to help and guide people with problems in their lives through care, counselling and protection within a framework of justice, equality, and empowerment. Social work practice consists of the professional application of social work values, principles, and techniques to one or more of the following ends: helping people obtain tangible services; counselling and psychotherapy with individuals, families, and groups; helping communities or groups provide or improve social and health services; and participating in legislative processes. The practice of social work requires knowledge of human development and behaviour; social, economic, and cultural institutions, and the interaction of all these factors. Core values of social work practice include, among other things, (1) Service, (2) Social justice, (3) Personal dignity and worth, (4) Importance and significance of human relationships, (5) Integrity, and (6) Competence. Social work is a practice-based profession and an academic discipline that promotes social change and development, social cohesion, and the empowerment and liberation of people. Principles of social justice, human rights, collective responsibility, and respect for diversities are central to social work.

As social work is more of an application than a theoretical discipline, it liberally borrows from many disciplines in its approach and method. Some of its approaches, though not an exhaustive list, are systemic, generalist, holistic, integrationist, empowerment, therapeutic, existentialist, behavioural, progressive, aboriginal and Gandhian (Simmon, 2016, Unpublished presentation at Bhopal School of Social Sciences available at https://www.slideshare.net/richisimon/approaches-to-social-work-66170592). As has been said, the variety of approaches and applications notwithstanding, it addresses human problems and relationships at the heart of everything. In doing so, it believes that social work clients create meaning and purpose in life. People are capable of controlling and changing their lives and are deliberate in their choices. Understanding the way in which people relate to their socio-cultural situation and their action problems will go a long way towards supporting the development of self-awareness and helping people assume self-responsibility, which is essential for achieving self-actualisation. There have been many studies (Chakrovorty & Chakrovorty, 2007; Whitman, 2007; Tandon, 2016; Rao & Burde, 2017; Nayak, 2018) which point to the variety of ways in which objective problems like health and diseases, inequality, poverty, democracy and decentralisation, good governance, crime, social disorganization etc. are understood, lived with, and responded to, and are determined by our tradition, values, social philosophy and worldviews. Whitman in the essay on 'religious coping' of suffering by patients with chronic pain, consider the way in which suffering is conceived in the Hindu religion. She uses the Hindu concepts of:

(1) *Attachment*: Over-involvement in this world, having desires for things that one does not have and clinging to things one has;
(2) *Detachment*: Turning away from over-involvement in the world and towards God/The Ultimate;
(3) *Dharma*: Guidelines for living one's life;
(4) *Karma*: The principle that governs the unfolding of events and is based on a person's integrity with which he has lived previous lives;
(5) *Moksha*: Complete release from the cycle of rebirths;
(6) *Samsara*: The process of successive rebirths until one reaches moksha, complete release from the cycle of rebirths.

Using these concepts, she finds that suffering is thought to be part of the unfolding of *karma* and a consequence of past inappropriate action. Suffering is also inherent in the cycles of life and rebirth. Hindu traditions promote three things—(i) the acceptance of suffering as being a just consequence under the laws of *karma*, (ii) the realization that suffering is transitory while in this world, and does not affect one's true Self; and (iii) the view that suffering is not solely negative. Attachment to this world, by wanting things to be different in some way, contributes to suffering. Detachment is a spiritual goal that allows one to turn toward God or *Brahman* (Whitman, 2007). This point to the importance of considering the traditional basis of Hindu society in treating patients by pain medicine practitioners and therapeutic social work counsellors. In a similar vein, Smriti Tandon in her study of followers of the Art of Living organization of Sree Sree Ravishankar, demonstrates the need for building a theoretical understanding of well-being based upon the cultural and cognitive categories of the people themselves. The chapter, while drawing from ethnographies, focuses on upper-caste Hindus and how well-being is achieved by them. It argues that well-being is a construct and that the idea of well-being is evolving. In contemporary times, well-being has been rediscovered and reinvented by the followers of the Art of Living in ways that align the material with the spiritual. Secular concepts of the modern nation-state, democracy, and good governance have their roots in the presumably *non-modern* Hindu world-views enshrined in the Vedas and later-Vedic literature. Jhumpa Mukherjee, in her essay, revisits the discourses on statecraft in our ancient scriptures like *Mahabharat*, *Arthashastra* and *Manusmriti* and argues that the earliest record of good governance is found in the Vedas. *Shanti Parva* in *Mahabharata* comprehensively covers the contours of a 'Welfare State' supposed to be unknown in those times (Mukherjee, 2010). There is, therefore, a need to reorient the discourse on governance away from Euro-centric trappings and graft it with our traditional ethos to make it more effective in contemporary times. Social workers fighting the crisis of democratic deficit and poverty of State Welfare need to learn lessons from the ancient resources and bring back the ancient political philosophy into the modern discourse on State and Government. Bhabani Shankar Nayak in his essay on 'Bhagbat Gita and Hindu Modes of Capitalist Accumulation in India' seeks to establish the roots of capitalist accumulation in *Bhagvad Gita* and expand the idea of capitalist accumulation process from social structures of accumulation theory to religious structures of accumulation within the Indian context. It analyses the philosophical tenets of Hindu religion as outlined in the *Bhagvad Gita*. It argues that the ideological narratives contained within the *Bhagvad Gita* are concomitant with the logic of capitalism. The Hindu economy has a sacro-social character (Nayak, 2018). This shows that ancient theories of (un)just production and distribution have many clues to sharpen the understanding of the dynamics of the poor as well as search for a poverty alleviation solution by the social workers, policymakers, and civil society.

Social problems are embedded in the cultural and spiritual milieu. Human sufferings or the way people feel about the existence of such sufferings are, though seemingly material, constrained by the meaning system rooted in the spiritual. Material failure or success itself borrows its standards from the religious-cultural system. Both are, in fact, more complementary than competitive. Material success or lack thereof has nothing in itself unless it is aligned with our spiritual philosophy and needs. Individuals and groups act in terms of the meaning they assign to their actions. Human meanings frequently come from tradition, mores, religion, and social philosophy. A social worker who is for example, dealing with the problem of beggary and their rehabilitation must understand what begging means to the beggar in question as well as the operational logic of the larger charity industry. Charity as a voluntary mechanism of redistribution has the important spiritual connotation of *Punya* (piousness). Poverty, for example, is not only an objective material condition of resource—lessens but also, to a Hindu poor, it is the aggregate consequence of bad *karma* (Unlawful action) in the past life. A social worker with such a nuanced understanding of social issues can better design his intervention programmes in an effective way. Such nuanced understanding demands accommodation of the study of our ancient and traditional moorings in the social work pedagogy and discourse. Social work deals with real objective conditions of a living being and can enhance its support through nursing, care and capacity building by drawing on resources from the tradition, ethical and moral system of values that lie underneath the problem itself. Sympathy for socio-spiritual values of life purposes, the concept of justice, terms of legitimation, organization of individual and society, gender and power relations, duty and responsibilities crystallized as *Dharma* etc. can multiply the social work competency in resolving human problems at the individual, family and neighbourhood, community as well as social level. There is urgency now that social work needs to reorient itself to an understanding of individual and social problem situations embedded in our traditional values and social philosophy of *Purushartha, Varna-Ashram, Dharma, Karma* and *Moksha*.

REFERENCES

Chakraborty, S.K. & Chakraborty, D. (2007). The economic function in the Hindu worldview: its perennial social relevance. *International Journal of Social Economics,* 34(10), 714-734. Retrieved from https://doi.org/10.1108/03068290710816856.

Dubey, S.C. (2005). *Indian Society*. New Delhi: National Book Trust.

Kane, P.V. (1990). *The History of Dharmashastra: Ancient and Medieval Religious and Civil Laws in India*. Poona: Bhandarkar Oriental Institute.

Kapadia, K.M. (1966). *Marriage and Family in India*. Calcutta. OUP: Calcutta.

Mukherjee, J. (2010). Revisiting Good Governance in Ancient Indian Political Thought. *The Indian Journal of Political Science*, 53-58. Retrieved from https://www.jstor.org/stable/42748367

Nayak, B.S. (2018). Bhagavad Gita and Hindu modes of capitalist accumulation in India. *Society and Business Review, 13*(2), 151-164. Retrieved from https://doi.org/10.1108/SBR-09-2017-0071.

Prabhu, P. H. (1979). *Hindu Social Organisation—A Study in Socio-Psychological and Ideological Foundation*. Bombay: Popular Prakashan.

Rao, C.N.S. (2004). *Sociology of Indian Society*. New Delhi: S. Chand & Company.

Sarkar, S.J. (1928). *India through the Ages: A Survey of the Growth of Indian Life and Thought*. Calcutta: M.C. Sarkar & Sons.

Sarma, D.S. (1971). *Essence of Hinduism* (Vol. 171). Bharatiya Vidya Bhavan.

Shama Rao, A. & Kamath Burde, J. (2017). A Hindu perspective to organizational learning. *The Learning Organization*, *24*(6), 386-391. Retrieved from https://doi.org/10.1108/TLO-05-2017-0042.

Shivananda, S. (2008), *All About Hinduism*. Rishikesh: Divine Life Society.

Tandon, S. (2016). Exploring Well-being in the Indian Context. *Indian Anthropology*, 46(1). Retrieved from https://www.jstor.org/stable/43899793.

Whitman, S.M. (2007). Pain and suffering as viewed by the Hindu religion. *The Journal of Pain*, *8*(8), 607-613. Retrieved from www.sciencedirect.com.

10

Baroda Experiment 1932

An Indigenous Model of Community Development

Jayalaxmi R. Mahanty and *M.N. Parmar*

Introduction

The genesis of Social Work in India is an age-old phenomenon. Though social work as a profession was recognized and developed by Western countries, the basis on which the profession rests upon very well existed in the foundation of Indian history. The seeds of the evolution of social work could be explored in world ideologies, i.e. secularism, humanism, Protestantism, rationalism, welfarism, liberalism, democracy, and utilitarianism. The notion of welfare stemmed from the roots of Dharma in India. The history of human suffering and selfish desire also persisted in human society, and so did the mutual assistance to provide protection to humanity. History speaks volumes of initiatives taken by kings, queens, landlords, foreign conquerors and invaders, and also under the system of diarchy, and later, under the constitutional reform of 1935, which ushered in a new era of a popularly elected government in the provinces. Social work emerged as a profession from the perspectives of social services, charity, reform and welfare. Social Work travelled a long way from welfare to empowerment and development, and the present emphasis of the profession is protecting and promoting people's rights.

Social work education in India, in the true sense of the term, dates back to 1936, when Sir Dorabji Tata Graduate School of Social Work (now Tata Institute of Social Sciences) was established in Mumbai under the leadership of Dr. Clifford Manshardt of the American Marathi Mission, with a view to preparing trained manpower adequately equipped with the knowledge and skills required for shouldering varied kinds of responsibilities in the field of social welfare. Obviously, the School was based on the pattern of schools of school work in the United States of America, but, at the same time, it had certain distinctive characteristic features, especially in respect of social work intervention in industrial organizations, directed towards improving the appalling conditions of workers in urban industrial centres. The school-sponsored a series of lectures on 'Some Social Services of the Government of Bombay', as a result of which major areas of governmental responsibilities in the field of social services could be finalized; and this led to a noticeable change in the functions of the state, which accepted that the promotion of welfare was its prime concern.

The philanthropic and religious charities of kings and elites notwithstanding, the very structure of Indian society has provided the means for taking care of the needy and the destitute through the institutions of family, caste, and community. The structure of Hindu society was such that the joint family used to look after the helpless members and the caste feelings created a strong bond of kinship. Aside from infrastructure development, Panchayati Raj provided a support system for the village community. The joint family system served as a useful social institution for taking care of the needy and destitute members; it protected child widows, the physically handicapped, mentally retarded, disabled people and unemployed members of the family without any consideration of individual contribution. The caste system as an institution has grown and developed over many centuries and is firmly rooted in the Indian social structure. As caste values were based on the ideals of service, caste played a significant role in looking after the interests of its own members and promoting their welfare. It has developed its own organizational structures, and provided social security to people belonging to 'own *birādarī*'.

The village community, which previously enjoyed local autonomy through the "Village Panchayat", has been another strong pillar of Indian social structure. It had both executive and judicial powers, and its members were treated with respect by the king's officers. The Panchayat also distributed the land, collected taxes out of the procedure and paid the government's share on behalf of the village. Other religious communities, such as Muslims and Jews, used the Zakat and Tithe systems to provide welfare services to the needy. *Daandakshina*, doles, and the establishment of institutions such as bridhashrams, dharamshalas, and the like were all regarded as religious obligations that were reinforced in a variety of ways in the Hindu religion. During the British period, Christian missionaries initiated the wave of social reform. The Serampore missionaries were the first evangelical Baptist missionaries in India, who identified the need for a series of reform measures necessary within the Indian social structure. They opposed child marriage, polygamy, female infanticide, Kulinism, self-torture, and Ghat murder. They worked for the abolition of *Sati* and advocated for widows' remarriage. The initiatives of Raja Ram Mohun Roy in the abolition of the *sati* system, Ishwar Chandra Vidyasagar in widow remarriage, Sashipada Banerjee and Kesab Chand Sen in women's emancipation from exploitation and discrimination, along with M.G. Ranade, Jyoti Rao Phule, D.K. Karve, Gopal Hari Deshmukh and Tilak in addressing a variety of issues crippling the then Indian society, have been some of the efforts that led to the social reform movement in India, which later on converged with political freedom under the leadership of Gandhiji.

Rural Development

The concept of rural development in India has existed since the Vedic times; it is not a newfangled concept. Rural development involves rebuilding every aspect of human life which includes the social, political, and economic condition of a human being. The development of a country is predominantly divided into two parts: urban areas and rural areas. Thus, the development of both areas is necessary. India mainly focuses on the development of urban areas instead of rural areas. Therefore, the government has taken an initiative to raise the standard of living of rural people. The government has recognized the needs and has adopted the development planning measures that have been implemented through Five Year Plans. Therefore, due to the development schemes, the people of the rural area have started to get the basic amenities needed to improve their vulnerable lives. As we know, the people of the rural areas have seen difficulties since time immemorial; the time has come to give them their deserving rights. Therefore, Article 14 of the Constitution provides 'Right to Equality and therefore, we should give them their respective rights. India cannot shine without the shining of rural India. National Development is almost synonymous with Rural Development.

Rural Reconstruction in India

In the Indian context, the village population has been growing without a proportionate increase in production or income. The average villager has a pitifully low standard of comfort.

Rural reconstruction implies the renovation of the villages for the total well-being of the ruralites. It is oriented towards their social, economic, and political development. The principal objectives of rural reconstruction include (a) eradication of poverty by means of regeneration of cottage industries, the establishment of cooperative societies, improvement of transport, (b) spread of education, (c) progress of health, and (d) abolition of social malpractices like casteism, untouchability, and the like. The non-violent Swaraj of Mahatma Gandhi was based on the idea of rural reconstruction.

Rural reconstruction has been advocated by three schools of thought, who are known as (i) The Philanthropic Group, (ii) The Reformist Group, and (iii) The Revolutionary Group.

The philanthropists offer a pragmatic approach. They plead for improving the condition of the rural population within the purview of the existing rural institutions and the structure of rural society. They attach supreme importance to purely humanitarian endeavour's like (i) the establishment of schools and hospitals, (ii) creation of charity funds to cater to the needs of the rural poor, and (iii) moral appeals to landlords or money-lenders to relax their pressures on the peasants and labourers. The Reformists assume that it is the malfunctioning of the existing social institutions that causes the economic misery and socio-cultural backwardness of the ruralites. They, therefore, stress the need for reformation of the social institutions for the healthy functioning of the social system in order to bring about the holistic development of the rural community.

The Revolutionary group supports the programme of the revolutionary transformation of the rural matrix. The thinkers belonging to this group are of the opinion that the evils of the rural community are not an outcome of the malfunctioning of the rural social institutions but are concomitant with the social system. These evils are the inevitable product of the normal functioning of the contemporary social order. Therefore, they recommend a radical transformation of the rural social institutions to bring about a revolutionary change in the social system.

Aspects of Rural Reconstruction

The Rural Reconstruction programme entails three aspects. They are material, intellectual and moral. So far as the material aspect is concerned, the rural reconstruction programme is oriented to improving the health and raising the standard of living of the realities.

The Importance of Rural Reconstruction

The importance of rural reconstruction cannot be gainsaid. Rural reconstruction puts an end to exploitation, diseases, illiteracy, gambling, drinking, corruption, or class struggle. It seeks to establish a socialistic system in the country and thereby brings about the social and economic development of the country. By establishing agricultural and cottage industries, rural reconstruction solves the food problem of the country and saves millions of rupees in foreign exchange, which goes towards the import of foodgrains. It also increases the national income.

Community Development Programmes in India

The Community Development Programme has been the biggest rural reconstruction scheme undertaken by the government of free India. It has been variously described as the Magna Carta of hope and happiness for two-thirds of India's population, the testament of emancipation, the declaration of war on poverty, ignorance, squalor, and disease under which millions have been groaning etc.

The Planning Commission has defined the Community Development Programme in these words: "Community development is an attempt to bring about a social and economic transformation of village life through the efforts of the people themselves."

According to Pandit Nehru the projects were of vital importance,"not so much for the material achievements that they would bring about, but much more so, because they seem to build up the community and the individual and to make the latter the builder of his own village centres and of India in the larger sense." It is intended to apply it to the concept of the village community as a whole, cutting across caste, religious, and economic differences.

Characteristics of the Community Development Programme

1. It promotes self-confidence among the ruralites.
2. It develops self-reliance in the individual and promotes initiative in the village community.
3. The community development programme has an impact on the psychological well-being of rural residents.
4. It seeks to create new administrative machinery suited to the manifold needs of the village.
5. It is predominately people-oriented.
6. Community thinking and collective action were encouraged through people's institutions like the panchayats, co-operative societies, Vikas mandals etc.

The programme of rural reconstruction was to be part of a wider programme to bring about a rapid increase in the standard of living.

Increased agriculture production lies at the root of all development. Therefore, the programme was progressively expanded to cover measures such as the provision of irrigation facilities, conservation of soil, production of nucleus seeds, their multiplication and distribution, education in agriculture and supplementary occupations.

The idea of community development is not new in India. The name is new, the prominence given to it today is new, but it has grown out of the experiences of the past, viz. the Sriniketan Movement (1921), Martandam Experiment (1921), Gurgaon Experiment (1927), Baroda Experiment (1932) and Experiments of Gandhian Tradition (1935). In pre- independent India, rural development was primarily the task of voluntary organisations set up by eminent people with selfless commitments to the rural poor (Dash, 2017). During the Second World War, the community development programme emerged as a technique of development for underdeveloped, agrarian-based countries. It was opted as an alternative to class struggle and people's violent demands for their own well-being. It was a method of accelerating the process of social, economic, and political growth in the under-developed regions of a country.

Among these programmes, one cannot undermine the efforts of the erstwhile King of Baroda State in pioneering development during his regime. A peep into the local historical context is necessary for proper and adequate understanding, as well as a critical assessment of Baroda's model for social work education. The erstwhile Baroda state was fortunate in being ruled by an enlightened, progressive, and able ruler, namely Maharaja Sayajirao Gaekwad. His constant quest and continuous zeal for the development of Baroda city is well-known. He was a pioneering educationist and the founder and builder of prestigious educational institutions. Baroda owes a great deal to his sagacity and vision. The founding of the Maharaja Sayajirao University of Baroda (popularly known as M.S. University or MSU) took place in 1949, along with several other universities in the country. It coincided with the ushering in of an era of constitutionally set, guided and striven for objectives of a good life for all the citizens of a newly created India. All thoughts and actions were in the direction of achieving the goals of speedy economic development and social justice.

Sayajirao ushered in progressive reforms and modern amenities and towered over the other princes loyal to the British Raj. Starting in 1893, he introduced free and compulsory primary education. By 1906, it covered the whole state. He was the first Indian ruler to embark on such an audacious mission—a target which independent India could not achieve until the Right to Free and Compulsory Education Act, 2009 was enacted. The

Maharaja opened hundreds of schools for Dalits as well as encouraged their admission to regular schools. But the Maharaja did not stop merely at sending boys and girls to schools. Under his aegis, colleges offering a plethora of subjects, including technical ones, were opened leading ultimately to the creation of a university that still bears his name—the Maharaja Sayajirao University of Baroda.

Baroda Experiment 1932

This movement was started by V.T. Krishnamachari in 1932 in the Baroda state, where he was Dewan at that time. In the first instant, its objective was to bring about a rapid increase in standards of living, industrialization, and the rapid expansion of the educational system. The second objective was to increase agricultural production through the provision of basic necessities for the development of the same. At first, some extension workers were taken on deputation by Dr. Spencer Hatch of Marthandam.

The first rural reconstruction centre commenced work in April 1932 in a group of villages around Kosambain, Navsari district.

After the centre had been at work for a year, the number of villages under it was increased, and Baroda state issued an order explaining the aims of the movement as follows:

1. The centre aims at effecting an improvement in all aspects of rural life-changing. The outlook of the agriculturist, the target is to create a desire for a higher standard of living.
2. Intensive efforts were made to achieve this goals. It was confined to a group of villages in which the superintendent and his trained co-workers could establish personal contact with all the agriculturalists.
3. Village leadership was developed.
4. Opportunities for Economic Development.

The entire Baroda state was divided into four main regions, and each region was supervised by the supervisors. They were expected to take care of the citizens and to support them in all good activities.

In 1908, Pandit Atmaram Antasari was invited by the Maharaja of Baroda. Maharaja was progressive, so he developed a special department for Antyodayas in the same year. The Maharaja used to give equal protection to the oppressed and disadvantaged sections of society and used to monitor their provisions and facilities personally. Secondly, in those days, finding teachers for Antyodya was a problem. Maharaja himself invited Arya Samaj people to the Baroda State and they were given special land to establish their ashrams and provide education to them.

Economic Programmes

1. Subsidiary occupations like kitchen gardening, weaving, poultry farming, silkworm rearing, beekeeping or any other trade may be found suitable.
2. In each village, the panchayat was made a live-body, discharging its function of providing drinking water, improving sanitation, and building village roads, in other words, adding to the opportunities for village life.
3. Farm improvements in cotton and other crops.
4. A co-operative society to inculcate thrift.

Maharaja used to give importance to people's participation and so every village got Panchayati Raj and Village Library. He was a visionary who always cared for the well-being of the people. He also established Baroda College. Earlier, it was part of Bombay University; later it became the Maharaja Sayajirao University of Baroda, a worldwide recognized residential University spread over 292 acres of land. It is now proudly imparting education in 111 departments, 14 faculties and 3 constituent colleges with a total of 41000 students, 1500 teachers and 1500 non-teaching staff. No affiliation was given to outside universities and now this university is a boon to all of us.

Moral and Educational Programme

Methods of work, self-help, the dignity of labour, self-respect, trust, and non-violence are given a lot of importance. The Baroda Experiment teaches many lessons for community development and the social work profession. It teaches us how to take all the communities together. The consultative approach of Maharaja is applauded. Maharaja strongly aimed to remove Untouchability from Baroda state, therefore, he used to invite people from all communities, community leaders for 'Samras Bhoj' where they could talk and interact with one another. He believed that action should begin at home, and so this initiative helped him to create the 'Samras' community.

Conclusion

Thus, the Baroda Experiment has its roots in creating a New India which is self-reliant and promotes all-round development. 'Atmanirbhar Bharat' is a vision that Maharaja had for our democratic India. It is a concern for the whole world's happiness, cooperation, and peace. It rests upon five pillars: the economy, infrastructure, system, vibrant demography, and demand.

The Baroda Experiment leads all the social workers to realize the roots of our work in a *Bharatiya* manner. It is a need of the hour to reflect on the work done by Maharajara for the development of communities.

Let's see the solution to the problems faced by people in India. Let's also see the possibility and opportunity to have social and economic life flourishing the way it was earlier. Above all, let's create our own indigenous model of social work by understanding and reflecting on the thoughts of projects run for community development like the Baroda Experiment and many more.

REFERENCES

Alatas, S.H. (2002). 'Autonomous Social Science Tradition in Asia: Problems and Prospects', *Asian Journal of Social Science* 30(1): 150-7.

Atal, Y. (1981). 'The Call for Indigenization', *International Social Science Journal* 33(1): 189-97.

Bhattacharya, S.N. (1970). *Community Development: An Analysis of the Programme in India*, Calcutta: Academic Publishers.

Dash, B.M. (2017). Revisiting Eight Decades of Social Work Education in India. *Asian Social Work and Policy Review*, 11(1), 66-75.

Desai, A.S. (1985). The foundations of social work education in India and some issues. *The Indian Journal of Social Work*, 46(1), 41-57.

Gray, M. & Fook, J. (2004). The Quest for a Universal Social Work: Some Issues and Implications', *Social Work Education* 23(5): 625-44.

Gray, M., Coates, J. & Bird, M.Y. (Eds.) (2008). *Indigenous Social Work Around The World: Towards Culturally Relevant Education and Practice*, Hampshire: Ashgate Publishing Limited.

Nagpaul, H. (1993). Analysis of social work teaching material from India: The need for indigenous foundations. *International Social Work*, 36(3), 207-220.

Section B

Indigenising Social Work Education in India, Nepal and Africa

11
Sanskar, Religion and Region
Indigenizing Social Work in Nepal

Pratik Sharma Lamichhane

Introduction

Nepal is a South Asian country with one of the world's oldest civilizations situated in the shadow of Mount Sagarmatha (Mount Everest). Nepal is predominantly a Hindu society, with the Hindu religion and culture being followed by the majority of its citizens. People here regard Hinduism as a way of life, as various ancient texts outline the activities that a person should engage in throughout his life in order to live a happy existence with his family.

Hindu texts are believed to be date back over 5000 years. According to astrologists, the age of the *Kali Yuga*, (*yuga*-age, literal translation) believed to be 5121 (Evidence in Nepal's calendar). As the present *Yuga,* which is 5121 years old we shall believe that the texts available here are old as the *Yuga* (Although people believe it is considerably older, we do not have evidence yet).

In Hindu religion, *Sanskar* is the collection of culture, rituals, actions that serve as a means of passage as well as the various *Ashram* stages of life. Ashrams are the stages of the human life-cycle. There are four ashrams that are mentioned in ancient texts, i.e. *Brahmacharya, Grihastha, Vanaprastha,* and *Sansyasa*. The sanskar is believed to aid people to attain peace of mind, spiritual nourishment and moksha.

Sanskars are life's turning points, which are thought to be commemorated with celebrations. Hence, celebrations are done in the major points of everyone's life since birth and also sometimes pre-birth. During the celebrations, people come together to convey their best regards and offer blessings to the concerned people giving sanskar the social character. This is a socio-religious ceremony that combines social and religious activities.

The sixteen Hindu rituals (sanskars) that are practiced and celebrated in almost every Hindu's life have been discussed in this chapter.

1. *Garbhadhan* (Conception)

The first sanskar of Hinduism is called *Garbhadhan* and the aim of this ritual is to produce a good child. To have offspring when physically matured female and male (Wife and Husband) are ready to have physical relation with each other, this ritual is celebrated. The most important thing is to have pure heart, good thoughts, and emotions are required. Negative energy is eliminated, resulting in healthy sperm and ovum. Parents are guardians of the child; they should be fully prepared to give birth to a child. This ritual is performed as parents must be fully prepared in order to produce healthily child.

प्रजां च धत्तं द्रविणं च धत्तम् (bestow upon us progeny and affluence)

—*Rigveda 8.35.10-8.35.12, Translated by Ralph Griffith*

2. *Punsavan* (Fetus Protection)

The second is termed *Punsava,* and the objective of this *sanskar* is to protect the fetus. It is generally done in the third month of pregnancy after the first signs of conception are seen. This *sanskar* is done when a couple desires a male child. *Punsavan* literally means "quickening a being or male, usually translated as "quickening a male fetus, bringing forth a male baby."[1] This *sanskar* is performed in *Shuklapaksha* and favourable *nakshatra*. The ritual is performed in diverse ways but involves the husband serving some to the expectant wife. In one version, she is fed a paste of a mixture of yoghurt, milk and ghee by her husband.[2] The roots of this ritual are found in section 4.3.23 and 4.6.2 of *Atharva Veda*, wherein charms are recited for a baby boy.[3] After this ritual is performed, horse riding, hiking, heavy exercise, running, biking, transportation in vehicles, salty foods, sexual relations etc. are restricted. This ritual is restricted to the core family members only.

3. *Simantonayan* (Satisfying wishes of the pregnant)

The third is called *Simantonayan*. According to *Vashistha*, this sanskar is done in the sixth or eighth month of pregnancy and sanskar also aims at protection of the fetus. Positivity and prayers are offered for the healthy physical and mental development of the child. Sanskar helps to keep the future mother stress-free in the last three months of pregnancy, so she can give birth to a peaceful and holy child. The ritual is also a socio-religious celebration that intends to keep a pregnant woman in a positive environment; *puja* is also performed aiming for the purification of the atmosphere. The hairs of the pregnant woman is combed forming *Juro* (A hairstyle). *Simantonayan* literally means "parting hair upwards".[4] Yajnavalkya Smriti, verse 3.79, asserts that the desires of the pregnant woman should be satisfied for the healthy development of the baby to prevent miscarriage and damage to her health.[5] After this rite, sexual relationship with husband is prohibited and husband is expected to keep his wife happy and in a peaceful condition.

4. *Jatakarma* (Birth Rituals)

The fourth is called *Jatakarma*. This is done after the birth of the child and the newborn's father would take cow ghee and honey and apply to newborn's lips in order to survive him on the earth. The child may face difficulty in adjusting to its new environment; nonetheless, this ritual aids it in surviving outside of the mother's womb.

Shasthipujan: Many consider *Jatakarma* as *Shasthipujan*. *Shasthipujan* is not considered as a *sansakar* as not being found in ancient texts. *Shasthipujan* is performed on the sixth day of the birth of a child. On this day people worship *Shasthi Devi*, a goddess considered as bringing fortune to the child. People in Nepal believed that the *Shasthi Devi* wrote a child's future, so it is practiced in Nepalese Hindu families.

5. *Namakarma* (Naming the Child)

The fifth is called *Namakarma*. With the birth of a child, the family is under *Sutak* till the tenth night. Hence *Namakarma sanskar* is done on the eleventh day. It is believed that the unhealthy child shall die within ten days hence this sanskar is performed after the end of the tenth day. The child will get his name as per the birth time position of 27 *nakshatras* and the moon. An appropriate name is given to the child on the basis of *Hora Shastra*. Astrology guides this *Namakaran* sanskar. Some writers also believe that the day to perform this sanskar is based on the traditional social caste system. For *Brahmin, Kshatriya, Vaisya,* and *Shudra* this ritual shall be done on the eleventh, sixteenth, twentieth and twenty-second days respectively. But to have uniformity in performing and avoiding social disputes this ritual is done on the eleventh day. Also, chanting the *Vedic Mantra* is vital in this ritual. Unpleasant, inauspicious or the world that means bad or evil must be avoided is mentioned in *Grihasutra*, while the preferred names are those affiliated with a deity, good quality, lucky stars, constellation, derivatives of the names of parents, and beautiful elements of nature.[6]

6. *Nishkramana* (Taking child outdoors)

The sixth is known as *Nishkramana.* The process of taking the child out of the maternity home to the outside is *nishkramana.* With the sound of chanting the *Vedic mantra,* the child shall be brought under the Sun which is supposed to increase the child's age, physical and mental development. Some scholars believe that this *sanskar* shows obedience to the sun, moon, water, fire, and wind—the *Panchmahabhut* (Five elements). According to *Grihashutra* the father shall bring the child outside and say "the brilliant sun has risen in the east, he is like the *hamsa* (Swan) of the pure worlds, let us salute him because he dispels darkness".[7] *Sanskar* is believed to be performed till the fortieth day after the twelfth day of the birth, the proper time calculations through astrological significance are necessary. However, in Nepali society during *Namakarma* the child is already brought outside performing *Nishkramana.*

7. *Annaprashana* (Feeding rice/solid food)

Annaprashana is the name given to the seventh sanskar. In modern times, this is frequently referred to as rice-feeding ritual. In Nepali society, it is also known as *Pasahni.* Since the birth of a child, she/he is surviving only on mother's milk, after a child has reached five months (daughter) or six months (son), this ritual is performed. Nepal's Hindu society performs this sanskar giving solid food (*Anna*) for the first time to the child. Although it is mentioned in the text that the fifth and sixth month is best for *Annaprashana,* some elders believe that the child's physical growth is equally important. Furthermore, the child's teeth should be seen to perform this ritual. Time is calculated with the help of astrologers for this ritual. In this ritual, sweet porridge or rice pudding is given to the child. Honey, curd and ghee are also given to the child based on the social practices in some societies reciting the *Vedic* chants.

Parallel to *Annaprashana,* in our society livelihood test is also done. In this test, books, pens, utensils, money, weapons, gold, silver etc. are placed in front of the child. It is believed that the first thing a child holds or touch will be the way how he survives on this earth.

8. *Chudakarma* (Hair Cutting)

Chudakarma is the eighth sanskar performed on a child. It is the ritual of cutting the hair on the child's head for the first time. On an auspicious day, within one year this ritual shall be performed. According to *Birmitrodaya Sanskar Prakash*, the time ranges from third to the fifth year, the seventh or *upanayana* ritual's time. Upanayana and Chudakarma have their own differences. I will mention *upanayana* in the latter part of this chapter. Many people believe this ritual is performed for the development and growth of power, better understanding, and long life. Brahmins chant *Vedic mantras* for the health and long life of the child. The hairs ought to be disposed of at the holy place, where no one can get it. The significance of this *sanskar* is the baby's cyclical step to hygiene and cleanliness.[8]

9. *Karnavedh* (Ear piercing)

The ninth sanskar is performed on a child, which is done in the third or fifth year. *Karnavedh* refers to the piercing of the ears. Both male and female child has to undergo this ritual in order to be protected against diseases. Although this is a religious ritual; it has huge significance for the physical health of a child. Many scholars have given their own time for this ritual to be done after *Namakarna sanskar*. *Sushrutsamhita* mentions the time for *karnavedh* as the sixth or seventh month, but *Paraskargrihashutra* mentions the third or fifth year. For a Brahmin to be eligible to perform any religious work, the sunlight must enter through a pierced hole in the ear. If not, he is regarded as an *Asur*. Hence, *karnavedh* is an important ritual to be performed. For a baby boy, the right earlobe is pierced first, and for a baby girl, the left earlobe is pierced. However, in the case of girls, the left nostril may also be pierced during this ritual.[9]

A. *Aksharambha* (Studying)

Aksharambha is regarded as the tenth sanskar in Nepali society, but it is not mentioned in any ancient text. As we can find the practice in our society, I have tried to mention it. In this sanskar, a child is taught the words and letters of the alphabet. It is done within three to five years, which some consider the seventh year of a child before *Upanayana Sanskar*.

10. *Upanayana/Vratabandh* (Wearing Scared Thread)

The tenth *sanskar* is popularly known as *Vratabandha* in Nepali society. The meaning of *Vratabandha* in the literal sense is to be bound by rules. This ritual is done only for a male child when he reaches the age of five. Although the practice is different in various places, we can consider that when a child reaches the age of five, he is eligible for the *Upanayana Sanskar*. In this *sanskar*, the sacred thread should be worn by a child who is performing this ritual. The sacred thread is known as the "*Janai*". After this ceremony, a child is authorized to perform all the rituals, which is also known as the spiritual birth of a child. During the completion of this sanskar, the child's education begins with the Vedas, regarded as the ancient form of education. This sanskar has the following parts:

(a) *Puja*: Worshipping god.
(b) *Havan:* Sacrifice.
(c) *Shiksha:* Teaching the duties and morality of life.
(d) *Bhiksha*: Begging as a renounced *Brahmachari* of *gurukul.*
(e) *Diksha*: Giving the most sacred *Gayatri mantra* to the child.
(f) Blessing: Child is blessed by elders, gods and goddess.

11. *Vedarambha* (Study of Vedas, texts and life skills)

The eleventh *sanskar* in Hindu society is *Vedarambha*. This simply means starting studying and learning the Vedas, Upanishads, Puranas etc. in a "*gurukul*" or "*pathsala*" (school). With a starting ceremony called "*upakarma*" and *Upasarjana* at the end of each academic year. This can be understood as taking examination after completing one academic year in a modern school. The child's academic career begins with the journey of learning Vedas. In modern days, we can somehow relate this to residential schools, which are prevalent throughout the globe. This ritual is performed after Upanayana sanskar for boys.

12. *Samavartana* (Completion of education)

The twelfth *sanskar* is called *Samavartana*, and it is related to the formal end of Vedic education in a gurukul. We can relate this to the graduation ceremonies of universities, which are still practiced today. After completing education, learning life skills, and following rules and regulations, a person returns to their home. Marking the end of the first ashram, called Brahmacharya. This ashram is associated with educating and learning the required skills for life. With this formal ending, a person is believed to be eligible to enter into the next ashram, which is the age of starting a family by marriage.

13. *Vivaha* (Marriage)

The thirteenth *sanskar is* known as *Vivaha* (marriage). This is also the entry point for the next ashram, *Grihastha.* Generally, this sanskar is performed at or after twenty-five years of age. Vedic Hindu marriage is regarded as sacramental, which is a lifelong commitment of husband and wife. *Vivaha* is regarded as the strongest bond between a man and a woman. Marriage takes place in the presence of parents, relatives, and friends. The bride and groom walk around the holy *Agni* (sacred fire) hand in hand seven times, symbolically for 7 future lives. The Vedic mantras are chanted throughout the ceremony. It generally takes around 7-9 hours for a Hindu marriage in Nepal. The auspicious time is calculated by astrologers, and the marriage should take place at that perfect time. Some benefits of *Vivaha* are mentioned in the book "*Hindu Sanskar parichaya ra bimarsha*" entry to *Grihastha Ashram*, religious right, duty, family responsibility, personality development, social prestige, morality, character development, love, happiness, peace, satisfaction, reproduction.

14. *Vanaprastha* (Preparing for renouncing)

The fourteenth sanskar is called *Vanaprastha*, and is meant to be performed at the age of fifty-sixty. This can be understood as the modern-day retirement age. The literal meaning of this sanskar is forest hermit. In this sanskara, a man withdraws himself from all the activities that he was doing and tends to detach himself from his family, possessions, and other activities. He is meant to prepare for the last stage of life and another ashram called sanyas. The aim of this sanskar is to prepare for the self-less satisfaction of human life.

15. *Sanyasa* (Last stage of human life)

The fifteenth sanskar of human life is *Sanyasa*. This is regarded as the last stage of a person's life; hence, before leaving the body, a person sheds all sense of responsibility and relationships to awaken in timeless truth. If we relate to Abram Maslow's hierarchy of needs, this stage can be regarded as the state of self-actualization. A Sanyasi (person who practices Sanyasa) renounces the world and leads a life of study and meditation by living on charity and alms.

16. *Antyesthi* (The Last Ritual)

This is the last ritual of a human being's life. This stage is called *Antyesthi*, also called *Antim-Sanskar*. This ritual in this sanskar is associated with a funeral. After death, a piece of gold, Tulasi leaf, and drops of water (Bagmati, and generally Holy River) are put in the mouth of a person lying in a Brahmanal (death bed on the bank of the Bagmati River, just below Pashupatinath temple). The body is laid on the ground with its head towards the Pashupatinath temple. The dead body is washed, wrapped in a new cloth, generally white cloth or yellow cloth, and decked with flowers.

After this, the eldest son performs the last rites at the *Chita*. For thirteen days following the last death ritual, the immediate families of the dead perform the last duty, called *Kirya.*

Conclusion

The above mentioned Sanskar is believed to be part of the concept of *karma* in the Hindu religion. *Karma* means deeds or actions; in addition, it also has a philosophical and technical meaning, denoting a person's deeds as determining his future lot.[10] The *sanskaras* are the character of dispositions, character or behavioural traits that are inherited. Sanskar is also believed to be a set of behavioural traits perfected over time through the conscious shaping of the inner self, one's desire, and sense of moral responsibility through practice.[11] In addition to this, Advaita Vedanta believes the sanskaras are the psychological concept called *Vasana.* Rituals are simply actions or activities that have been practiced since the origin of civilizations. As mentioned in this chapter, Hindu civilization is believed to be five thousand years old, the rituals today that we practice in our society is learning from those thousands of years of experience of doing things.

However, the rituals that you practice must empower you and help others live as well as their lives. In social work practice, there is a common belief that "social workers help people to help themselves." If we look closely at this definition, we could reflect on empowering clients through the social work profession. If the rituals of Hindu society help the social workers in the Hindu community understand and help solve the problems of the society, I believe that Nepali social work professionals should understand the sensitivity of it and indigenize those practices in Nepali society.

In the Hindu tradition, the rituals are regarded as the traces that evolve through the refinement of a person's inner consciousness and personality development. The rituals are believed to prepare people for future life and hence they are performed. The development of a person's moral character, behaviour, and attributes is also shaped by these rituals. The Sanskrit term for this is *Guna*. The Sanskar is not only the end but the beginning of social recognition as well as the passage from one stage of life to another[12] which aims to make the life of a person easy and peaceful. During social work practice and social work education in Nepal, a social worker must be aware of this cultural factor, which helps him understand the social value. This chapter also aims to believe to negotiate the demands of culture, social work values, ethics, and social law. And also, for the educators and practitioners to develop an understanding of their context and to use that understanding to explain social work concepts in ways that a layman can understand and relate to. After all, the social worker's intervention plan shall work with the client.

NOTES

1. Mary McGee (2007). *Sanskar, The Hindu World.*
2. *Ibid.*
3. Maurice Bloomfield. *Hymns of the Atharva Veda.*
4. Rajbali Pandey (1969). *Hindu Samskaras: Socio-religious study of Hindu Sacraments.*
5. Mary McGee (2007). *Sanskar, The Hindu World.*
6. *Ibid.*
7. P.V. Kane, *Sanskara, History of Dharmashastra,* Vol. II, Part 1.
8. Rajbali Pandey(2013). *Hindu Sanskaras: Socio-Religious Study of Hindu Sacraments.*
9. Mary McGee (2007). *Sanskar, The Hindu World.*
10. *Encyclopedia Britannica*, 11th Edition, Volume 15.
11. Stephen H. Phillips (2009), *Yoga, Karma and Rebirth: A Brief History and Philosophy.*
12. Joyce Flueckiger, (2015). *Everyday Hinduism.*

REFERENCES

Bloomfield, M. (2019). *Hymns of the Atharva Veda*, Oxford: Oxford University Press.

Encyclopaedia Britannica, 11th Edition, Volume 15, New York: Encyclopaedia Britannica, Inc.

Flueckiger, J. (2015). *Everyday Hinduism.* West Sussex: Wiley-Blackwell.

Kane, P.V. (1974). *History of Dharmasastras*, Vol. II, Part I, Chapter VI—Samskara. Pune: Bhandarkar Oriental Research Institute.

McGee, M. (2007), *Samskara in the Hindu World.* London: Routledge.

Pandey, R. (1969). *Hindu Sanskāras: Socio-religious Study of the Hindu Sacraments,* Delhi: Motilal Banarasidass Publication.

Panthi, B.S. (2007). *Laxmikanta Hindu Sanskar Parichaya Ra Bimarsha*, Jawalakhel: Shree Press.

Phillips, S.H. (2009). *Yoga, Karma and Rebirth: A Brief History and Philosophy.* New York: Columbia University Press. http://espiritworld.com/home/?p=404, accessed, July 2, 2020.

12

Challenges of the Use of Social Work Models among Students of the University of Nigeria, Nsukka, Nigeria

Charity Ngozi Uzuegbu

Introduction

The International Federation of Social Workers (2014) defined Social work as "a practice-based profession and an academic discipline that promotes social change and development, social cohesion, empowerment, and liberation of people." Principles of social justice, human rights, collective responsibility, and respect for diversities, are central to social work. Underpinned by theories of social work, social sciences, humanities, and indigenous knowledge, social work engages people and structures to address life challenges and enhance wellbeing. Social work is a profession that helps people to help themselves using approved theories and models. It aims to help people solve problems that they encounter in life. IFSW (2014) stated the purpose as "facilitate the inclusion of marginalized, socially excluded, dispossessed, vulnerable and at-risk groups of people; addressing and challenging barriers, inequalities, and injustices that are in society; forming short and long term working relationships with and mobilizing individuals, families, and communities to enhance their well-being and their problem -solving capacities; assisting and educating people to obtain services and resources in their communities...Plan, organize, administer, and manage programmes and organizations dedicated to any of the purposes delineated above.

In the course of helping people, social workers function on three levels. These are the micro, mezzo, and macro levels. At the micro-level, the activities are directed at individualistic interventions. The Social worker engages the individual in addressing his problems. The focus of micro-level practice is to help individuals, by giving one on one support and providing skills to help manage challenges (Johnson & Yanca, 2010). The Social worker addresses the problems of the individual to enhance the person's social functioning. Mezzo social work involves direct practice with small groups to promote change (Gilbert, 2018). Intervention is focused on smaller groups such as neighbourhood businesses, religious centres, and local communities, schools, and organizations. The macro-level addresses problems that focus on the societal level. Macro social work addresses large-scale problems on a societal level or problems that affect entire systems or communities. A social worker interested in this kind of work pursues social policy and change, activism, advocacy, and social entrepreneurship (Gilbert, 2018). The responsibilities for social workers on a macro level typically are to find the root cause or the why and effects of citywide, state, and/or national social problems. Macro-level social workers often advocate encouraging state and federal governments to change policies to better serve vulnerable populations (Kirst-Ashman & Hull, 2015).

To be a social worker, a person has to go through social work education. Classroom work and field education, also known as field work practice, are two components of social work education. These two components provide the students with the all-around training and development needed for effective practice. Social Work fieldwork practice is a supervised internship at an organization that provides social services. Tippa and Mane (2020), quoting Hamilton and Else (1983) defined it as a consciously planned set of experiences occurring in a practice setting designed to move students from their initial level of understanding, skills, and attitudes to levels associated with autonomous Social Work practice. Dhemba (2012), quoting Hamilton and Else (1983) views it as "a consciously planned set of experiences occurring in a practice setting designed to move students from their initial level of understanding, skills and attitudes to levels associated with autonomous social work practice." Social Work field practice is a component of Social Work education that allows students to put what they have learned in class into practice under the supervision of supervisor.

Field work education has various advantages. It enables students to have a real-life experience of what they learn in class. It also allows students to apply the theoretical concepts, principles, values, and ethics they learn in the classroom to a community practice setting under the supervision of a professional social worker. Through field experience, students learn to apply clinical skills to clients and become familiar with the many roles social workers play in agencies and communities. Mohinuddin (2019) further stated that the field work practicum gives students the opportunity to take on professional roles in order to learn skills, render services, and participate in the provision and development of social work services. The hands-on experience reinforces the student's identification with the purposes, values, and ethics of the profession fosters the integration of empirical and practice-based knowledge; and promotes the development of professional competence. In summary, field work practice provides an opportunity for students to apply the theoretical content in the classroom to real-life situations, enabling them practically to learn how to solve human problems, develop skills in solving human problems, and take the ownership of decisions they make.

Social work field practice generally has two patterns, namely concurrent field placement and block field placement. Dehemba (2012) said, concurrent field placement is the model where field placement occurs concurrently with classroom education. Each student is referred to a prospective agency during the semester. The students are expected to be in the agency for two or three days per week and take classes two or three days per week. In block placement, the student first completes all coursework and then spends four or five days per week working at an agency, for a specified period of time.

Social workers have various models that they use to treat clients. Some of these models are: behaviour modification, family therapy, crisis intervention, psycho-social model, client-centred therapy, play therapy, and reality centred therapy. In the course of their training, the students are taught various social work models and they use these models in the treatment of their clients.

Treatment Models

Behaviour Modification

The behaviour modification model was developed by B.F. Skinner. It was developed from a learning theory. It focuses on helping a person to change their behaviour (drop bad behaviour or learning new behaviour). It uses various techniques to help an individual change their behaviour. Some of these techniques are reinforcement, covert-reinforcement, shaping, systematic desensitization, aversion therapy, conditioning, and biofeedback.

Crisis Intervention Model

The crisis intervention model is a model used in treating people who are in a crisis situation. Crises have been defined by various authors. MacDonald (2020), quoting Caplan, 1961:18, described it as a state when people face an obstacle to important life goals—an obstacle that is, for a time, insurmountable by the use of customary methods of problem-solving..." Saunders (n.d.) defined it as a situation that involves a disruption of an individuals' normal and stable state where the usual methods of coping and problem-solving do not work; and Alexis (2020) defined it as a situation that is difficult for anybody to cope with. A crisis situation can, therefore, be seen as one in which an individual cannot handle his normal coping ability. The normal individual experiencing a crisis situation is unable to solve the problem using their normal coping capacity. A crisis situation is characterized by hopelessness, anger, despair, and grief, denial, conflict, difficulty in sleeping, depression. Crisis intervention helps a person to restore his normal problem-solving capability. Death, loss of job, divorce, and examination failure are all examples of crisis situations. The steps involved in the use of Crisis intervention are to plan and conduct a thorough bio-psychosocial and lethality/imminent danger assessment, establish a collaborative relationship, identify the major problems including the precipitants, explore of feelings, explore new coping strategies, implement of an action plan and follow-up (Roberts, 2005). The Social Worker assesses the client's crisis situation and helps them in resolving their problems and regaining their stability.

Family Intervention

Family therapy was developed from systems theory. It is a treatment process where the family is treated as a whole and individuals are treated as parts of that whole. The family is seen as a system with the members being components of it; the components are interrelated and mutually influential. Family therapists do not focus on an individual family member during treatment, rather; family therapists address problems within the family system. The goals of family therapy are to establish healthy boundaries, improve functioning, change negative patterns of interaction, and, build positive relationships among family members (Herbele, 2003). Some of the common problems treated under family therapy are parent- child conflict, problems between siblings, the effects of illness on the family, adjustment problems among family members, inconsistency in parenting skill etc. and handling expressed emotions (Verghese *et al.*, 2020). There are many types of family therapy. They include Structural therapy, which aims at identifying and re-ordering the organization of the family system; Strategic therapy which focuses on patterns of interactions between family member; Systemic/Milan therapy which focuses on a belief system, Narrative therapy with its major technique of restoring of dominant problem-saturated narrative; Trans-generational therapy, which focuses on trans-generational transmission of unhelpful patterns of belief and behaviour and co-joint family therapy, which focuses on teaching family effective communication.

Theoretical Framework

This work is anchored on the Afro-centric theory of Marcus-Garvey, proposed in 1950 (Chawane, 2016). The theory proposes that blacks must look at knowledge from the African perspective. It enables scholars to capture and incorporate African civilization and ideals into their works. Developing treatment models based on African background will enable scholars to capture and integrate cultural practices into the treatment models where African interest, values, and perspectives dominate. Further, the African value system and knowledge will also be captured, which will make the application of the models in treatment scenes more practical, effective, and easy. Indigenization of the treatment models will make the Social Work profession more practical and enhance the acceptability of the profession in the country.

Methodology

The study was carried out by social work students from the University of Nigeria's, Nsukka department of social work. The Department of Social Work was established as a unit under the Department of Sociology/ Anthropology of the University of Nigeria Nsukka in 1989 and later became a full department in 2006. The Social Work students have been involved in field work practices as per the requirements of study. The students are placed in agencies for their field work, where they work for two days (Tuesday and Thursday) each week throughout the semester. The agency of placements is changed from year to year. This is to enable the students to have experience of working in different settings and situations in life. The writer has been a field work instructor since 1994 till date. During this period, she has taught both undergraduate and postgraduate students. Within this period, she has held seminars with the students where they share experiences correct their mistakes, and learn from each other. Data for the study was collected from the experiences shared by the students over a period of eighteen years (from 1994 to 2020). During the course of the discussion, the students shared the problems and challenges they experienced using the Social work treatment models in assisting their clients. These problems greatly affected their ability to work effectively with the clients. In the course of the discussion, the need to indigenize these models became apparent. It is in line with this that the writer examines these challenges. It is hoped that this will provide a basis for African Scholar Workers to think of developing African-oriented models for Social Work Practice.

Results

Social Work Treatment Model—Challenges

Data collected from the students during the fieldwork seminars shows that they encounter the following problems in the use of the foreign-oriented models in treatment of the clients: These problems are:

Foreign background: One of the problems encountered is that the models have a foreign background. This arises mainly from the fact that the models were developed in Europe and America, thereby making them difficult to use in the African setting. As one of the students noted during the seminar,

> *I find it difficult to use the models to treat my cases because they do not suit us. I try to adapt it to our traditional setting, but it is difficult.*
> *Another said I have tried several times to use these models to treat cases, but they do not work, and I use some of our traditional methods in treating the cases.*

Due to the foreign background of these models, they do not suit our environment and it is, therefore, difficult to use in Nigeria.

Culture: Another challenge is that the models and techniques are not culturally appropriate. The models can work effectively in foreign cultures. The Nigerian cultural setting differs from European and American culture, and attempts to use the technique in the African setting prove to be difficult and counter-productive.

> *An example cited by one of the students is the case of using Co-joint family therapy in teaching families appropriate communication. Co-joint therapy entails the family sitting together and discussing the problems of the family, the children tell the parents where the parents have gone wrong; the parents*

> *do likewise to the children; and the social worker will teach them an appropriate mode of communication. However, this approach is culturally inappropriate in the Nigerian culture, where children are not expected to look at their parents and talk to them. Rather, children are expected to keep quiet in the presence of their parents and only talk when the parents allow them to. Thus, to use this technique and teach families effective communication is difficult, almost impossible.*

Inappropriate Setting

Another challenge experienced in the application of the models by the student is an inappropriate office setting. As one of the students said,

> *The social work offices are not well-equipped with the required office gadgets required for the effective use of these models.*

Another said the management does not understand the nature of our work and does not bother to equip the offices.

> *And another student said the offices are in the way they are because the management does not understand the nature of our work and it makes it difficult for me to do meaningful work in society.*

The inappropriate office setting makes it difficult for the social workers to have a conducive environment to work in. This may arise from poverty or lack of knowledge by the management staff of the appropriate nature of what the social worker office should be.

Poverty

Poverty is the last factor that makes it difficult to apply foreign models in African settings. Most of these models require equipment and tools for effective use. Most of the social work agencies in Nigeria are not able to buy the gadgets because of a lack of resources, making it difficult to use the models. An example is the use of play therapy for the treatment of cases. The student social workers could not use this model to treat their clients because of the unavailability of the required toys.

> One of the students said, "I do not have anything to work with".

This assertion was supported by another student who also said that I do not have the things I need to work effectively in the offices.

The lack of equipment and gadgets may also be linked to the fact that these gadgets are alien to Nigerian culture and the management may find it difficult to install.

Discussion

Data gathered from the seminars shows that social work students and, by extension, social workers in Nigeria face challenges in using the foreign-based model in the treatment of cases in Africa. The major problems are that the models have a foreign base and do not fit into the cultural setting of Nigeria, thereby making them ineffectively used in the country. This finding is also confirmed by the works of (Denov & Shevelle, 2019, Spitzer (2019) who asserted the need to use treatment models within the context of the client's culture. These assertions point out the fact that foreign-based models lacked the cultural contents and ingredients needed for effective intervention in the African setting. There is a need for African social workers to develop African-based models for social work practice in Africa to be more effective and enable the indigenization of Social work. This problem is not peculiar to Nigeria but also too many other African countries, like Tanzania, Rwanda, Uganda, and South Africa (Spitzer, Twikirize, & Wairire (2014); King, Bokore, & Dudziak (2017); Masoga & Shogane (2019). The finding on the Euro-American background of the treatment models is in line with the works of King *et al.* (2017) in Rwanda, who noted that the foreign models did not capture and note that there is a disconnect between the learned theories and local practices hence making it difficult to treat people who experienced genocide and other forms of trauma in Rwanda. The work advocated for a treatment model based on local concerns, knowledge, and practices. Spitzer and Twikirize (2014) stated that locally relevant cultural practices, indigenous knowledge systems, and African ethical concepts are very important elements for the success of any social work intervention in the African continent. This will help in furthering the Indigenization of social work. Indigenization of Social Work is very essential as it will increase the acceptance and relevance of Social Work in African nations.

The problem of an inappropriate office setting and the inability of the management to be properly equipped may also be linked to the fact that the tools and equipment required for the effective use of the models are alien to our culture, so the office management may not comfortably install them.

Recommendations

In view of these problems, the following recommendations are made. African scholars should develop techniques that are African based, bearing in mind the cultural practices and values obtainable in Africa. This model will be developed with the local modes of play, practices, and techniques used in the Nigerian settings in mind; this recommendation will not only make the intervention techniques appropriate to our cultural situation but also addresses the problems of an inappropriate office setting. It will also enable the management to equip the social work offices with the appropriate culturally appropriate tools.

REFERENCES

Chawane M. (2016). The Development of Afro centricity: A Historical Survey. *Yesterday and Today*, Number 16. December.

Dehemba J. (2012), Fieldwork in Social Work Education and Training: Issues and Challenges in the Case of Eastern and Southern Africa. *Social Work and Society.* Vol. 10, No. 1.

Denov, M. & Shevelle, M.C. (2019). Social Work practice with war-affected children and families: the importance of families, culture and arts, and participatory approaches. *Journal of Family Social Work*, Vol. 22, No. 1, 1-16.

Gilbert, N. (2018). What is the Difference between Micro, Macro and Mezzo Social Work? https://www.noodle.com/articles/micro-macro-mezzo-social-work-examples-and-differences

Heberle (2003). What is Family Therapy? Techniques and Concepts Available at https://study.com/academy/lesson/what-is-family-therapy-techniques-lesson- quiz.html

International Federation of Social Work (IFSW) (2014). Global definition of Social Work. Available on www.ifsw.org 17th August, 2020.

Johnson, L.C. & Yanca, S.J. (2010). *Social Work Practice: Ageneralist Approaches* (10th ed.). Boston, MA: Allyn & Bacon.

Kirst-Ashman, K.K. & Hull, G.H., Jr. (2015). Generalist practice with organizations and communities (6th ed.). Pacific Grove, CA: Brooks/Cole.

King, R,U., N. Bokore & Dudzick, S. (2017) The Significance of Indigenous in Social Work Response to Collective Recovery : A Rwandan Case. *Journal of Indigenous Social Development.* Volume 6, Issue 1.

MacDonald, D.K. (2016). *Crisis Theory and Types of Crisis.* Available at http://dustinkmacdonald.com/crisis-theory-types-crisis/

Masoga, M.A. & Shoganne, A.L. (2019).Viewpoint: Indigenous knowledge systems and environmental Social Work Education: Towards environmental sustainability. *South African Journal of Environmental Education,* Vol. 35.

Saunders, M. (n.d). Crisis Intervention and De-escalation Techniques. Available at http://www.cit.memphis.edu/modules/De-Escalation/presentations/FL%20-%20De%20Escalation%20Techniques.pdf

Spitzer, H. (2019). Social Work in East Africa: Amzungu perspective. *International Social Work,* Vol. 62 (2), 567-580.

Spitzer, H., Twikirize, J.M., & Waririe, E.E. (2014). Professional Social Work in East Africa: Towards Social Development, Poverty Reduction and Gender Equality. *Fountain*, 373-84.

Tippa, N. & Mane, N. (2018). Problem and prospect of field training in Social Work Education: A Review. *Innovare Journal of Social Sciences,* Vol. 6, No. 1.

Verghese, M., Kirpekar, V. & S. Loganathan (2020). Family Intervention: Basic Principles and Techniques. *Indian Journal of Psychiatry,* Vol. 62(2): S192-S200.

13

Building a Crime-free Society Using African Traditional Parenting Model

Titilola A. Adebowale

Introduction

A crime is an illegal act for which someone can be punished by the government for a gross violation of the law. It can also be a serious offence, especially against morality. The causes of crime are endless, such as poverty, parental neglect, low self-esteem, alcohol, drug abuse, neglect, lack of love, violence on television, and deprived neighborhoods, and so on. All of these can be said to be an offshoot of poor parenting skills. Crime does not spring up in a day; it is the accumulated misbehaviour of people over a long period of time. Many people have criminal tendencies that develop with individuals and escalate into real crimes as a result of not being controlled over a period of time during childhood. The family is the nucleus and smallest unit of the society that nurtures the primary relationship between parent and child (Landry, 2014), as well as other members of the family. One of the primary responsibilities of the parent is to bring up the child with the family and societal values that will make him useful to him, the family, community, and society at large. When the child goes against this wish, he is most likely to have problems that can lead him to crime. On the other hand, if the parent refuses to carry out their responsibility in giving the child the right parenting, the child bears the brunt while the parent also partakes in the consequences. A child, who is involved in crime, will surely bring shame and stigma to the parents while the family's name is spoiled. The right form of parenting is the solution to crime. Parenting is the process of raising and educating a child from birth until adulthood (Bernie *et al.*, 2010). It is also the process of taking care of or supporting a child from birth to adulthood, involving their physical, emotional, social, and intellectual capabilities. It can refer to the process or state of being a parent, carrying out responsibilities for the child to achieve a positive and definite goal. Parenting can be interesting and, at the same time, complex, depending on the interpersonal skills an individual parent possesses (Santrock, 2006). Parenting is like a planted seed that can only bear fruits of its kind, reaping what it has sowed. Parenting is not to dominate or intimidate the child, but to nurture and add values.

Baumrind's Parenting Styles Theory

Parenting has been found to be very important in developmental psychology. This is well established in the work of Diana Baumrind, a developmental psychologist at the University of California, Berkeley, in the 1960s, while Maccoby and Martin also reviewed the model in the 1980s. She studied pre-schoolers and discovered that they exhibited distinctly different types of behaviour based on the different types of parenting styles they encountered, which suggests what they become in life. The three developmental psychologists (Baumrind, 1967; Maccoby & Martin, 1983) came up with four parenting styles on which others can build. They are: authoritative, authoritarian (disciplinarian), permissive (indulgent), neglectful (uninvolved). The common dimensions of these parenting styles are *demandingness* (the level of control the parents have on the behaviour of their children) and *responsiveness* (the level of acceptance of their children's developmental and emotional needs).

However, looking into these four common parenting styles can lead us to some innate discoveries, as expounded by Steinberg, Blatt-Eisengart, and Cuffman, (2006). The authoritative style is characterized by warm and responsive attitudes, clear rules, high expectations, and supportive and valued independence (Nyarko, 2011). The child is happy, capable, and successful. The above characteristics can produce the following behaviours; high academic performance; more self-esteem; better social skills; less mental illness; and lower delinquency, that is, reduced criminal tendency. The authoritarian type is characterized by unresponsiveness, strict rules, high expectations, and blind obedience (Baumrind, 2012; Smith, Dishion, Shaw, Wilson, Winter & Patterson, 2014). The child tends to be obedient and proficient, but ranks lower in happiness and social competence. The likely associated outcomes of this style of parenting are lower academic performance; lower self-esteem; poorer social skills, mental illness, drug/alcohol abuse; and delinquency. The third type is permissive parenting which connotes warmth and responsiveness, few or no rules, indulgence and lenience (Miklikowska & Hurme, 2011). It ranks the child low in happiness and self-regulation. Such a child in this parenting style is more likely to experience problems with authority and tends to perform poorly in school. The consequences of this style are impulsive behaviour, egocentric attitude, poor social skills and problematic relationships. The fourth type is a neglectful or uninvolved style which is characterized by cold and unresponsiveness, no rules, being uninvolved and indifference (Davids, Roman & Leach, 2015). The child has less self-control, self-esteem and competence than their peers. This type of parenting can lead to the following behaviours: impulsiveness, delinquency, drug or alcohol abuse, and suicide.

Most parents would prefer the authoritative style of parenting; which is adequate depending on the skills possessed by the individual parent (Spera, 2005). There are some hurdles that need to be cleared with active skills to allow this adjudged best style to be favourably achieved. Such hurdles are in the area of peer pressure, poverty, neighbourliness, social influences birth order and so on. Peer pressure is a very serious factor that easily affects children's behaviour especially adolescents even in the face of the best parenting style. During this stage, the adolescents believe highly in their peers opposing the responsiveness of their parent. The parent needs high parenting skills beyond what one can read in textbooks. Poverty is another problem that can truncate the goodwill of authoritative parenting. Poverty is a disease that cannot easily be treated and can indirectly affect authoritative parenting. When a child is in serious need and if it is not met, it can lead to unprecedented behaviour if the parent is not skilled enough. Birth order is another factor that can easily militate against the best type of parenting. The position of a child in the family may play a negative role in the success of authoritative parenting. If the child is the only child of the parent or the first born or the last or the only girl/boy, the relations, grandparents or some other individuals who happen to be involved in the training of the child might introduce some indices or parameters that are not authoritative parenting friendly. Neighbourliness is another factor that can be injurious to this parenting style. In most cases, neighbours try to impress themselves; as a result, they tend to deviate from the roles and norms of this type of parenting when the parent of the particular child is momentarily not available.

Parenting in African Setting

In light of the above, there are other methods that can help the authoritative parenting style be achieved. Cultural factors also play an important role in parenting so there is no universally best style of parenting (Amos, 2013). Africa is a continent rich in culture and tradition that takes care of values, rules, and norms to achieve parenting goals. The interference of modern and Western culture has watered down parenting in the African context. Some decades ago, when Africans were more like extended family, when the idea of looking for greener pastures outside their fatherland was not in vogue, there was discipline. Crime was a strange phenomenon. Everything possible to foster discipline was used. Folklore, moonlight tales, proverbs, even taboos were used to inculcate discipline. An oral tradition that could easily send a message of reality into the child's subconscious mind in every sphere of life was used (Amos, 2013). According to African culture, it is not true that a child should not ask questions. He can, the onus lies with the parents to use their skills to answer him correctly without watering down the lesson he needs to learn. The parent makes good use of oral tradition to tell stories that could create fear in the child to guide him to conform to societal norms (Adinlofu, cited in Amos, 2013). There are societal and family values that do not contradict but support each other. The culture and traditions of the Africans tend to support these values. When these values are held up in high esteem, they serve as boosters to the moral standards and behaviours of the child.

The child is also taught critical thinking skills in order to be assertive and not be spoon-fed (Hart, Nwell & Olsen, 2003). The child is being given riddles to solve to learn some facts about life that can gradually bring him up to face life's reality; this invariably teaches the child to be resilient, an advantage to face adversity and still come out strong. Proverbs were often used to create awareness of life situations in the child. Proverbs often teach and educate children. It is a way of giving expert advice on life issues. They contain common sense that may not be easily accepted naturally. It is used to teach wisdom beyond a child's imagination. Many proverbs are commonly used by many races, such as English, Asians, and Africans. They are commonly used colloquially, which makes them unique. It is widely used in Africa to the extent that important points are backed up by proverbs. It gives a child the opportunity to critically think and make references to this critical thinking, making it part of the experience of life.

Parenting in Africa can be very interesting because choice of the parenting style made by the individual parent usually revolves around the best three parenting styles postulated by Baumrind (1961) but well supported and guided by cultural heritage and African beliefs. The various cultures and beliefs usually help in the training of the children, strengthening the desired behaviour. Parenting cannot be perfect outside of the culture of Africans. Africans are known for having many wives and children, and they ensure that all their children are well-trained because they regard their children as their pride. There is keen competition among the wives in the polygamous home in regard to their children's success. Parents, especially mothers, take the raising of their children as their priority so as to avoid unnecessary shame and disgrace from their children's misbehaviour (Simons & Conger, 2007). There is an adage common to most countries in West Africa that says a good child belongs to the father, while the bad one belongs to the mother. Why? The belief is that serious parenting is done by the mother because she holds forth for the man who must have gone in search of daily bread for the family. This has always been the orientation of traditional African settings, where the major role of a mother is to bring up the child in a proper manner that will earn her honour in the future (Mckinney & Renk, 2008). Modern parents have grown up with this belief. Even when the family is a nuclear one, the entire community is still perceived as a big family.

African values include communalism and community, which include neighbours and kinsmen. This type of relationship also supported good parenting in Africa. In an African setting, a child belongs to every older member in the community, either extended family or unrelated neighbours, family friends, and important members of the community (Boyd-Franklin, 2013). There is an adage that says, "It is only one person that gives birth to a child, but the parenting is done by many people". In such a situation, it will be difficult for a child to be involved in crime because no community will want a child to give them a bad identity. When a child misbehaves, the child and parents will not bear the brunt alone. Even their community will share in the shame. Extended family and friends play a large role in disciplining children (Ndofirepi & Shumba, 2014). If a child got into trouble, many people would be ashamed of the child's actions. Hence, everyone protects him by disciplining him so as not to get into trouble. When a child's criminal tendency is being noted and the community tries to put him right, meeting with opposition from the parent and child, who eventually commits a crime, that entire family can be excommunicated from that community. In African communities, if the parent dies, the children will not automatically go to the orphanage, but instead to live with aunts, uncles, or grandparents rather than with godparents. They mostly feel comfortable with grandparent, uncles and aunts because of the close relationship that had been established in the extended family system before the demise of the direct parent. They believe that there is continuity of parenting in that family. It is believed in Africa that breast milk is the best for a child's brain development. Africans believe that a child that is not breastfed but cow milk will behave like an animal with criminal tendency, while breastfed baby behaves normally, warm, and compassionately. Due to this belief, if a woman dies during childbirth, while the baby lives, and a very close member of that family will take care of the child and breast-feed the child to be able to have compassion and be responsible for parenting the child.

Africans place important value on child-rearing, beliefs and attitudes. Africans cherish their values greatly. Value is what is held up as the most important thing in life, can always build one's attitude and behaviour. It is believed that a child that is not well trained will sell off the house that the parent might have valued most. Africans value good parenting because of the belief that a well-trained child will later take good care of them. The raising of a child in the African context is like investment and the child is like a security measure because the government does not really take adequate care of the aged, as much as what the children would do. If a child is involved in crime, he cannot go far in life; the future may be at stake. There are many things parent value and inculcate in their children such as beliefs that can build up the attitudes and behaviours of their children that will always rule out crime. Parent emphasizes cleanliness, family ties, independence, obedience, religion and moral personal values such as behaving well and respecting others (Thomas, 2017). The child's values are expected to run along with the parent's and that of the community, in such a situation the child is not likely to be involved in crime.

Punishment is also used to enforce messages of obedience. Even though it is viewed as a crude way of disciplining a child, it is a good way of curbing misbehaviour and standing as a deterrent to others. Researchers have shown that modern parents use physical punishment to reduce deviant behaviour (Berlin, Ispa, Fine, Malone, Brooks-Gunn, Brady-Smith, & Bai, 2009; Ispa & Halgunseth, 2004). Punishment can be very effective depending on the skills and the nature of the punishment and the gravity of the offence. Corporal punishment is sparsely used. Withdrawal of a child's rights or freedom for a short period until the assignment expected from him is carried out is an example. Stories that show terrible consequences of behaviour that can scare a child from that behaviour is also used. Making references to individuals' cases, positive or negative, depending on what the parent is emphasizing. Parents also use both verbal and non-verbal cues to communicate with their children the exact moral behaviour they are passing across to them. There are several songs in different dialects that frown against crimes; they are more meaningful and impactful when rendered to address any issue at hand. They also make use of taboos, which superstitious traditional beliefs are meant to scare children away from any behaviour that negates family and societal norms and values. This would be able to shield them from crime.

Education has been found to play a big role in the training of children (Gershoff, Lansford, Sexton, Davies-Kean & Sameroff, 2012). Education has and is still making an impact in helping parents make use of adequate parenting from all the styles and African methods available to them. Education is the bedrock of development and a means of enlightenment. Parent, through education, are able to sieve good ideas from the parenting styles their parents used to train them. This type of development cuts across all spheres of life, including behaviour and relationships. The type of education offered to the child in the school is good enough to uphold the type of parenting he is receiving at home, so home and school training synchronized will prevent crime in the life of a child. When the home, school and environment are of one voice with the same values and goals, there will be no place for crime. Many of the children lack monitoring; they will leave the house for school, but will not enter the classroom to learn. They have a criminal group they belong to, so they go to school to learn about criminal activities. There are too many for the teachers to do the monitoring alone. No parent will ask about the work done in school; the child would have been asleep before the arrival of such a parent from work. They can easily become criminals because nobody is monitoring them.

Education is received through different channels; there is no one-way traffic to having an education. Good behaviour that is devoid of crime is education. An education that is of no benefit to oneself or society is no education. Adverse education could be obtained from different angles unknowingly to a child except there is an adult monitoring the source of such education. One such source that people usually overlook or underrate is Information and Communication Technology (ICT). It is a good source of education but carelessly handled by children. Unfortunately, the parents that should censor what is being learned on the internet, phone, and television are not alive to their responsibility. Most children who get themselves involved in crime learn the act from these gadgets because they lack control (Steele, 2011). Some children get entangled in crime through the influence of their peer group. Parenting involves knowing and checking on the friends, their children move with so that they can all have adequate behaviour. Many parents are lacking in this area. Some may not even see their children for the whole working days except on weekends, and the children are left in the hands of maids or nannies. Such parents are after the money they will make in their business. Parenting is more of a sacrifice for the upbringing of the child, especially at the reformatory stage. In such situations whereby the parent neglects the role of parenting, the child can fall victim to "free teachers" outside the home environment. Such teachers are not being paid because the children they train in the act of crime will, later on, feed them with the money made from crime. The free teacher will automatically disown the child as soon as the child is caught.

Effects of Modernity on Parenting in Nigeria Today

The error Africans make today is trying to parent their children with a foreign culture that is alien to them entirely. The custodian of this type of parenting understands its roots, which they can easily work upon when they run into troubled waters. Their adjustment and errors will be hidden from those who blindly imitate such parenting. Viewing this incident critically, most African parents today look down on the traditional way of parenting their children through which they (the parent) were raised as being primitive and local. One can then clearly ascertain that neo-colonialism has taken over the average African, making them think the foreign way of parenting is better than their own. Many Africans do parent their children in a foreign way, claiming that is where they live, but foreigners do not parent their children according to the African culture where they reside while in Africa. Even in situations whereby some Africans try to raise their children according to their own culture in a foreign land, the foreigners usually kick against it and summon them to the court of law. In some cases, the social work department of that foreign country is made to retrieve those children from their parents for the government of that country, against the wishes of the parents. It is important to note that many Africans who were raised with an authoritative parenting style in addition to cultural and traditional ways are making impacts in their respective professions in the foreign land they reside. Some of them are usually celebrated for their remarkable and outstandingly pleasant behaviour.

Nigerian parents currently believe there are two types of parenting, the old and modern parenting schools of thought. The old school type of parenting is termed too strict; they use too heavy a disciplined approach. They classify this type as the authoritarian type of parenting where a parent feels things must be done in their own way. The Nigerian modern parenting style is seen as being more lenient; it is authoritative, warm and loving with clear boundaries. This produces a great result because the child is made to understand why he is being beaten. At the order of leniency, permissive parenting comes into play where the child can have everything he wants and not only what he needs. At times, it may be difficult to distinguish between present-day authoritative and permissive parenting. Nevertheless,

Nigerian parents still manifest a high degree of discipline that is already wired in them. The issue is, will their own children be able to discipline the generation coming behind them? if care is not taken, crime will surely increase. The major contribution to this is that modern parents are no longer using the different African ways of parenting with their children; and also, not much discipline is being wired into the current children compared to what was wired into the current parents. However, if the so-called Nigerian "modern parenting style is cautiously attended to, adding skills in African parenting, it can be a suitable one, if it can be devoid of over-indulgence which can be disadvantageous to the child. If the parents are able to control what their children have access to and spend quality time imparting values to them, then modern parenting can be highly esteemed.

Parenting today can be traumatic regardless of which approach one takes, because all of the enabling environments that were helpful in the past are no longer available, and where they are available, they are very weak. The question that needs to be asked is what is the level of parenting in Africa today? The high level of crime all over Africa can show a low level of good parenting.

Implication for Social Welfare Counselling

Parenting commences from the cradle; it has to be handled with care. Curbing crime has to be done right from an early age while the behaviour is being formed. Counsellors should emphasize the right parenting that could curb crime. This is very necessary to make the job of the counsellor easy and smooth, because good behaviour is the nucleus of a peaceful society that is devoid of problems.

There is no fixed parenting. All types of parenting can be blended and enhanced with the African model of parenting, making use of local and traditional means such as proverbs, songs, folklore, and so on, should be encouraged by the counsellors for a parent to use.

Information is power. All stakeholders, such as parents, teachers, neighbours and extended family, should be rightly informed about parenting, embracing it with African culture.

Parents need to possess parenting skills in both normal parenting styles and the African model, which they can acquire by joining a parenting group where they can share ideas and learn from their various experiences.

Parents need to be available for the children. They need to know their children very well and monitor them beyond the comfort zone of their home. Parents need to observe their children in the midst of their peers and neighbours, and the kind of relationship that exist among them.

Counsellors should look into all factors that may contend with African parenting styles and consider the positive effects on the adherents.

Conclusion

There are no fixed rules to the parenting style that should be used, they can always be blended and mixed up with the rich African culture and tradition making parenting natural, interesting and easy to manage. Many foreigners are now deviating from their normal ways of parenting because of the loopholes in the rigid parenting style. Some of them are now imbibing the natural setup of the African way of parenting. Unfortunately, Africans are adopting foreign parenting that is not as rich as their own. Few Africans now send their children to their homes country for better parenting due to the weak parenting in foreign lands which often sends their children to correctional home because of the crime usually committed. It is very essential for parents to let their children perceive their system of parenting as part of parental treatment born out of love for the children. Crime has been on the increase because parenting generally has been under-estimated.

REFERENCES

Amos, P.M. (2013). *Parenting and Culture: Evidence from some African Communities*. Doi. 10.5772/56967.https://www.intechopen.com/books/prentingin-south-america=and-african on texts/parenting-and-culture-evidence-from-some-african-communities

Baumrind, D. (2012). Differentiating between Confrontive and Coercive Kinds of Parental Power Assertive Disciplinary Practices. *Human Development.* Doi.10.1159/000337962

Baumrind, D. (1967). Child care practices anteceding three patterns of preschool behaviour. *Genet Psychol Monograph.* 75(1):43-88. https// www.ncbi.nlm.nih.gov/pubmed/6032134

Berlin, L.J., Ispa, J.M., Fine, M.A., Malone, P.S., Brooks-Gunn, J., Brady-Smith, C., and Bai, Y. (2009). Correlates and consequences of spanking and verbal punishment for low-income white, African-American, and Mexican American Toddlers. *Child Development*, 80(5), 1403-1420.

Bernier, A., Carlson, S.M., Whipple, N. (2010). From external regulation to self-regulation: Early Parenting Precursors Functioning. *Child Development*, 81, 326-339.

Boyd-Franklin, N. (2013). *Black families in therapy: Understanding the African American experience.* New York : Guilford Publications.

Constantine, M.G., Blackmon, S.M. (2002). Black adolescents' racial socialization experiences their relations to home, school and peer self-esteem. *Journal of Black Studies* (3), 322-335.

Davids, E.L., Roman, N.V., Leach, L.L. (2015). Decision-making styles: A systematic review of their associations with parenting. *Adolescent Research Review*, 1, 69-90. 32 Doi:10.1007/s40894-015-6003-y

Gershoff, E.T., Lansford, J.E., Sexton, H.R., Davis-Kean, P., and Sameroff, A.J. (2012). Longitudinal Links between spanking and children's externalizing behaviours in a national sample of White, Black, Hispanic and Asian American families, *Child Development*, 83, 838-843.

Hart, C.H., Newell, L.D., Olsen, S.I., (2003). Parenting skills and social-communicative competence in childhood. in: J.O.Greene and B.R. Burleson (Eds.), *Handbook on Communication and Social Interaction Skills.*753-797. Mahwah, NJ: Eribaum.

Ispa, J.M., and Halgunseth, L.C. (2004). Talking about corporal punishment: Nine low-income African-American mothers perspectives. *Early Research Quarterly*, 19 (3): 463-484

Landry, S.H. (2014). The role of parents in early childhood learning. Children's Learning Institute, University of Texas, Health Science Centre, USA, Revised Edition.

Maccoby, E.E. and Martin, J.A. (1983). Socialisation in the context of the Family: Parent-Child Interaction. In: P.H. Mussen & E.M. Hetherington (eds.), *Handbook of Psychology.* Vol. 4. Socialisation, Personality, and Social Development (4th ed.) pp. 1-101, New York: Wiley.

Mckinney, C. and Renk, K. (2008). Differential parenting between mothers and Fathers: implications for Late adolescents. *Journal of family issues*, 29, 806-827.

Miklikowska, M., Hurme, H. (2011). Democracy begins at home: Democratic parenting and adolescents' support for democratic values. *European Journal of Developmental Psychology*. Published online June 2011:541-557. Doi:10 .1080/17405629.2011.576856u

Ndofirepi, A.P., and Shumba, A. (2014). Conceptions of a child among traditional Africans: A philosophical purview. *Journal of Human Ecology*, 45 (3), 233-242.

Nyanko, K. (2011). The influence of authoritative parenting style on adolescents' academic achievement, *AJSMS.* Published online. 278-282. Doi:10.5251/ajsms.2011.2.3.278.282

Simons, L.G. and Conger, R.D. (2007). Linking Mother-Father differences in parenting to a typology of family parenting styles and adolescent outcomes. *Journal of Family Issues*, 28,212-241. 10.1177/01925 13x06294593

Smith, J.D., Dishon, T.J., Shaw, D.S., Wilson, M.N., Winter, C.C., Patterson, G.R. (2014). Coercive family process and early-onset conduct problems from age 2 to school entry. *Developmental Psychopathology*. Retrieved in July 2020. Doi:10.1177/109019819802500307

Spera, C.A. (2005). Review of the Relationship among Parenting Practices. Parenting Styles and Adolescent School Achievement. *Educational Psychological Review*. 125-146. Doi:10.1007/10648-005-3950-1

Steele, C.M. (2011). *Whistling Vivaldi: And other clues to how stereotypes affect us (Issues of our time)*. www Norton & Company.

Steinberg, L., Blatt-Eisengart, I. and Cauffman, E. (2006). Patterns of competence and adjustment among adolescents from authoritative, indulgent, and neglectful homes: A replication in a sample of serious juvenile offenders. *Journal of Research on Adolescence*, 16, 47-58. doi:10.1111/j.1532-7795.2006.00119.x

Stevenson, H.C. (2013). *Promoting racial literacy in schools: Differences that make a difference.* New York: Teachers College Press.

Thomas, A. (2017). *Promoting culturally affirming Parenting in African-American parents. Positive Parenting in African-American families*. Retrieved on 5th August 2020 from https://www.apa.org

14
Social Work Practice
African Feminist Perspectives

Geeta Sahare

Introduction

Feminism internationally aims to realise the liberation of women from all types of oppression and provide solidarity among women of all countries. However, the remarkable difference is the growing gap between different parts of the world. Women from one continent are harvesting the fruits of capitalism and the global economy, whereas women from the other continent are all too often confronted with poverty and terrible labour conditions. In the Indian context, it is gaining more strength among Muslim women from the ban of "*Triple Talaq*" and would empower more women from all spheres of society after reforms in the form of the new National Education Policy of 2020. Such majors by the centre would certainly help in empowering the younger generation, especially women.

Feminist theories generally explain the basic structure and dynamics of women's experiences within their socio-political and inter-personal sexual hierarchies. To enhance flexibility and responsiveness in applying different theories of African feminism, social workers should be conversant in various branches of feminism. Most social workers generally adopt five branches, namely liberal, cultural, postmodern, womenist, and radical feminism, of feminist theories and apply each one to their social work practice, using group work examples.

This chapter has two objectives: The first one is explaining variations in feminism and providing examples of how the theories can be applied to group work practice. This important goal is to encourage the incorporation of feminist theories into social work practice. This will provide several branches of African feminist theories, and each one is based on different socio-political and philosophical perspectives. Another aspect is to review the major laws and beliefs of a theory and apply each one to social work practice, using some social worker group work examples.[1]

Using African feminist theory in social work is a very important and useful way of contacting the gender biases of many traditional conservative theories since African feminist theories, unlike many familiar traditions, structure and dynamics of women's experiences, draw attention to the ways in which day-to-day actions can be stored up as discriminatory social structures. To enhance the social worker's flexibility and responsiveness to women's social and personal problems, practitioners should be familiar with various branches of feminism. Most of the feminist theories suggest different ways to help in eliminating misperception, sexual inequalities, social restrictions, and oppression faced by women, which many researchers and writers have pointed out are shared by social workers, but the goals of each branch of feminism vary according to the perspective on the forces that impede women. Different situations, different women and different times call for different approaches to problem solving, with grounding in several branches of feminism, and any social worker can select wisely among all these theories.[2]

To achieve excellence in their work, social workers must observe and review feminist material in a sophisticated manner, avoiding trendiness and resisting the desire for a simple and elegant type of theory that will suit the needs and solve the social problems of all women in society. Without a perfect and smooth understanding of a broad range of African feminist theories, the social worker would be poorly equipped to function at that level. This chapter draws on the actual use of feminist theories in the social work field. It is further hoped that doing so helps elucidate the ways feminism can be practiced and demonstrates why a particular branch may be more suited than others to solving a particular problem or the set of problems, because many of the clients with whom social workers come into contact suffer from multilevel forms of marginalization and oppression, and as a feminist social worker, we favour the branches that call for more comprehensive change in society, whether it is radical feminism or womanism.

Theories of Feminism

There are many ways to describe the multiple forms of feminism that have emerged since the 1960s, though many of them overlap with one another on key points. The following descriptions represent one way to categorise them and draw on a variety of sources. While these terms are contested, we try to summarise some of the main elements of each that will allow a basic understanding of their differences and commonalities.

Liberal Feminism

This kind of feminism works within the structure of mainstream society to integrate women into it and make it more responsive to individual women's rights, but does not directly challenge the system itself or the ideology behind women's oppression. The suffragist movement is an example.

Of key importance to liberal feminism is that a dividing line is drawn between the public realm, which the state is expected to regulate, and the private realm, which is expected to be free from state control. The traditional liberal values of independence (*vs*. interdependence), equality of opportunity (*vs*. equality of outcome), and individualism (*vs*. collectivism) are so ingrained in Western society that they are now accepted as standard social functioning, rather than viewed as a particular ideology.

These traditional liberal values are central to liberal feminist thought. Liberal feminists point out that society violates the value of equal rights in its treatment of women, primarily by restricting women as a group, rather than treating them as individuals. They argue that women should have the same rights as men, but they often fail to examine the *de facto* inequality in the distribution of men's rights by race, socioeconomic status, and other factors.[3]

Liberal feminists contest such public issues as women's lack of political equality and their lack of access to certain social services needed to ensure equality between the sexes. Battles for equal education, equal employment opportunities, and equal pay for equal work have been the hallmarks of liberal feminism. Successful campaigns in these areas continue to support the separation between the public and private spheres. For example, in *Roe* v. *Wade*, the U.S. Supreme Court upheld a right to privacy; that is, it affirmed the inappropriateness of state interference in the private decision between a woman and her physician regarding abortion. It did not provide equal access to abortion nor require the states to ensure equality, for example, by funding abortions for poor women. Besides its inadequate attention to poverty, liberal feminism often excludes the interests of women of colour by insisting that sex, rather than race, is the major source of oppression of women.[4]

Liberal feminists do not seek an end to the meritocracy, nor do they seek other fundamental changes in society; rather, they hope women will merit more of society's current rewards. Women's lack of training in skills thought to be necessary for men's success, such as assertiveness, is frequently seen as exacerbating, if not causing, inequality. Liberal feminists are more likely to examine interpersonal interactions and encourage women to behave more like men who are successful in their careers rather than training women to dismantle structural supports of power imbalances. Despite the theory's limitations, liberal feminists have achieved significant victories, primarily through the use of formal policy as a mechanism of social change. These successes include outlawing sex-discrimination, improving maternity leave, achieving educational reforms, improving economic rights within marriage, increasing the likelihood of women obtaining child custody after divorce, and even achieving woman suffrage.[5]

Radical Feminism

Radical feminism views patriarchy and sexism as the most elemental factors in women's oppression, cutting across all others, from race and age to culture, caste, and class. It questions the very system and ideology behind women's subjugation. The term often refers to the women's movements emerging from the second wave feminism in 1960s.

At a time when people were increasingly questioning different forms of oppression and power, civil rights, peace and other liberation movements were born. Radical feminists, seeking to understand the roots of women's subordination, have provided the major theoretical understanding that has served as the basis for the inspiration and analysis guiding women's movements around the world. Radical feminists argue that individual women's experiences of injustice and the miseries that women think of as personal problems are actually political issues grounded in power imbalances. They insist that separating public from private issues masks the reality of male power, a system of domination that operates similarly in both spheres. Furthermore, they insist that the public and private systems of male control function in dynamic interaction. What happens "out there" in the bastions of male political arenas affects women as individuals on an extremely personal basis. So, for example, dismissing claims of sexual harassment by public figures devalues individual women's experiences of sexual harassment. Public-private division isolates and depoliticizes women's oppression.[6]

Radical feminists characterise society as patriarchal. Like in India, most societies are patriarchal. By this, they mean both that, historically, families have been organised according to male lines of inheritance and dependence and that society has been constructed in a way that accrues a disproportionate share of power to men. By characterising contemporary society as patriarchal, radical feminists assume that the most fundamental and significant social division is by gender. Patriarchy is described as a cultural universal, with all institutions reinforcing that social order. The patriarchal structure consists of a system that privileges men through the complex political manipulation of individual identity, social interactions, and structural systems of power. It is not only legal systems that create and reinforce the sexual hierarchy, but all human interactions are permeated by male privilege. Radical feminists have developed a psychological analysis of male supremacy that has two main themes. Supporters charge that women are damaged psychologically by the internalisation of oppressive patriarchal messages, and they argue that psychological control of women is a significant component of patriarchal systems.[7] Some radical feminists see women's personalities and their sexuality as having been constructed to meet men's needs rather than women's. Furthermore, women are so limited in their roles that psychological problems are almost inevitable. Rigid sex-role prescriptions not only distort people but also lead to sex-based oppression. Radical feminists suggest that men become oppressors not by virtue of biology, but by rationalising supremacy on the basis of biological difference. It is also thought that women are conditioned to serve men and that it is because patriarchal ideology permeates the culture that women are assured of being confined to their caste-like status. This psychology of sex-role conditioning accounts for women's apparent complicity with patriarchy, evidenced in their subservient behaviour. Radical feminists have studied the appalling prevalence of violence against women, particularly in the forms of physical and sexual assault, and they define violence as political in nature. They argue that violence against women is motivated by a desire for dominance and control; men are more likely to abuse women, and battering is typically associated with woman abuse.The only dismantling of patriarchal structures that will be an effective response.[8]

In the Indian context, it becomes rather more oppressive due to the hierarchical pyramidal caste system of Brahmins, Kshatriyas, Vaishyas, and Sudras in descending order. In a patriarchal society, there is a higher prevalence of violence as men belonging to lower castes are viewed as inferior to those belonging to higher castes. The women belonging to the Shudras are viewed as the most inferior by the upper caste, especially in villages, and face more forms of physical and sexual assault.

The radical feminist analysis of sexism is purposefully comprehensive. Sexism is described as a social system consisting of "law, tradition, economics, education, organised religion, science, language, the mass media, sexual morality, child-rearing, the domestic division of labour, and everyday social interaction," the purpose of which is to give men power over women. It is this very pervasiveness of sexism that necessitates fundamental social change. Radical feminists are sometimes impatient with the notion of reform, and they doubt the ability of a patriarchal state to legislate in the interest of women. Instead of demanding equal pay, more women professors, legalisation of abortion, and an increase in childcare services, radical feminists critique the basic structure of work systems, support a radical analysis of universities, insist that child care should be viewed as a social rather than an individual responsibility, and maintain that the nuclear family is an unworkable social system. The most basic institutions need fundamental change.[9]

Cultural Feminism

Cultural feminism emphasises essential differences between men and women in terms of biology, personality, and behaviour. Women are seen to have different and superior virtues that provide the foundation for shared identity, solidarity, and sisterhood. Since by nature, women are viewed as kinder as and gentler than men, it follows that if women were in power, the world would be a better place.

In the Indian context, it is not a new thing. There have been many "women" as goddesses in the past, such as mother Sarasvati, Parvati, Lakshmi, Durga, Kali, and many more.They were held in very high esteem and worshipped. However, it is not known when their status deteriorated in the Indian society.

However, some of the worst customs like child marriages, Sati pratha (burning widows living on the pyres of the deceased husbands), untouchability, and the Varna caste system have deteriorated the whole social system, and women are the worst affected. Female foeticide, the dowry system, and illiteracy amongst women are some of the other reasons for women's worsening status in Indian society.

In the 1960s and 1970s, some women supported the idea of forming separate women—only cultures. According to cultural feminist theory, the difference between women and men is privileged over class, race, and other sources of inequality. According to this theory, the difference between women and men is celebrated because it considers those aspects ascribed to womanhood superior to, or more valuable than, opposing aspects in men.[10] For example, women are said to be nurturing and altruistic, and these aspects are privileged over the competitiveness ascribed to men.

The development of knowledge through emotion and intuition is valued, as is a sense of community among women. Social workers such as Jane Addams, Crystal Eastman, and Sophonisba Breckenridge, who practiced in the late nineteenth and early twentieth century's, are often connected with this branch of feminist thought. Cultural feminists often stress the spiritual potential of the women's movement. Although there are several approaches to feminist spirituality, many cultural feminists are interested in the development of a specifically woman-centered religion or spirituality.[11]

In the process of creating a new system of thought and language through which women could free their minds from patriarchal chains, theologian Mary Daly (1978) revived the romantic tradition of depending on intuition to uncover the "patriarchal reversals" of language that obscure meaning. Cultural feminists celebrate "the feminine principle in women. The essentialist's arguments concerning women's goodness challenge dominant assumptions and foretell a revolution in which women will achieve power. Women's and men's natures are seen as changeable. Still, differences between women and men are thought to be significant, and cultural feminists often speak of women as being more closely connected to natural forces, thus seeming to accept as positive the association of men with culture and women with nature. This is especially evident in ecofeminist strains of cultural feminist theorizing, where it is assumed that women are nonviolent and in tune with the earth.[12]

There is a strong call for supporting women's "voices" or perspectives. The goals of eco-feminism are peace, ecology, the development of women's spirituality and women's culture, and the restructuring of society to increase the social valuation of women and women's culture. Generally, cultural feminism seeks to coalesce feminists and eliminate splits among women.

To accomplish these goals, they use claims of universalism and downplay differences, including very important differences such as racism, experienced by some but not all women. There is a strong emphasis on building women's culture, often using separatism as an approach, sometimes as an end in itself.[13]

Post-modern Feminism

It borrows heavily from post-modernism, which is an epistemology, that is, a theory of knowledge and understanding. The use of language is a central concept. Words, whether spoken or written, are said to lack fixed and intrinsic meanings, so one must always know the context, speaker, and the social processes that contributed to the use of words in order to understand their meaning. They need to be replaced with a plurality of different notions of a plurality of *resistances*, or sites from which one can argue against an oppressive power. Post-modern feminists seek multiple ways to deconstruct the culturally construed ideology of male superiority.[14]

Kristeva argued that the word "woman" is a social rather than natural construct, and neither can nor should be defined. By taking a *woman* as the starting point, given the term's existence only oppositional *difference* to the notion of man, feminist practice based on the notion of "woman" could only be negative, formed in reaction to the concept of woman. This added that a conception of gender as basic in the sense of inescapable or over-determined is warranted, however, given the pervasiveness of cultural and social gender structuring. But, this does not mean we must declare gender differences inherent or fixed. To do so is to "naturalize" and excuse oppression. According to Flax, the tasks of postmodern feminist theorists are: (1) to articulate feminist viewpoints in society; (2) to analyse how women are affected by the social world; (3) to examine the role of power and knowledge relationships in shaping the way women think about the social world; and (4) to imagine ways in which the social world can be transformed.[15]

Womanism

African-American women have contributed significantly to the development of all of the divisions of feminist theory discussed here. In addition, black female writers and theorists have developed a new branch, often referred to as "womanism". Race is an all-encompassing and powerful determinant of people's lives.

Race and gender are experienced, however, quite differently by black and white women, because gender identity is constructed and is often represented in polarised and antagonistic ways for black and white women. For example, white women, for example, are frequently unaware of their own experiences with race or the privileges accorded to them as members of the dominant group. As a result, it can be difficult for white women to understand the importance that many black women place on race or the relative constancy of the effects of social perceptions of racial differences. However, because both are experienced concurrently, race and gender cannot be separated. Because of this, black women who work toward feminist goals tend to focus their efforts at the intersection of sex and race, and usually on class struggles as well.[16]

Womanists have argued that additive models of oppression in which oppressive systems are seen as parallel and only occasionally intersecting, hide from view, and therefore from change, interlocking systems. Because of categorical thinking, it is difficult to conceive of race, sex, and class as a single consciousness with a single struggle needed to overcome them. Womanists argue, however, that it is necessary to examine all these aspects so that neither race, nor sex, nor class is hidden or discounted. That means we cannot consider one system of domination and then move on to the next without exploring the intersections. It also means we need to revamp theories of oppression as we learn more. When we expand our understanding of racism, we need to reexamine our understanding of sexism and classism in light of what we know about how racism operates.[17]

Besides failing to account for the mutual dependencies of systems of oppression, additive models do not account for people of mixed racial and ethnic identity. When our categories become blurred, for example with biracial or multiracial people, or with bisexual people, we often see how limiting the study of a single category of dominance can be. Instead, womanism proposes a "both/and" worldview. Rather than posing race and gender as contradictory opposites, where a woman is expected to identify either as black or as a woman, womanism allows for a unified whole. Working from the assumption of an interlocking system is a paradigmatic shift away from focusing on separate, interacting systems. It is a move towards an inclusive view of mutually dependent oppressive systems. Womanism starts with the perspective of black women rather than white men and centres on the *complex matrix* of oppression. Both action and articulation are emphasised in womanist theory. Womanism uses racial consciousness to underscore the positive aspects of African-American life. But womanism does not focus solely on a social agenda.

Self-healing is among the goals. To survive, despite racist and sexist valuations, black women need to define themselves quite differently from the way they are viewed by those in power.[18]

Black Feminism: School of thought, which argues that sexism, class oppression, gender identity, and racism are inextricably bound together. The way these concepts relate to each other is called inter-sectionality. The term inter-sectionality theory was first coined by legal scholar Kimberlé Crenshaw to discuss Black Feminism, which argues that the experience of being a black woman cannot be understood in terms of being black or being a woman. Each concept is considered independently but must include the interactions that frequently reinforce each other. Combahee River argued in 1974 that the liberation of black women entails freedom for all people since it would require the end of racism, sexism, and class oppression.

Marxist and Socialist-Feminism: Feminists grounded in Marxist and socialist analysis, attributes women's oppression principally to the capitalist economic system where global corporate power prevails. Many other feminists believe that this form of power seen in the class system is a crucial factor in women's subordination but see patriarchy as the major force behind women's subjugation.

There are various ideologies associated with the feminist movement. For instance, social feminism sees women's oppression from the Marxist perspective of exploitation, oppression, and labour. They see the women as being held down as a result of their unequal standing in both the workplace and the household. Women's oppression is seen as a part of a larger pattern that affects everyone involved in the capitalist system.[19]

Eco-Feminism: This form of feminism views patriarchy and its focus on control and domination not only as a source of women's oppression but as being harmful to humanity as well as destructive to all living creatures and the earth itself. Combining a more comprehensive analysis of power, often with a greater spiritual vision, eco-feminists see women's rights and empowerment linked to political, economic, social, and cultural factors that benefit all living creatures, including Mother Nature herself.[20]

Transnational or Global Feminism: This approach to feminism is concerned mainly with how globalisation and capitalism affect people across nationalities, races, ethnicities, genders, classes, and sexualities and has reinforced a range of global movements. It recognises inequalities across different groups of women and the importance of inter- sectionality as a way to understand and engage difference. While global issues do not affect women in the same way because of these differences, the impact of these issues and power dynamics is seen to be crucial to feminist social justice agendas. This vision understands the need for comprehensive approaches that integrate multiple issues and movements to find common cause across agendas to ensure long-term social transformation.[21]

Visionary Feminism: The notion of visionary feminism, as seen in the many writings of the African-American feminist, Bell Hooks, combines the need to challenge patriarchy, class, race, and other forms of oppression such as imperialism and corporate control. She also focuses on love and the role of man. "Visionary feminism is a wise and loving politics. It is rooted in the love of male and female beings. The soul of feminist politics is the commitment to ending the patriarchal domination of women and men, as well as girls and boys. Love cannot exist in any relationship that is based on domination and coercion. In a patriarchal culture, males cannot love themselves if their very self-definition is based on submission to patriarchal rules. When men embrace feminist thinking and practice, which emphasises the value of mutual growth and self-actualization in all relationships, their emotional well-being will be enhanced. A genuine feminist politics always leads us from enslavement to liberation, from apathy to love.[22]

Conclusion

What has revolutionised the conduct of treatment for women has been the awareness of the explicit connections between the conditions in which most women live, their social status, and their mental health. Feminist theories can guide the application of this new knowledge to social work practice. Identifying when to apply which theory requires the ability to make distinctions among theoretical perspectives and a minimum level of comfort in operationalizing the theory. Here we have discussed a variety of options available to those who wish to pursue feminist approaches to intervention. Feminist theories present viable alternatives to traditional intervention, particularly for women who are interested in focusing on their needs as women. Social group work and feminist practice both promote liberating modes of human endeavour. The approaches used in the example groups corresponded with the feminist orientations of the facilitators. There were distinctions, and there was some overlap. Several women talked about using empowerment in the groups. Empowerment of women is sometimes offered as a reason for providing women's services, although it is not always clear what is meant by empowerment.

The use of a range of feminist theories seems to contribute to meeting a breadth of women's needs. It is gratifying to be able to provide examples of the progress that has been made in understanding the wide variety of experiences of women and in terms of successful outreach to marginalised populations. While it is encouraging to realise the dual focus on changing both the person and the environment is being used, perhaps greater attention to training social workers in how to incorporate both types of goals into social work practice would be beneficial. Becoming familiar with feminist theories can help social workers incorporate both personal and environmental goals into social work practice. It is important to use the tools we have, including feminist groups, to help social workers help their clients to promote a more just society. In the Indian context, some of the theories may apply, but a comprehensive approach would be more suitable.

NOTES

1. Leena Dominelli (*2002*). *Feminist Social Work: Theory and Practices*. pp. 23-40.
2. Bryson, B.L. and Lawrence, C-Webb, Race, (2001). *Social Work Practice and Profession: The Utility of Black Feminist Thought.*

3. N. Akbar, *Afrocentric Social Sciences for Human Liberation.*
4. *Op. cit.* Race, (2001). *Social Work Practice and Profession: The Utility of Black Feminist Thought,* pp. 7-17.
5. Janet A. Nes, Peter Iadicola, (1989).Toward a Definition of Feminist Social Work: A Comparison of Liberal, Radical, and Socialist Models, *Social Work*, Vol. 34(1). pp. 12–21.
6. Janet A. Nes, Peter Iadicola, (1989).Toward a Definition of Feminist Social Work: A Comparison of Liberal, Radical, and Socialist Models, *Social Work*, Vol. 34(1). pp. 12–21.
7. Eisementein, Z. (1981). *The Radical Future of Liberal Feminism.*
8. Koedt, A. (1973). *Lesbianism and Feminism* in Radical Feminism.
9. Echols, Alice. (1989). *Daring to be Bad: Radical Feminism in America 1967-1975.*
10. Echols, Alice. (1989). *Daring to be Bad: Radical Feminism in America 1967-1975.*
11. Jaggar, A.M. (1983). *Feminist Politics and Human Nature.*
12. Cannon, K. (1996). *Womanism and the Soul of the Black Community.* pp. 124-135.
13. Hooks, B. (1981). *Black Women and Feminism.*
14. Scott, J. (1980). *Deconstructing Equality* vs. *Difference* and Foucault, M. (1990). *Power/Knowledge: Selected Interviews and Other Writings 1972- 77.*
15. Josaf, G. (1981). *Women and Revolution.*
16. *Ibid.*
17. Campbell Erica, A Black Feminist Approach Towards Engaging Social Work Students in Social Justice Collaboration, *Journal of Urban Social Work*, Vol. 3, Issue S1, pp. S29-S39.
18. NASW. (1996). *The National Association of Social Work Code of Ethics*, pp. 12-30.
19. Armstrong, E. (2020). *Marxist and Socialist Feminism*, pp. 11-24.
20. Gaard, G. (2011). *Eco-feminism Revisited in Feminist Formation*, Vol. 23, No. 2.
21. Molatokunbo Seunfunmi Olutay, (2019) *Feminists Across, International Journal of Humanities and Social Science*, Vol. 9, No. 8. pp. 35-40.
22. Nkealah, N. (2007). Conceptualizing Feminism in Africa. *Journal of English Studies*. Vol. 23, Issue 1. pp. 133-141.

REFERENCES

Akbar, N. (1984). Africentric Social Sciences for Human Liberation, *Journal of Black Studies*. Vol. 14.

Armstrong, E. (2020). *Marxist and Socialist Feminism*, North-Hampton: Smith College Faculty Publication.

B.L. Bryson and Claudia Lawrence-Webb, Race, (2001). Social Work Practice and Profession: The Utility of Black Feminist Thought, *Gender and Class Journal*. Vol.-7(4).

Campbell, E. (2019). A Black Feminist Approach Towards Engaging Social Work Students in Social Justice Collaboration, *Journal of Urban Social Work*, Vol. 3, Issue S1, Springer Publishing.

Cannon, K. (1996). *Womanism and the Soul of the Black Community*. New York: Continuum Publishing Company.

Dominelli, L. (2002). *Feminist Social Work: Theory and Practices,* New York: Palgrave Publishers.

Echols, A. (1989). *Daring to be Bad: Radical Feminism in America 1967-1975*. Minneapolis: University of Minnesota Press.

Eisementein, Z. (1981). *The Radical Future of Liberal Feminism*. Boston: North-Eastern University Press.

Foucault, M. (1990). *Power/Knowledge: Selected Interviews and Other Writings 1972-77*. New York: Pantheon Books.

Gaard, G. (2011). Eco-feminism Revisited in Feminist Formation, JSTOR, John Hopkins University Press, Vol. 23, No. 2.

Hooks, B. (1981). *Black Women and Feminism*. Boston: South-End Press.

Jaggar, A.M. (1983). *Feminist Politics and Human Nature.* New York: Rowman and Littlefield Publishing.

Jane, T.A., Nes, P.L., (1989).Toward a Definition of Feminist Social Work: A Comparison of Liberal, Padical, and Socialist Models, *Social Work*, Vol. 34(1).

Josaf, G. (1981). *Women and Revolution* Boston: South End Press.

Koedt, A. (1973). *Lesbianism and Feminism* in Radical Feminism, Anne Koedt, Ellen Levine, and Anita Rapone, (Eds.), New York: Quadrangle Books.

Molatokunbo, S.O. (2019). *Feminists across International Journal of Humanities and Social Science*, Vol. 9, No. 8.

NASW (1996). *The National Association of Social Work Code of Ethics*, Washington DC: NASW Press.

Nkealah, N. (2007). Conceptualizing Feminism in Africa. *Journal of English Studies*, Vol. 23, Issue 1.

Race (2001). Social Work Practice and Profession: The Utility of Black Feminist Thought, *Gender and Class Journal*, Vol. 7(4).

Scott, J. (1980). *Deconstructing Equality versus Difference*. London: Routledge.

15

An Analysis of Social Work Intervention and People Participation in Community Mental Health Promotion

Pavithra, A.V. and *Lokesha, M.U.*

Introduction

Today, health has become a multifaceted issue. Mental health is an integral part of health and well-being. It fundamentally affects physical health, and the two are inseparable in terms of achieving a complete state of wellness. Mental health moves into the realm of the relationship between the individual, the group, and the environment. The term "mental health" encompasses a variety of human aspirations: rehabilitation of the mentally disturbed, prevention of mental disorders, reduction of tension in a conflict-laden world, and the achievement of a state of well-being in which the individual functions at a level congruent with his mental and physical potential.

The term "community", when simplified down to its most important element, is all about association. It is not just an entity or a group of people, it is a feeling. It is a feeling connected to others, as human beings are social beings. Every individual thrives when they are part of a community. This is especially true for someone with mental illness who is already experiencing the common symptoms of loneliness and isolation. The community provides many elements that are critical to mental health, namely belonging, support, purpose etc.

Community mental health denotes the context in which the organisation and functioning of the community determines or is conducive to the mental health of its members. Therefore, health services should be available to all sections of the community. It is possible if there is a will and widespread engagement. This means the participation of individuals, families, and communities in the promotion of their mental health. It also implies that the community should actively participate in the planning, execution, and maintenance of health services. If we move farther from the individual to the family, to the village, and further still to the entire community, the interplay of the factors becomes even more obvious. This becomes all the more important when we are working for the community and we have to cater to services, keeping in mind that large number of people are benefited. Hence, all our efforts have to be directed in such a way that the greatest good for the greatest number is attained. So, for social workers, it is important to recognise the determining factors or predictors of community mental health, social environment, natural environment, and political environment.

Unique Contribution of India to Community Mental Health

In the last three decades, many reforms have been initiated in mental hospitals in India by involving the family members of the people admitted and those attending the outpatient services. The strength of joint family, religion, marriage, the close-knit community, greater tolerance of deviant behaviour in the larger community, and faith-based coping and healing have all contributed to a large number of people with various mental disorders being taken care of in the community in India.

Family participation in taking care of the patients under the care of mental health services has been a unique contribution from India. It was initiated by Dr. Vidyasagar in the 1950s at Amritsar Mental Hospital, followed by the mental health centre of a Christian College, Vellore, and the All India Institute of Mental Health, Bengaluru, in the 1960s. Family members would actually be admitted along with the person with mental illness to be a part of the care for the patient. This initiative has been continued in most of the general hospital psychiatric units (GHPUs), which developed from the 1960s onwards in India. During the 1970s and 1980s, efforts were also made to understand the functioning of families with an ill person in the family and their needs.

The Significance of the Study

In India, family and community always play a key role in the management of chronic mental illness. More than 70 per cent of the people in India live in villages. An estimated 150 million people across India are in need of mental health care interventions, both short-term and long-term, according to India's latest National Mental Health Survey 2015-16. The National

Mental Health Survey of India-2016 conducted a study of 34,802 individuals, who were sampled from 12 states of India using tablet-assisted personal interviews. The results demonstrated that the prevalence rate for any mental disorder is 10.6 per cent, and approximately 150 million Indians are in need of active intervention. Despite a large number of people who need care, mental health has been truly neglected in India, rooted in stigma, taboo, and myths. Lack of awareness about the symptoms of mental illness, stigma, and the lack of mental health services available has resulted in a massive treatment gap with inadequate numbers of trained mental health care professionals.

According to the World Health Organisation, there are just 0.3 psychiatrists, 0.07 psychologists, and 0.07 social workers per 100,000 people in India. To compare, the ratio of psychiatrists in developed countries is 6.6 per 100,000 and the average number of hospitals globally is 0.04 per 100,000, while it is only 0.004 in India. The numbers highlight the crisis of proper mental health facilities, workforce, and infrastructure. Proper mental health models to create a better scenario for mental health patients is a need in the present society. All these show that there is a need to develop a unique model for community mental health in India.

Mental Health and Social Work

Social work is a unique profession that emphasises promoting the health and social well-being of individuals, families, groups, and communities. Social workers believe in the rights and dignity of all people and work to achieve social justice.Social workers work with people to assess, resolve, prevent or lessen the impact of psycho-social, physical, and mental health-related issues. Social workers are a perfect fit for primary care because it is about public participation, accessibility of services, relevant technology, interdisciplinary collaboration, and health promotion.

In India, the three broad categories of health care services in the mental health field include prevention, treatment, and rehabilitation. Specific to the domain of social work, some of the typical and important roles that social workers carry out in community mental health centres include:

- Imparting prevention education on a range of topics related to mental health issues like depression screening, sleep hygiene, self-care, stress reduction etc.
- Organizing a functional assessment and actively working towards restoration using motivational interviewing.
- Training the patients on evidence-based skills.
- Educating home-based self-management.

- Providing medication education and supporting adherence is key.
- Imparting education about welfare schemes of the government for different sections of society.
- We are collecting information about local meals, camps, community events, and resource distribution programmes.
- Decision-making ability: quick, precise, and clear during times of crisis, suggesting the best suitable referral service, taking action at times of urgent need.
- Emphasizing early intervention, individual and public education, advocacy, and improving access to services, resources, and information.
- Critical thinking-ability to evaluate client needs, the effectiveness of interventions, needs and issues of associated family members.
- Planning, organizing, and documentation.

Ways to Promote Mental Health Literacy in the Community

The majority of people with mental health issues remain untreated in the community. This untreated mental illness increases the disability associated with mental illness. So it is necessary to identify them in the early phase and connect them to the mental health system. If the detection and treatment were initiated at the early stages of the illness, the recovery would be better and the disability could be prevented to a large extent.

The most commonly used approaches to detect mental health issues in the community are organising mental health education programmes for the community through initiating capacity building programmes, sensitisation programmes and organising community mental health camps (camp approach). Mental health education programme activities are aimed at enhancing awareness about mental illness, which helps ordinary people identify people with mental health problems in their community. It comprises methods like face-to-face talk, public meetings and lectures, pamphlets, street theatre, folk dance and drama. These programmes increase treatment and help-seeking behaviour among ordinary people by increasing awareness about mental disorders. For example, SCARF (Schizophrenia Research Foundation) Chennai initiated a programme in 2011 in which a bus with multiple facilities travels from village to village spreading awareness about mental illness using TV and other means, along with psychiatric consultation and medicine.

Another way to identify and treat people with mental health problems is by training an adequate number of mental health professionals or volunteers in the community. So capacity-building programmes can be used to develop and strengthen the skills, abilities, and resources needed to handle mental health issues in the community. Groups of professionals or semi-professionals like NGO staff members, health workers, ASHA workers, school and college teachers, NSS volunteers, village leaders, and Self-Help Group members can be trained to identify and refer people with mental health issues. They can work as mediators between the mental health care system and victims of mental health problems. These trained personnel can identify people with mental health problems in the community and perform an initial screening by using simple screening tools developed for the purpose of community-level workers. For example, a research trial named MANAS (Manasanti Sushar Shodh) was conducted in Goa, where it was found that the trained counsellors' led intervention can lead to an improvement in the recovery from common mental disorders (CMD) in the community.

Another effective way to detect mental health problems in the community is by extending mental health services from the hospital to the community through organising community mental health camps or psychiatric camps. The NIMHANS community mental health camp is an example. A mental health multi-disciplinary team will go to the community and render psychiatric services. These types of camps are beneficial for extending services to a vast number of people in the community.

Social work has a long and distinguished history of service to people with mental disorders and their families. At the same time, the field of community mental health gives social workers a unique opportunity to practice collaboratively with other mental health professionals, and at the same time, it helps to maintain the integrity of their knowledge and skill base. As a result, community social workers must be knowledgeable about various types of mental health problems and disorders, how to identify them by understanding the symptoms, and other aspects related to both medical and psychosocial interventions, as well as the rehabilitation of people with mental disorders.

Review of Literature

According to Gerald Corey, problems such as depression, anxiety, substance abuse, and stress commonly affect individuals, their families, co-workers, and the broader community. In addition, they have a direct impact on workplaces through decreased productivity and increased costs. Mental health issues are the result of a complex interplay between biological, psychological, social, and environmental factors. There is increasing evidence that both the content and context of work can play a role in the development of mental health problems in the workplace.

In their study, Sini Mathew *et al.* described the role of psychiatric social workers in community mental health settings. They stressed that social-cultural factors shape a patient's ability to cope and adjust. A biomedical model is not adequate for treating mentally ill patients. Thus, psychiatric social workers have a major role in community mental health services. According to their study, the role of social workers in the multidisciplinary team in community mental health services can be broadly classified into two levels, namely micro and macro. Macro-level interventions include working with individuals, groups, and families, whereas micro-level or individual interventions comprise brief psycho-social assessments, brief therapies, and placement services. The psycho-social assessments and interventions help to diagnose the problem and to expand the management scope from the individual to family and societal levels. In addition to this, the study also found that there is a wide scope for group work methods in community settings. Social workers can be involved in group psychotherapy and group psychoeducation programmes for mentally and neurologically ill patients and families. At the family level, social workers also provide information on different benefits to mentally ill and mentally retarded people and help them get those benefits. At the macro level, psychiatric social workers perform the roles of trainer, consultant, case manager, advocate, resource mobilizer, organiser, administrator, collaborator, activist, and researcher. Finally, the study concluded that through the provision of tangible services, resource mobilization, and psycho-social intervention at the individual, family, and societal level, social workers help mentally ill people and their families achieve optimum social functioning.

In their investigation, Rangawsamy Thara *et al.*, elaborated on the emergence of community mental health services in India. According to them, due to family involvement and the unavailability of institutions, community care of the chronically mentally ill has always been prevalent in India. Some mental health clinics became functional in some parts of the country in the 1980s. Several community studies have found that one-third of the chronically mentally ill people in the community go untreated.The need to "reach the unreached" was the prime motivating factor for the community mental health movement. As a part of this effort, the Schizophrenia Research Foundation (SCARF, India) initiated a community-based mental health programme at Thiruporur in 1989 that was functional till 1999.

In their study, Chadda, R. *et al.* (2015) explained that community mental health is the treatment of people with mental disorders in the community. According to them, in ancient periods, treatment of patients with mental illness was limited to mental hospitals or asylums. The present chapter further traces the beginning of community psychiatry in India by popular social reformer Dr. Vidyasagar, where he experimented with treatment of mentally ill patients along with family members in tents outside the mental health hospital in Amritsar. The chapter also explained the role of the National Mental Health Programme and the District Mental Health Programme. The authors critically evaluated the merits and demerits of the Mental Health Care Bill as related to recent developments in community mental health in India. In addition to this, they proposed community mental health interventions in settings where services are scarce, for example, in rural areas by non-specialists. The investigation used a 3-tier model for the delivery of mental health services, consisting of an outpatient programme, the deployment of mental health workers for community care, and involvement of family members and key people in the community in the form of local health groups.

Research Methodology

Aim of the Study

The study aims to analyse social work intervention and people's participation in community mental health promotion.

Universe of the Study

The study area is at Marody village, which is located in Belthangady Taluk, Dakshina Kannada District, Karnataka. The total population of this village is approximately 5000.

Definition of Key Terms

Social Work Intervention includes participatory rural appraisal techniques, community camps, one-day workshops for lay counsellors, school mental health programmes, awareness programmes on mental health, fieldwork placements of social work students, and referral services.

People's participation is the process of engaging people in programme planning, implementation, and evaluation. These programmes are intended to promote community mental health.

Community Mental Health Promotion involves actions that improve the psychosocial well-being of the community.

Lay counsellors include school teachers, ASHA workers, SHG supervisors, Panchayat members, interesting homemakers of Marody Panchayat and social work students of Alva's College, Moodubidire.

Objectives of the Study

- To identify the prevalence of mental illness among villagers.
- To raise awareness among people regarding mental health services.
- To promote mental health literacy among people in the community.
- To analyse the role of social work intervention and people's participation in community mental health promotion.

Sample Technique

- The researcher used a convenience sampling technique for data collection.

Methods of Data Collection

- The researcher collected data from both primary and secondary sources.
- Primary data was collected through the use of a structured questionnaire constituted of closed-ended questions.
- Secondary data has been collected from books, journals, websites etc.

Data Processing

- After data collection, it was edited, coded, classified, and tabulated.

Analysis and Interpretation

The data was analysed with the help of tables, charts, and diagrams. The analysed data was interpreted accordingly. Based on the findings of the study, social work intervention was planned and implemented.

Analysis, Interpretation and Findings

The researcher conducted a survey of 100 families to identify the prevalence of mental illness among the villagers of Marody Panchayat. According to the findings of the study, more than 20 per cent of the population is dealing with a variety of mental health issues. In addition, the majority of them have poor knowledge of mental illness and are not seeking any mental health services.

Consolidated Result of Community Mental Health Survey

Sl. No.	Variables	Yes	No	Sometimes	Total
1	Specific Learning Disorders	21	79	-	100
2	Anxiety features	15	83	2	100
3	Developmental disorders	07	93	-	100
4	ADHD features	03	97	-	100
5	Mental Retardation	01	99	-	100
6	Behavioural addiction	14	85	1	100
7	Depression	12	88	-	100
8	Insomnia	19	80	1	100
9	The problem in daily routine	07	93	-	100
10	Depressive cognitions	04	96	-	100
11	Disappointment	03	97	-	100
12	Suicidal thoughts	01	99	-	100
13	Other Substance abuse	27	72	1	100
14	Family drinking	09	91	-	100
15	Compulsive thoughts	03	97	-	100
16	Cleanliness	01	99	-	100
17	Severe mental disorder	05	95	-	100
18	Paranoid ideas/ delusional disorder	01	99	-	100
19	Anxiety disorders	07	93	-	100
20	Hallucinatory behaviours	02	98	-	100
21	Delusion disorder	01	99	-	100
22	Severe Mental illness	03	97	-	100
23	Undergoing Treatment	06	94	-	100

Analysis of the Findings

The study shows that about 21 per cent of the children are victims of learning disabilities, and about 15 per cent of the children have the problem of hesitation. It is imperative to note that nearly 7 per cent of the children have problems with developmental issues, and it is even evident that 3 per cent of the children have problems with regard to concentration. Among all the families under study, one child was found to be mentally challenged.

As far as addiction to TV and mobile phones is concerned, the study shows that nearly 14 per cent of them are addicted to the same.

The study shows that about 12 per cent of the respondents are experiencing depression and another 19 per cent of the respondents are suffering from sleeplessness. Another 19 per cent of the respondents have problems with their daily routine.

In connection with the total respondents under study, nearly 4 per cent feel meaninglessness in life and about 3 per cent of them have the feeling of disappointment. It is to be noted that one of the total respondents has a suicidal tendency.

It is clear from the table that 27 per cent of the population are diagnosed with alcohol disorders, of which 9 per cent show family drinking.

It is also evident from the above table that compulsive thoughts prevail in the community as 3 per cent of respondents are diagnosed with this problem. It is also clear that 5 per cent are victims of convulsions and 1 per cent are of suspicious nature.

A serious look at the findings also reveals the presence of anxiety among 9 per cent of respondents; 2 per cent of informants are experiencing hallucinations; 1 per cent are victims of delusions in the community; and 3 per cent of respondents are experiencing severe mental illness. It also shows that a very small percentage, namely 6 per cent, of people are receiving treatment for mental health and related issues.

From the above findings, it is essential to note that there is a very limited amount of care and treatment given to people who are facing the challenges of mental health and other related issues. Immediate action is needed to prevent and reduce the burdens of mental disorder as well as death to promote mental health in the community.

Social Work Intervention and People's Participation in Community Mental Health Promotion

After a preliminary study, an initial meeting was conducted with the key people of the community. The participatory rural appraisal method was also initiated to identify and feel the needs of the beneficiary community as

well as build rapport with localites. Based on this information, researchers initiated and organised many programmes to address mental health issues prevailing in the community. Some of the important programmes are mentioned and explained here.

Community Camp: Awareness is critical in community mental health programmes. The camp approach is mostly a popular method of reaching out to the people in the community. As a part of the social work curriculum, based on the findings of the study, a community camp was organised on the theme of community mental health for 3 days. The objective of the camp was to spread awareness regarding the importance of mental health among villagers of the Marody panchayat area.

The programme targeted specific groups such as school children, adolescent girls, women, high school students, and Panchayat villagers. Experts in the field of mental health like psychiatrists, psychiatric social workers, professionals from the health department, faculties from social work, and the department were invited as resource people for the camp. Children were taught memory techniques, study methodology, relaxation techniques, and the difference between good and bad touch at the programme school programme was also organised for adolescent girls where the resource person elaborated on the importance of menstrual hygiene, common adolescent issues like physical and psychological changes, and how to deal with these kinds of changes.

The awareness session was organised for rural women folk by experts in the mental health field like psychiatrists and health professionals, who explained the common mental health issues faced by women, the stigma attached to them and also created insights about the importance of mental health. In the camp, another interesting workshop was organised for 50 high-school students (both boys and girls) on the topic of stress coping mechanisms for adolescents. In the workshop, stress coping mechanisms, effective study techniques, dealing with emotions, how to overcome suicidal thoughts and mobile addictions were taught in a participatory mode. Mediums like street plays, puppetry, and folklore traditions were used in the awareness programmes as a medium of information dissemination.

Training Programme for Lay Counsellors: As a part of community mental health promotion, a one-day workshop on mental health issues for lay counsellors was organised. School teachers, ASHA workers, SHG supervisors, Panchayat members, interested homemakers of Marody Panchayat and social work students from Alva's College participated in the programme. The vision of the programme was to build a community where everyone has the first aid skills to support people with mental health problems. The lay counsellors team was formed with the objective of creating awareness in the community, encouraging help-seeking, organising mental health camps regularly, reducing stigma and involving the community in general in the rehabilitation of the patients.

In the programme, resource people highlighted that lack of knowledge and stigmatising attitude towards mental illness may prevent people from seeking help early and also providing appropriate support to colleagues and family members. They elaborated on various kinds of mental health issues, their symptoms, and remedies. Ineffectiveness is also explained as the role of family and community in the treatment of mental illness.

In order to address mental health needs at an early stage, a programme was initiated by the social work department of Alva's College. The primary motto of the programme was to ensure the skills to assist people with mental health problems and to spread awareness beyond mental health professionals. The programme was highly interactive; the participants were made to participate in role-play, group discussion, case analysis, and other activities.

School mental health programmes were also organised in two schools in the community, which included a teacher's orientation programme where teachers were provided with the skills to identify mental health issues in the initial stage and address mental health issues. The programme also had educational enrichment programmes that covered a gamut of issues like effective study methods, preparing for the examination, taking care of mental health. A life skills training programme was also included as a part of the school mental health programme.

Field Work Placement of Students in the Community

In order to have continuity in efforts and to maintain contact with the community, social work students were placed in Marody Panchayat for a field work practicum. In the fieldwork, students were conducting home visits, studying local CBOs like Panchayats, youth clubs, SHGs, and schools, and identifying problems in the community.

Along with this, during the field work, students were facilitated to practice all the methods and techniques of social work like group work, casework, social work research, home visits, Panchayat visits, school visits, programme planning and organising based on the felt needs of the community on mental health issues.

Referral Services

In order to assist victims of mental health issues, referral services are also given by social work students to avail proper mental health services by professionals.

Analysis of Social Work Intervention

Community intervention approaches have been successfully used in this model to promote community mental health in the Marody Panchayat area. From the study, it is clear that social work intervention strategies are an effective approach for early detection and intervention of mental health issues. Community mental health programmes can be used to enhance mental health literacy in the community. Awareness and educational programmes have helped the community in allaying their fears and disseminating the right knowledge and information regarding mental illnesses. The present study explored the potential of social work intervention in the community for identification of mental illness, de-stigmatization, and awareness-building in regard to mental health problems through a series of educational programmes. All the programmes had active support from the youth, the Panchayat and school authorities. Here, community involvement proved a boon in the community mental health programme. Awareness-building and community mental health promotion were major IEC (Information, Education, and Communication) activities. It is evident from the study that interventions focusing on raising awareness of mental health issues and mobilising efforts in support of mental health are necessary and effective for addressing the present situation.

Way Forward

1. More empirical study of the factors affecting people's mental health problems needs to be carried out in the future.
2. Government and non-government programmes to enhance the quality of life of people with mental disorders need to be strengthened.

Conclusion

Social work has a long and distinguished history of service to people with mental disorders and their families. Since its inception, it has focused on the social contributions of emotional well-being and mental health. Because of the high degree of congruence between the conceptual framework through which mental health services are now provided, the value base, and the practice of social work, it is expected that the profession will play a strong leadership role in this field in the decades ahead. As a result, it is necessary to redefine social workers' current roles within the spectrum of community mental health services, identify the necessary education and knowledge base, and consider future directions. The concept of community mental health is accorded greater prominence as it requires us to think of health as something experienced not only individually, but also collectively. Community-based initiatives in the management of mental disorders will not be sustainable unless the family and community are involved in the intervention programme with constant support and guidance from mental health professionals. So, ensuring popular participation is a must in community mental health programmes.

REFERENCES

Acuin, J., Firestone, R, Htay, T.T., Khor G.L., Thabrany, H., Saphonn, V., Wibulpolprasert, S. (2011). Southeast Asia: an emerging focus for global health. *Lancet*. 2011 February 12; 377(9765): 534-5.

Chadda, R.K., Patra, B.N. and Gupta, N. (2015). Recent developments in community mental health: Relevance and relationship with the mental health care bill: *Indian Journal of Social Psychiatry,* Vol. 31, pp. 153-60.

Directorate general of health services, Ministry of health and family welfare, government of India and National Institute of Health and Family welfare: (2016). *Manual of Mental Health for Social Workers.*

Deva, P. (2007). Mental health care in Asia. *World Psychiatry*; 1: 118-20.

Gerald Corey, G. (2013), *Theory and practice of counselling and psychotherapy*, Wadsworth.

Isaac, M. (2012). Introduction. In: Chavan, B.S., Gupta, N., Arun, P., Sidana, A., Jadhav, S. (editors). *Community Mental Health in India*. New Delhi: Jaypee Brothers Medical Publishers (P) Ltd.

Kala, A. (2013). Time to face new realities; Mental Health Care Bill-2013. *Indian J Psychiatry*, 55: 216-19.

Maj, M. (2008). The WPA Action Plan 2008-2011. *World Psychiatry*, 7:129- 30

Maj, M. (2011). Report on the implementation of the WP Action Plan 2008- 2011. *World Psychiatry*, 10:161-64.

Murthy, R.S. (2004). Mental health in the new millennium: Research strategies for India. *Indian J Med Res,* 120:63-66.

Murthy, R.S. (2012). The relevance of community psychiatry in India. In: Chavan, B.S., Gupta, N., Arun, P., Sidana, A., Jadhav, S., (eds.). *Community Mental Health in India*. New Delhi: Jaypee Brothers Medical Publishers (P) Ltd., pp. 3-22.

Ruchiwit, M.A. (2016). Study of the holistic health status of the peoples in the Greater Mekong Sub-region Countries. *Ponte, 72*(5):100-118.

Secretariat A.S.E.A.N. ASEAN economic community blueprint.http:// www.asean.org/wp-content/uploads/archive/5187-10.pdf

Mathew, M. & Sekar, K. (2007). Community mental health care programmes at NIMHANS-*Handbook of Psychiatric Social Work*, Bangalore.

Rangaswamy, T. (2012).Twenty-five years of schizophrenia: The Madras longitudinal study, *Indian journal of psychiatry*, 54, 134-7.10.4103/0019-5545.99531

Thara, R. (2002). Community mental health in India: Avision beckoning fulfilment? *Can J Commun Ment Health*, 21: 131-137.

Thara, R. & Padmavati, R. (2013), Community mental health care in South Asia, *World Psychiatry*,12:176-177.https:??doi.org? 10.1002?wps.20042

Varma, V.K. & Gupta, N. (2009). Changing mental health services, In: Varma, V.K., Kala, A.K., Gupta, N. (eds.). *Culture, Personality and Mental Illness*. New Delhi: Jaypee Brothers Medical Publishers (P) Ltd.; 2009.

Wickramage, K., Suveendran, T. & Mahoney, J. (2009). *Mental health in Sri Lanka. Evaluation of the impact of community support officers (CSO) in mental health service provision at the district level*. Colombo: WHO Country Officc,

World Health Organisation (1997). *Health for All the Twenty-first Century*. Geneva: World Health Organisation.

Young, M.E. (1992).*Counselling Methods and Techniques: An Electic Approach*. New York: Macmillan.

16

Challenges and Concerns in Indigenising Social Work Education and Practice in India

Pankaj Kumar and *Jaspreet Singh*

Introduction

The term "indigenous" is primarily used to refer to First Nations, Inuit, and native people. Historically, public policy and law referred to natives and Indians (Choate, 2019). Indigenous knowledge implies that knowledge has to take into account the socio-economic conditions and culture of the region in which it is to be applied. In addition, the field experience of professionals involved in imparting knowledge should also focus on the need to find a place in the knowledge base. According to Khinduka (1987),

> "*The knowledge base of social work is a composite of knowledge produced indigenously in the local, socio-economic and cultural context by social work professionals and knowledge derived predominantly from other disciplines by professionals after analysing and evaluating it with reference to their own practice experiences.*"

The meaning of "indigenous knowledge" is not clear. In its literal sense, the word "Swadeshi" refers to people or things originating from or originating from a particular geographical location. The word has two meanings. Firstly, it is related to a person or something that either rises from the root in one place or lives there. The current understanding of "indigenization" is that knowledge of social work must originate from within the culture, reflect local practices and practices, and be interpreted within a local frame of reference, thus locally relevant. It should be culturally relevant and address context-specific problems. It invokes indigenous research, which adequately represents and reflects on the cultural context in which problems arise. As a result, the development of indigenous knowledge is reversible, and researchers and social workers must incorporate their perspectives on local cultures, society, and history into their work (Yang, 2005). Proponents of indigenous education say that no discipline has the necessary tools or principles to address the complexity of the society in which we live (Hertel, 2016).

Indigenous knowledge should also be developed more independently. Some scholars argue that this feature restricts the discussion to knowledge that precedes "modern" influences, but most argue that due to the permeability of the boundaries of knowledge through trade, travel, and colonization, indigenous knowledge should be recognised as the knowledge that has arisen systematically. For example, while very high-standard basket weaving is indigenous to northern Botswana, its symmetrical designs are not because Swedish, not local, consultants introduced them to increase the appeal of baskets to the tastes of Western consumers. In social work and social development, indigenous knowledge can be an element, as new ideas and models can be incorporated as part of the new models if they fit existing practices, beliefs, and understanding. Certainly, many of the social problems in India can be solved.

Indigenous Social Work

Indigenous knowledge is local knowledge, unique to a given culture or society (Langill *et al.* 1998; Dumbrill and Green, 2008). Indigenous social work emphasises cultural relevance and culturally specific knowledge and education, which may or may not be universal or cross-indigenous. (Hart, 2002). The two streams of literature deal with indigenous social work, and both relate to contexts where there is a history of colonization. One region is born in developing countries in Africa, Asia and South America, and the other is born in developed Western contexts such as the United States, Canada, and Australia, where it is primarily concerned with vocational education and practice that is tribal or belongs to the people of the First Nation. However, regardless of origin, it is not necessary that the knowledge that originated from its place of origin under the indigenous process should be only for the tribal or people of the First Nation, nor is it a social function for developing countries. Indigenous social work refers to a form that will seek effective, culturally appropriate research, education, and practice. Indigenous social work will be instrumental in mainstreaming developed Western countries, helping to develop models that are relevant to countries with culturally diverse customer populations.

To strengthen the social work profession, knowledge for social work education and training has to be rooted in the local cultural context. The teacher who is using the teaching material for learning should keep in mind that the praxis knowledge is at the local level and at the grassroots level, it is in line with socio-economic and cultural realities. Incorporating indigenous knowledge into the profession of social work learning is important because it includes the knowledge that service users and careers bring to the profession.

It has been customary to date the beginning of professional social work in India to 1936, when the first school of social work was established in Bombay. But those who have studied the history and philosophy of social work in India know that there has been a long and ancient tradition of social work practice in India. The motivation for this can be varied; it can be religious, humanitarian, secular, or rational-secular. There were several streams, including donations, relief, social reform, and institutional welfare services. Most of it was a voluntary effort, and in the intervening history, the state got some support from it. It was extended under official orders or administered with legislative support. It is very long and even history has been briefly examined.

In the social work occupation, Indigenous people are often viewed through the same lens, working with people from outside these cultures. Not surprisingly, social work literature views its work with indigenous peoples from a cross-cultural, anti-oppressive, or structuralism point of view.

However, the status of social work education in India remains a matter of debate even today as it has still not achieved its professional status. Kulkarni has written a note in the *Indian Journal of Social Work*. This article is a response to some of the assumptions and comments stated in the "note". In all fairness, those assumptions etc., can be quoted first:

1. The models of social work education that have developed in the developing countries seem to have been imported from Western social work education. (Kendall).
2. "These (developing) countries, which were predominantly rural, had adopted the American urban models of education" (Brigham).
3. The note then quotes Kendall again (1986) and adds, "particularly in Asia, the efforts towards indigenization of the curriculum to increase its relevance to the local situation seem to move rather slowly. Equally important is the slow process of indigenization of the body of knowledge in these countries, which is the key to the indigenization of social work education and practice.

4. The note finally sums up by saying that "the distinguishing features of Asian social work professionals do not emerge."

This article is limited to social work education and practice in India only. An attempt has been made to outline the origins and development of social work education and practice in India. Reviews and analysis are presented in a continuous flow. Therefore, it does not necessarily coincide with the sequence in which the points quoted from the search editor's note are listed above. However, it hopes that it will adequately indicate clearly if the social work profession in India is indigenous and, if so, its nature and extent. It was important to understand the ideas of great Indian thinkers like Mahatma Gandhi, Swami Vivekananda, Rabindranath Tagore, and Dr. Ambedkar who had access to the Western world and also the experiences of colonialism. He strongly felt that the indigenous orientation of Indian education was a must. According to Tagore, narrow utilitarianism was not the ultimate aim of education. For him, education that was rooted in the society's history, economy, and culture was important in ensuring social equality (Mukherjee, 1962). Swami Vivekananda, who first got his recognition in America, said "We shall add to our stock what others have to teach, but we must always be careful to keep intact what is essentially our own." According to Dr. Ambedkar, there was a vision to bring equality in society through education. According to him, "It is education that is the right weapon to cut social slavery and it is education which will enlighten the downtrodden masses to come up and gain social status, economic betterment, and political freedom."

These ideas of our great thinkers underscore the importance of making local knowledge relevant. According to these thinkers, the literature emanating from the West was not irrelevant but needed to be made relevant in view of the history, culture, and society of India. Knowledge generators always test their knowledge formation through social interactions. According to role theory, social work teachers have a role in developing new knowledge over time. According to role theory, social work teachers are knowledge bearers to strengthen social work education with indigenous knowledge. To understand the importance, one has to search a lot for the visionary's vision and practice to make it more relevant.

Global Influence on Social Work in India

Social work education in India is offered at Bachelors, Master, M.Phil., Ph.D. level and also various other diploma and certificate courses offered through the various universities in India but the social work curriculum in India is highly dominated by the West (Baikady and Shengli, 2020,

Dash, 2020). The biggest challenge in India in identifying and using social work practice is that Indian social work education is usually associated with other disciplines and has gone through identity issues that need to be re-examined. Social work education in India requires review and radical changes (Nadkarni and Joseph, 2014). Social work in India is interdisciplinary in nature where the theories and approaches are borrowed from different disciplines like psychology, sociology, anthropology, philosophy, women's studies, economics, education, medicine, law, and administration. And this interdisciplinary study and approach contribute to a better understanding of overall human behaviour, issues, and concerns (Singh and Crawley, 2011). The global curriculum cannot be used to justify local issues and requirements.The magnitude and depth of the problem in one place differ from the other (Baikady & Channaveer, 2020). The curriculum structure is unique and different in all the schools of social work in India. There are a few schools that have attempted to incorporate indigenous, regional, and local context-specific content into the curriculum, but the majority of schools continue to use Western-influenced methods such as casework, group work, and community development (Dash, 2018).The other thing is the lack of a professional identity. Social work in India is still struggling to create its own space and identity. It is very common that many times, social work is linked with other disciplines like psychology, sociology, and so on.

Global Perspectives on Indigenizing Social Work Education and Practice

Globalization is a highly competitive concept. Globalization is interpreted as a long-term, complex, and multi-phased historical process, less than a reliance on the subtle and shifting between local and global, or universal and particular. Global globalisation holds that non-Western societies modernise in specific and selective ways relative to the West. It is important for indigenous people that the first wave of globalisation be called "germinal". In the second phase, Europe extended its influence from the mid-15th century to the middle of the eighteenth century. The third stage take-off sees a strong articulation of the principles of national self-determination and identity, and the fourth—struggle-for-hegemony—the creation of the Third World. In the fifth phase of uncertainty—from the late 1960s to 2000, global "civil society" perceptions and global citizenship were exposed to contemporary "risks" (Gray & Hetherington, 2013). This is the phase in which the indigenous struggle began with the formation of the International Working Group for Indigenous Affairs (IWGIA), an international human rights organisation formed in 1968 by human rights activists and anthropologists, which has led Indigenous organisations worldwide. This all shows that there is a highly complex interplay between the global and the local in many ways (Grey, 2005).

An Indian Perspective on Indigenizing Social Work Education and Practice

The social work curriculum in Indian universities includes history and philosophy of social work, human society, dynamics of human behaviour, Indian social problems, areas of social work, welfare services, social work practices in different fields etc. As previously stated, Western social work practices and theories dominate the Indian social work curriculum. Indian civilization is considered to be around 3000 years old, whereas Indian society is a pluralistic society which is rich and diverse in history and philosophy. This philosophy can become a precursor to professional social work and will play an important role in giving a new direction to the indigenization of the practices of social work in India. It has also been noticed that the courses in social work in Indian institutions are not local-centric. Many of the theories and practices have neither been practiced nor do people believe that there is a need to adopt these practices into the field. As mentioned above, India is a diverse culture, and the issues and challenges faced by the people are far different to those of Western people. To understand the issues and challenges, the first thing that is needed is good research that focuses on local context and problems, that is, regional and national level problems. The second is action research, which should be oriented towards the solution of concrete problems, and the third is a practical approach to problems. It is more concerned with local and cultural relevance than with universal variables or principles (Gray & Ceates, 2020).

The Indigenization Movement in the Social Sciences

Globally, indigenization is the process in which third-world countries are re-establishing their birthplaces for better use in social science and social work. Due to imperialism and the inspiration to be modern, Third World countries and cultures have invoked Western values and ideals of liberalism, democracy, and freedom in the past. But their faith could not last long, and the Third World countries aroused their indigenous cultural confidence, and they began to aspire to reclaim their traditional cultures and values. There has been rapid development in the areas of post-colonial, de-colonial, and indigenous research paradigms, which has attracted everyone's attention towards the discourse of indigenization. This is a concept that is clearly reflected in post-colonial paradigms.

In the field of social science, the indigenization movement is one such movement that has been started to promote our indigenous knowledge. The indigenization movement has emerged rapidly in the last 5 decades. Because many social scientists claim that third world countries are facing political colonialism as well as academic slavery. India's social work curriculum seems to require changes and updates in order to meet the needs of the present day (Baikady *et al.*, 2014). According to Shukla and Dash (2020), Indian social work has not been adequately modified to address local cultural contexts and problems.The cultural diversity present in India, along with the diversity prevailing in India, is becoming a challenge for the development of the curriculum. Students in India have to reflect on caste and class to a large extent. Attention to diversity and cross-cultural training is mandated by the Indian Association of Social Workers for social work education. However, there is some empirical evidence that suggests progress by individual schools of social work in explaining diversity and incorporating it into their programmes.

Sociologists who support indigenization believe that Western countries have done the work of transplanting knowledge slavery to our countries. With this view, Third World countries gave birth to the indigenization movement and sparked the debate on indigenization. Some proponents of indigenization began to challenge the beliefs of Western philosophy and also attacked Western principles. As such, the cause of purpose, cultural knowledge, dualism between religion and science etc., began to be increasingly criticized. Proponents of indigenization argue that a new concept needs to be developed based on indigenous intellectual tradition, history, culture, food etc. to formulate the principle of social science. Some proponents of indigenization believe that social science is universal, but they argue that concepts and principles derived from Western civilization cannot be the same for everyone.The indigenization of social science has given rise to many new theories and models. Chang (2005) developed three new models that strengthened indigenization: the Transnational Model, the Theoretical-reasoning Model, and the Grounded Model. The Transnational Model attacks the blind application of Western concepts and theories to non-Western societies and strongly supports the study of new theories created by indigenous scholars. The Theoretical-reasoning Model focuses on socio-cultural criticism and attacks the dominance of empiricism in the Western social sciences. Grounded Modĕl emphasises the importance of ground research along with fieldwork and focuses on problem-solving and developing agendas for indigenous society from indigenous scholars (Yunong & Xiong, 2008). The benefits of indigenization in the social sciences started to come in the 1970s. And it is said that indigenization has become an important factor for the development of social science in third-world countries. Despite the development of many theories, principles, and models of indigenization, many sociologists have believed that social science should not be indigenized because the concept of indigenization cannot be applied to science (Alatas, 2002).

Debate on Indigenizing Social Work

Why do Indian and African countries, in particular, need to build their brand? Usually some questions are raised, such as the first being that the social problems of the two countries are quite different from the Western countries, the second being that both these countries are poor, the third being that the administrative and organisational structures of these countries are quite weak, and the fourth being that leaders of these two countries require strong commitment to deal with social problems. Fifth, Western theory has not been developed keeping in mind the culture of these countries, and so many principles do not apply. Most of the social scientists in India argue that the problems of India are very different from the problems of Western countries. Like homelessness, domestic violence, drug abuse, negative attitude towards women, poverty, unemployment, population explosion, communalism, youth dissatisfaction, elder abuse, bonded labour etc., there are many major social problems. Whereas Western countries have very few social problems of this type. Therefore, indigenization in the context of Indian society should go to the root of these social problems and try to find a solution.

The term indigenization has been used in almost the opposite sense, which means increasing the local stake in the indigenization of foreign-owned companies or creating new knowledge by adopting local methods such as beliefs and customs. The notion of indigenization first emerged in relation to social work in 1971, when the United Nations international survey of social work training was used to refer to the inappropriateness of American social work principles. At this conference, the importance of its socio-cultural, political, and economic characteristics was also emphasised for each country, and it was said that in the indigenization of social work, each country has to respond to the specific social problems, needs, and values of their country. Western social work principles can be amended (Yunong & Xiong, 2008). Social scientists from developing countries, in particular, began to argue that the principles and skills of socialism apply in Western countries because their societies are compatible with it, but underdeveloped countries began applying Western social work theory and techniques without first examining their applicability. Midgley accused Western countries of establishing a new colonialism in a more subtle and effective way to assert their dominance over developing countries in the name of serving individualism, humanism, and liberalism in developing countries (Midgley, 1981). Cheung and Liu (2004) in their literature review suggested five guidelines to promote indigenous social work in developing countries. In the first, he explained the indigenous basis of social work education, in which it suggested the creation of philosophical basis, theory, work, and new approaches. The second is to solve social problems and formulate strategies in the context of indigenous social development. The third is to redefine the basis of knowledge and value, the central focus of social work practice in Western countries, and to develop an indigenous conceptual framework and methodologies for it. In the fourth premise, it was accepted for indigenous people to accept historical and cultural experiences and realities as they were. The fifth describes conducting social work practice in the context of local community expertise and resources (Cheung & Liu, 2004). Yip (2005), in his chapter "A Dynamic Asian Response to Globalization in Cross-Cultural Social Work", gave five suggestions for social work practice, the first involving adaptation to Western social work practice, the second implementation in the local context, the third local indigenous criticism of the effects of professional imperialism and colonialism, and the fifth skill involved the engineering of technology (Yip, 2005).

Sociologists of Third World countries believe that the principles, models, etc. used in social work fail to help those who need tangible and immediate help because the principles and models of social work are not relevant. The principles and models of social work do not work to eliminate structural problems. Therefore, all sociologists and social workers criticise the theory and models of social work as well as the whole of social science, and hence social work education is called "Eurocentric." Those who solve the problems of the individual and society on the basis of local knowledge and indigenous culture are dismissed as "witchdoctors" or "traditional healers" or "underdeveloped". (Bar-On, 2014).

Criticism of reconstructing social functions to fit different societies takes three forms. The first is what can be called a "We are all human and so we are the same" thesis. This idea does not mean that all people are equal, but that their nature is. It can be said in a form, but can it be valid for all societies that we are all human beings in common? Thus, we assume that by employing the same principles, models, and technology for all, we can manage all at once, but can it be possible while the nature, culture, language, and social problems of all societies are also different? Clarkson's (1974) made an announcement to all that "a spirit of adventure" is needed among Western teachers to teach in developing countries (Clarkson, 1974). Also, those who believe that social work is a science and therefore, supernatural in nature, and conversely, those who believe that it "to convey a sense of human warmth and build up the dignity of those with whom it deals."

The second category is ideology. To challenge the social work models of Western countries, arguments have to be made against them. One such argument derives from the practicality of social work, which not only emphasises the need to explain the beliefs and structures of society, but also emphasises its justice. It is argued that endeavours of this nature do not have universal standards because the values and behaviour of particular societies are limited to them and therefore, have no trust with outsiders. The argument stems from the New Right's belief that, according to this situation, collective problems do not occur but are the problems of an individual, and that such problems can only be controlled at the individual level.

Finally, a third school of thought denies the need for indigenization as it already is. For example, most social scientists have suggested that since there are different societies all over the world that have different cultures, social work training should be different across the world and hence its practice should be different. Furthermore, social scientists in the West believe that the idea of indigenization is very insulting because it suggests that the individual's concerns are "too weak to resist opposition to foreign perspectives."

In short, social work works with people; people are well connected with their surroundings, and culture is an important contributor to the development of the personality of any society. The social worker of any country should resolve that social work in that country should be based on "multi-dimensional empowerment," which includes everything personal, social, educational, economic, and political. Social workers should intervene in every aspect of human existence, possibly because, at least in India, they know better than anyone else how to advance the human condition. Those who do social work on the basis of righteousness, it has to be noted that religion works to spread all kinds of good qualities—good thoughts, good words, good works—and, as a result, all the work should be the same. Yes, it must be written against any form of discrimination, and it should always be rectified.

Why Indigenous Social Work in India?

In simple terms, indigenous means something that is native, local, or more of its own (Islam, 2018). Indigenous social work is the change or transformation of some services, approaches, models, ideas, and theories into the local context and also in accordance with the culture, beliefs, ideas, and needs of the particular society. For instance, in India, there are problems like the caste system, dowry system, poverty, terrorism, illiteracy, unemployment, population explosion, drug abuse, violence against women, tribal unrest, and so on. The rapid change in societies and the social economic position in society need interventions that are more local or indigenious to the people of the community. The other challenge is that the nature, magnitude, or depth of the problem in one state or district is totally different from that in another. India is a diverse social, cultural, economic and political milieu and it is not easy to take a single model or approach to tackle the entire problem. Even India's problems and issues are vastly different from those of any other country in the West.To address these problems, there is a high need for professional social workers in India trained in Indian indigenous methods and approaches. Social work education in India is not new and it is eight decades old. Social services and charity are deeply rooted in Indian society. Social work practice in India has gone through a drastic change from a religious to welfare to a right-based approach.

Indigenous social work in India is the need of the hour. But the high preference for Western theories and practices in social work education makes our profession invisible. To make it possible, we first need to build the framework and the approaches relevant to contemporary Indian society (Yip, 2006) stated three approaches to indigenous social work, i.e.

> There are many practices in social work which are assumed to be universal and are called "Eurocentric Social Work Practices." It is not applicable to all possible cultures. On the other hand, there is a need to redefine or reshape the meaning of social work in a local context. This is more about culturally specific, culturally competent and authentic to the culture.

Dominance: Minority: There are various disciplines which tend to be dominant towards the discipline of social work. The other thing is that in all societies, there is one culture that is dominant towards others, and this dominant culture has a great extent of influence on the minority, which leads to the suppression and negligence of the culture of the minority. There is a need to give equal importance to all the cultures in society. For this, we need to have a bicultural or multicultural practice of social work. The social worker has to be aware of social exclusion, social inclusion, and oppressed ethnic groups in society. Social work also has to learn about the empowering process of minority ethnic groups in the larger society.

Many times, there are chances that a client may be influenced and confused between their past experiences and the current situation. This may be because of their ethnic culture and tradition, as well as their new or current exposures. This social worker has to be sensitive towards the traditional culture, customs, and norms of the client.

Challenges in Social Work

Lawyers and medical practitioners believe that social work is similar to them and treat their clients with great demeanour during their work. Is it necessary for social work students and practitioners to be able to critically question the practice, the principles, in order to determine whether the practice is morally serving the population of that country? In the last few years, many efforts have been made to indigenize social work education and practice in India. It is not right to say how far this effort will be successful. If it is successful, then it is very important to consider the problems of indigenization. Some of the following problems may occur:

1. Since social work is an interdisciplinary field, psychology will be needed to understand the personality of the person. Thus, it is difficult for students to relate to the local socio-economic and psycho-social conditions of India.
2. For indigenization, a lot of changes have to be made in the curriculum and new courses have to be adjusted, which is not so easy.
3. Students mostly have to depend on foreign textbooks, so students do not understand the practical situation of the country properly and fail to solve the problems.
4. As the subject of social work in India has still not been professionally recognised and there is no separate system for admission to the university for studying social work in India, even though it is different from other subjects, such as social work programmes in other countries, separate test arrangements have been made to select students for admission.
5. And finally, India lacks financial and other resources, such as education equipment, infrastructure etc., for indigenization.

Way Forward

1. The educational reading material and instruction are available in English only, and in India, most people do not know English language as English is not their first language. So, the books and reading material need to be available in the regional languages so that they can be approachable by every individual.
2. There is a dearth of literature available on indigenous social work. Efforts should be made to develop more indigenous literature.
3. Indigenous practices' approaches and models should be developed to tackle the local concerns and issues.
4. There is an urgent need to review India's current social work education curriculum.

REFERENCES

Alatas, S.H. (2002). The Development of an Autonomous Social Science Tradition in Asia: Problems and Prospects. *Asian Journal of Social Science, 30*(1), 150-157. Retrieved on July 19, 2020, from www.jstor.org/stable/23654629

Baikady, R., Pulla, V., & Channaveer, R.M. (2014). Social Work Education in India and Australia. *International Journal of Social Work and Human Services Practice*, 311-318.

Baikady, R. & Channaveer, S.I.C. (2020). Eight decades of Existence and search for Identity: Educators perspective on social work education in Contemporary India. *Social Work Education the International Journal*, 1-16.

Bar-On, A. (2014). Indigenous practice: Some informed guesses—self-evident but impossible. *Social Work/Maatskaplike Werker, 39*(1), 26-40.

Cheung, M. & Liu, M. (2004, January). The self-concept of Chinese women and the indigenization of social work in China. *International Social Work, 47*(1), 109-127.

Choate, P. W. (2019). The Call to Decolonize: Social Work's Challenge for Working with Indigenous Peoples. *British Journal of Social Work*, 1081-1099.

Clarkson, E.M. (1974). The contribution of casework to Social development. *International Social Work, 17*(3), 43-49.

Dash, B.M. (2020). Movement towards Indianisation of Social Work Education. In: S.M.S., Baikady, R., Sheng-LiC., Sakaguchi, H. (eds.), *The Palgrave Handbook of Global Social Work Education*. Palgrave Macmillan, Cham., pp. 393-405.

Dash, B.M. (2018). Revamp Social Work Education, *The Pioneer*, March 14, retrieved from https://www.dailypioneer.com/2018/avenues/revamp-social-work-education.html

Gray, M. (2005). Dilemmas of international social work: Paradoxical processes in indigenization, universalism and imperialism. *International Journal of Social Welfare*, 231-238.

Gray, M. & Ceates, J. (2020). Indigenization' and knowledge development: Extending the debate. *International Social Work*, 1-15.

Gray, M. & Hetherington, T. (2013). Indigenization, indigenous social work and decolonization: Mapping the theoretical terrain. *Decolonizing Social Work*, 5.

Hart, M.A. (2002). Seeking mino-pimatisiwin: an aboriginal approach to social work practice. *Native Social Work Journal, 2*(1), 91-112.

Hertel, A. (2016). Applying Indigenous Knowledge to Innovations in Social Work Education. *Research on Social Work Practice, 27*(2), 1-3.

Islam, M.F. (2018). *In Quest for Indigenous Social Work Education and Practice in Bangladesh: Complexities and Prospects*. Retrieved July 22, 2020, https://www.researchgate.net/publication/327535239_In_Quest_for_ Indigenization_ of_Social_Work_Education_and_Practice_in_ Bangladesh_ Complexities_ and_Prospects.

Midgley, J. (1981). Professional Imperialism: Social Work in the Third World. *Heinemann Educational Books, 28*(1), 191.

Singh, S., J.E. & Crawley, G.B. (2011). Predicting India's Future: Does it justify the Exploration of US Social Work Education? *Social Work Education: The International Journal*, 861-873.

Shukla, S. & Dash, B.M. (2020). Colonial legacy and professional imperialism in social work: Calls for Bharatiyakaran/Indianisation of social work education in India, *African Journal of Social Work, 10*(2), 16-22.

U.G.C. (2001). *UGC Model Curriculum on social work education.* New Delhi: University Grants Commission.

Yang, R. (2005). Internationalization, Indigenization and Educational Research in China. *Australian Journal of Education, 49*(1), 66-88.

Yip, K.S. (2005). A Dynamic Asian Response to Globalization in Cross-Cultural Social Work. *International Social Work, 48*(5), 593-607. Retrieved July 22, 2020, from Social Work Education? *Social Work Education: The International Journal*, 861-873. https://www.researchgate.net/publication/249729970_A_ Dynamic_Asian_ Response_to_Globalisation_in_Cross-Cultural_Social_ Work.

Yip, K.S. (2006). Indigenization of social work an international perspective and conceptualization. *Asia Pacific Journal*, 43-55.

Yunong, H. & Xiong, Z. (2008). A reflection on the indigenization discourse in social work. *International Social Work, 51*(6), 611-622. Retrieved July 19, 2020, from https://journals.sagepub.com/doi/pdf/10.1177/0020872808093340.

17

Indigenous Model of Intervention in Coping with Ruins of COVID-19

Yugal Jha

Introduction

During the present time, the whole world is fighting and facing the mishap and downfall due to coronavirus infection. The present pandemic COVID-19 has shattered the schedule of world affairs and India as well. With the outbreak of COVID-19, we have to take necessary precautions to combat COVID-19. The Indian Government has outlined many of her policies to make its impact lesser till its end. The scenario is presenting a very pathetic picture that compelled the world people to struggle with its infections altering to lives and beliefs of the whole society.

The coronavirus pandemic is an infectious disease that has created respiratory illness. COVID-19 has infected and sickened millions of people in the world. It is having a capability of transmission to infect the people in a chain. The best way to prevent the slowdown of its transmission is to keep oneself away from the infected chain of persons. However, there are many ongoing clinical trials evaluating potential treatments and vaccination has also been developed recently. The coronavirus impact will remain an endemic disease such as malaria and dengue for many years. The impact of this has necessitated for adoption of new life style.

Now, we have to adopt some basic principles for a new lifestyle with the physical distancing, behavioural changes in life conduct and cultural set of preservation are the positive effect of novel corona that paved us for the modern lifestyle and culture from many guilt of pollution and guts of diseases. We are not at all caring about hygiene during travel time in metro, trains, and in true sense with a set of unhealthy life-style just to win the race of this worldly life. Even we are not caring about nature, animals and living and non-living organism surrounding life. The new era just peeped into the walk of human life a new kind of life with modified dignity, purity, and security coping with the new pillars of crisis management to overcome the corona effect. Due to the shockingly poor state of implementation for the well-being of rural migrant workers to save them from the heat of COVID-19, the entire set of system needs to be much more comprehensive and vibrant as watching dog check the proper implementation of the different schemes for their livelihood, health care sanitation and accommodation.[1] The gist of these indicators drive one to conclude main objectives of good governance is to remove the hurdle of the distressed people under the impact of this COVID-19. Today the entire world and India are mitigating the challenges with the commitment as an exemplar model of human service that can be replicated in the whole world. The Government of India's actions are being praised by WHO (World Health Organization) for facing a global epidemic that is challenging the existence of human civilization. Likewise, India has given relief to the sufferers of this epidemic of 55 countries of the world by lifting the export ban on essential medicine for the curative measures of the human population. In this unprecedented situation, lockdown, isolation, and distance are the only preventing measure for lesser impact of this pandemic and get the people ready for their routine of day-to-day life and to restore the livelihood system being stay blessed in their original home places.

Let us think about our governance to enkindle the humanitarian approach on public health care system and food supply system within the boundary of natural vegetation based on local governance on the vocal system of decentralization through Panchayati Raj Institution to combat issues and challenges under the impact of COVID-19 in India. This is the time to initiate a dialogue on how to build a sustainable and climate-friendly future India facing how many lockdowns are unnoticed to all under the impact of post-coronavirus till the normal deliverance of the system of the country. The structure of the democratic republic could be rebuilt to face any disaster management with the enforcement of existing rule and regulation strengthening local communities, institution and local bodies, resilience, rethinking power sector project a nd agriculture, good governance and green job in order to attain sustainability and vibrant India with their huge demographic human capitals which are facing great hardships in overcoming the impact of COVID-19.

Some misconception that Indian society is inflicted with narrow consideration like religion, caste, prejudices, and ideology as well as socially and economically fragmented, therefore, it will be major challenges to handle the impact of this COVID-19 crisis successfully. Government of India has been trying its best for the marginalized people of the nation to overcome this pandemic. The stunning scenario is that Indian society is trying to cope with challenges with a commitment of fellow-feeling through its social organization in a time of crisis. Most of the organization are formed by the volunteer is of a very subtle label formed out of their love and self-motivation for the care and well-being of marginalized sections of the victims of COVID-19. The purpose of these thousands of groups is completely unique Indian model of service that is generated by society for society and from society. As a result of these million humanitarian activities serving the needy affected people who are also self-reliant and not dependent on anyone rather fully competent in providing local resources in achieving the social purpose of their service.

The slogan of the present government 'vocal for local' is just the revision of gram swaraj—the perfect Indigenous model of village government, many times uttered by Mahatma Gandhi and many social reformers like Dr. Lohiya, Loknayak Jay Praksh and Pt. Din Dayal Upadhyay which has been neglected in the governance of the democratic system of India. Today, the government is bound to design a profile of development paradigm for self-governing village or village republic and not merely a village panchayat to constitute the bricks of new India that incorporates with the indigenous approach of the farming set of the governance where the village autonomy[2] will provide every input and output for the good fortune of the community. The impact of coronavirus had ruined the total accommodation set of migrant labour in India. Thus an alternative village government system with its quality governance based on local resources and resistance must be designed to overcome the restless livelihood system of the present pandemic affected miliions of unorganized labourer of the nation.

The global vision of human liberty for the human society is the village republic system based on the autonomous rural economy, signifying with the sense of equalitarian society, social justice and peace. The vocal agency of local system has proven its best configuration with Panchayati Raj Institution. The Panchayati Raj Act of December 1992, easily constitute a milestone in the history of 'Gram Swaraj' as Gandhi spoke "freedom from meanest of our countrymen."[3] The amendment, in fact, aimed at enhancing the capabilities of the rural people to evolve themselves in the planning process with the respect to their priorities. It also exercises decentralization of the execution of all types of development of activities with the active participation of the masses. Today, the impact of COVID-19 and its prevailing cycle of post COVID-19 paved a new channel for the entire system of this nation to redesign the people voices into the policy choices. The prevailing situation compelled the set up for a societal change with their mindset for the economy, ecology and cultural constructive social reconstruction with their affirmative and formative direction of local boosted planning. Prof. Shekhar Sharma, Director CSIR, said 'The horrible situation of globalization can be revamped by the affirmative movement of Swadeshi'[4] which has been a movement of the visionary of India for their local governance in quality assignment into action for small scale industry and innovative skill of the self-reliant the village Republic of India.

One of the agro-scientist Mr. Prabhu in his writing 'Indigenous farming and local governance gave his findings of the traditional method of the water storage system of habitat and habitation of India in its remote village with participatory community approach for the development of a new ideology called eco-feminism with the gist of the green economy is one of the most important tools to design the new prosperous area of village republic to lessen the impact of coronavirus from the domain of urban and rural people of India.

The specific feature of Indigenous society has been sketched in the book of 'Santhal Village Government' by W.W. Hunter, 1868 and by the settlement officer John Rid, in the report of irrigation and canal commission 1901-1903 about the traditional resource inventory of seasonal farming of the pageantry set of agricultural input which has been a great source of local governance to develop new design of innovative skill to recapitulate the basic amenities of huge humane capital with the attachment to water, forest, land, and its street, open field, trees, hills and sacred grooves that surround their settlements and protect their well-being in the different remote corner of India. As one of the Sarvodaya saint Vinoba Bhave explains the concept of village government to signify people's democracy without any expensive election with the participatory approach of Lok Niti. It was late 1951 when Vinoba Bhave launched Bhoodan Movement to share equal land from each and every zamindar of Indian village for the Gandhian way of Gram Rajya in which every family must have an equal share of their livelihood in their peasantry culture. This governance of *lok-niti* has given an aura of a great communitarian set of governance that inspired Lok Nayak Jay Prakash (JP) for a party-less democracy in Indian governance of the village system. JP's call for the construction of Indian polity advocated a self-governing village or a village republic not merely a village panchayat. Such village could at once become centres of struggle and resistance during a revolution and would constitute the bricks with which structure of the rural economy of village governance could be built in the Indian republic system. The Great social scientist Vinoba Bhave explains it in his book 'Sarvodya', the single motto of Gram Raj[5] is the genuine set of Indian visionary that involves each and entire 'villages' configuration in its decentralized collaboration for political, cultural, moral and economic power at all levels.

Like the concept of Sarvodaya, the Antyodaya is also a fine blend of configuration for village republic which has been designed and initiated by its mentor Pt. Din Dayal Upadhayay with its ideology of integrated humanism that refers to wipe out tears of each and every man who are in fear, hunger and still lagging behind to fulfil their square-meal of the day. Like his guide and mentor, Nanaji Deshmukh has also made experimental agenda of village governance to strengthen the self-reliant (*atmanirbhar*) village Republic of India (Dash, 2021). One of the champions of rural local governance, Nanaji Deshmukh was a great exponent of updating the rural economy by the village reconstruction campaign in the context of nurturing the concept of integral humanism from Sarvodaya to Antyodaya. Before Nanaji Deshmukh, one of the social reformers Loknayak Jay Prakash has experimented with the Indian model of configuration of village government during 1970s in one of the districts of Bihar for the self-reliant republic village of India. Unfortunately, the two great stalwart Dr. Lohiya and Pt. Din Dayal passed away at an early age. Really the two great champions of Indian polity was the crusader of village republic system which India had to lose in a very premature time of making Indian democracy vibrant and successful. Had they alive, the Indian democracy could have been the *bona-fide* shield of village autonomy of Indigenous governance and self-reliant peoples planning.

It was the period when Nanaji Deshmukh crafted the design of rural village economy with the socialist group by bringing together Dr. Ram Manohar Lohiya and Pt. Din Dayal Upaydhayay—two great stalwart committed to the welfare of weaker sections of society from Sarvodaya to Antyodaya to uplift the rural areas of India where 'Bharat Mata Lives'.The Chitrakoot experiment of Gramodaya is a great initiation for the structural training programme for the activist grooming them into a professional social worker. Chitrakoot model for social work and practices was his great inspiration that he learnt from his torch bearer like Pt. Din Dayal Upadhyay and Jay Prakash Narayan, through the Jay Prabha Gram Project in U.P. Beed (Maharashtra) for surroundings village of farmers. Nanaji Deshmukh launched an Integrated Programme for the development that covered health, hygiene, education, agriculture, income generation and conservation of resources that were both sustainable and replicable. His design of a participatory approach for total transformation envisioned his self-governance campaign to make the rural area and their configuration strengthened with local resources and planning. Thus, the challenge of this pandemic, COVID-19 is meted out by upgrading the sufferer, distressed and marginalized workers who are returning to back their village with the new design of agricultural harvesting plan. The new innovative skill for the SME groups must be supported and financed with the new package of different economy generating programmes for their empowered and well-equipped future-oriented life-system.[6]

Agenda into Action: Some Thoughtful Experiments, sharing experiences of India under this lockdown period has opened new challenges to scuffle the menace on various measures providing precautionary preventive and curative health services, economy, governance, sanitation, water, pollution, and maintaining law in the country. The lockdown period for interdicting all the means of communication aggrieved ourselves by mentioning the agony, loss of life and also the economy, however, issues related to governance and politics be spoken like this. A sudden and unexpected large number of affected people have created enormous governance problems in the area of providing medical equipment and staff on a large basis in a short period. Containing lawless groups of people who fasten the spread of corona infection and who posed hindrances to the corona warriors, sometimes shamelessly.[7] Meeting the needs of a standard jobless stranded workforce, students and others who are in depression to go back home. Facilitating scientists, pharmacists, manufacturers and trader of equipment and medicine etc.

All these are few challenges before the government in tackling the menace that requires making right and appropriate policy as implementing them. In this process, the role of police, para-military and defence forces need to be underlined. Further, the provision of safety, security, and properly equipping the medical personnel became an urgent imperative process. The provision of an adequate number of PPE Testing devices, well-equipped quarantine infrastructure and Ventilators etc. became the challenge before the government. Not only had this there emerged necessity to make policy in order to bring the economy back on track.

During the lockdown period, we have observed chaos and anarchy in the Indian democratic polity due to the impact of COVID-19. Thus, this is the time to switch over to the sharing humanitarian shift to overcome the low down economy with the design of an attitudinal change for establishing an agro-economy based agriculture planning of farming to revive the local economy shifted to green economy[8] with all collaboration of community farming with co-operative responsibility to survive with the inevitable bond of post-coronavirus pity. We should explore all the possibilities to promote and revive the (MSMEs) scheme in the urban areas. This scheme of Micro, Small and Medium Enterprises will essentially support the lifestyle of a vast number of workers who have stayed on in towns. They all have to be provided with employment and income after our proposed cash transfers run out. The best way to overcome the problems of urban unemployment with local bodies of urban planning for a caring economy including old disabled and ailing person. The humanitarian crisis of the post-lockdown period reveals the imperative for more, not less labour protection. Such measures far from reviving investment or employment would also further reduce domestic demand.[9]

The post-pandemic period must see significant increases in public expenditure on education, health, especially for urban and rural poor. The growing economy can be sharpened by the fiscal stimulus to finance the institution of five universal justice and fundamental economy rights: the right to food, the right to free public health care, the right to free public education, and the right to living old age pension and disability benefits. We must improve their status, treat them decently, give them proper remuneration and associated benefits and greatly expand their coverage in the settlement of the urban poor. During the lockdown period, the disaster of COVID-19 has presented horrible devastations which are locally, regionally and globally affected the huge chunk of the human population either urban or rural. So, we have learnt the lessons to provide a sustainable and affordable system of governance, command and control[10] to bring this transformation to survive with the post-coronavirus period. People have also seen that drastic changes in the system are not always bad. But this type of hardship has paid many socially, economically, culturally fruitful remedies to cope up with the challenging obstacles.

Conclusion

What we need today is the process of developing the leadership quality with the sharing experiences of world and India to overcome this novel coronavirus impact. This task is not so easy but not impossible because human history has been the workshop of great visionary trump by the galaxy of talented leadership that recorded unprecedented solidarity to overcome this type of catastrophic shocks. We have discussed many alternatives paradigm to suit the indigenous design, models and opinion to access the challenges of this pandemic. We have also discussed how stimulus of the economic package can practically be survived the agenda of comprehensive road map of suppressing transmission, restoring livelihood and presenting the priority of agro-economy set up with a strong infrastructure for the vibrant[11] democracy of India. No doubt public health challenges of confronting the novel coronavirus has dashed terrible human crisis into the life bed of migrant workers, marginalized groups and leach gatherer of the downtrodden society. Our thoughts and salutes are with all those corona warriors who played their marvelous role to save them and provide all the possible testing kits and services to the grieved and affected people. We call all the effective missionaries of research and development to explore the medicine and effective vaccine to access the root of the pandemic. We recognize the risk of life must be ensured with the better health care system and countdown of COVID-19 with the developed clinical trial is the agenda of the governing authority of the world. It is a heroic show of solidarity collaboration, and the progressive opening of some concrete agenda of local planning for business of eco-friendly behaviour of the governance to safe and save life and livelihood of the world people. We hope that after succeeding phase of post-lockdown period we can start alternative knowledge system of social engineering for further promotion of self-governance with their own productive patterns of local farming—a boost of the innovative skill of indigenous farming and formative planning. Thus, the purpose of writing this chapter is to provide an academic platform to academician, scholar, stakeholders, bureaucrats, civil society and corporate sectors representatives to discuss, deliberate and contribute an idea for the alternative natural management and reminding traditional tips to restore and retain the values of green politics and for the biosphere of the local surroundings. Needless to think about the proper timing of lockdown before or later, the better choices are to explore all the technical devices to access the menace like coronavirus and strong sustainable affordable configuration for village uplift to ease the woes of a hundred beautiful feat of endurance and love[12] that has captured the cravings of siblings of migrant labourer either to be carried on the luggage with a suitcase or to save the life of their father. If we would have a strong habitat and habitation for their livelihood, the huge human capital of workforce must be oriented with their artisan skill to explore a better developed paradigm for village governance and urban local industrial corridor. Baba Saheb Ambedkar rightly quoted, "No constitution is good or bad but its significance depends on the mindset of policymakers to shoot the hurdles of taboos to herald the life system of the people of the nation for their total development suited to circumstances and social reconstruction into the cultural ethos of the country."

NOTES

1. Taijal Kantikar, 'Life after lockdown', *Hindustan Times,* 22 May, 2020.
2. Mahatma Gandhi, Swadeshi Movement, *Young India*, 7 August, 1921.
3. Mahatma Gandhi, Trusteeship and Village Economy, 2 October, 1925, *Young India.*
4. Shekhar Sharma, 'Swadeshi and Self Governance', *Webinar* Organized by Bhartiya Karyakaram Mandal, 21 May, 1920.
5. Vinoba Bhave, 'Sarvodaya evam Gramdam',Wardha, 1950.
6. Smt. Purnima Sinha (Chairman NIESBUD, Delhi), 'SME and Entrepreneurship *Webinar*, 21 May, 2020.
7. Prof. Jitendra Narayan, "Covid-19 and Governance Politics", *Webinar*, 17 May, 2020, Bihar Regional Branch Patna.
8. Vandana Shiva, Environmentalist, Pandemic and Lockdown Crisis Management, *Webinar*, 15 May, 2020.
9. Jayant Goshal, The economic fallout of COVID-19, 14 May, 2020, *Indian Express.*
10. Dr. Priyadarshawni Karve, Director Samuchit Infotech, Pune, The thought Experiment after Lockdown Period, *Webinar*, 22 May, 2020.
11. Prabhat Patnaik, 'The care Economy after COVID-19', *Indian Express*, 20 May, 2020.
12. Ivanka Trump, The Daughter of Bihar, Symbol of Endurance and Love, *Times of India*, 23 May, 2020.

REFERENCES

Bhave, V. (1950). *Sarvodaya and Bhoodan.* Wardha: Pavnar Ashram.

Dash, B.M., Kumar, M. & Shukla, S. (2020). *Social Work in India: Indigenous Approaches and Model.* New Delhi: Concept Publishing Co. Pvt. Ltd.

Dash, B.M. (2021). Social Work Practice: The Nanaji Way, in Nanaji Deshmukh: *An Epitome of Indian Social Work* (Dash, B.M. & Kumar, M. (eds.), Concept Publication, New Delhi, pp. 33-41.

Gandhi, M. (1940). *Hind Swaraj*, Ahmadabad: Navjiwan Publication.

Narayan, J.P. (1964). *Three Basic Problem of Free India*, Delhi: Asia Publishing House.

Narayan, J.P. (1970). *Communitarian Society and Panchaayti Raj*, (ed.), Brahmanand, Varanasi: Navachetna Prakashan.

Pradhan, B. (1980). *The Socialist Thought of Mahatma Gandhi.* Delhi: GDK Publications.

Index